Service at the

Heart of Learning

Teachers' Writings

Edited by

Emily Cousins

Amy Mednick

Expeditionary Learning
Outward Bound

New
American
Schools

The etchings included throughout the book were made by sixth-grade students at I.S. 30 in Brooklyn, New York, for a learning expedition on water. As part of this science and humanities expedition, students initiated a water-conservation campaign.

Cover Etchings: Yuann Trinidad, Dilruba Aklher, Taan Alawie, and Minerva Zenteno.
Interior Etchings: Jilan Byloun, Sofia Chernyak, Mohamed Belakhdar, Dilruba Aklher, Yuann Trinidad, Taan Alawie, Lev Belyavskiy, Sead Bajraktarevic, Stas Kudryashov, Akkas Mahmood, and Minerva Zenteno.

Cover and interior design: Carroll Conquest, Conquest Design

Expeditionary Learning℠ is a Service Mark of Outward Bound, Inc.
Outward Bound® is a Registered Trademark of Outward Bound, Inc.

Copyright© 1999 by Expeditionary Learning Outward Bound®.

ISBN 0-7872-6030-4

Library of Congress Catalog Card Number: 99-62811

Printed in the United States of America

10 9 8 7 6 5 4 3 2

DEDICATION

To Joshua Minor,

who exemplifies the highest standard of service in his stewardship
of Outward Bound's ideals, as illustrated by his bringing Outward
Bound to the United States in 1962 and his continued advocacy
of Expeditionary Learning Outward Bound today.

SERVICE AT THE
HEART OF LEARNING
TEACHERS' WRITINGS

CONTENTS

Foreword
Greg Farrell   VII

Acknowledgments   XI

Introduction
Meg Campbell   1

✳ **Humanities**
Seasons of Life: Biography as Service (Middle School)
Deb Fordice   9

"What Can We Do About It?" Busing Ends In Denver
(Middle School)
Sally Carey   37

Snapshot: Do a Greater Deed
Michelle Brantley   50

Tuskegee Airmen Touch Down in Dubuque (High School)
John Adelmann   53

"We Have No Heroes" (Middle School)
Paola Ruocco   85

Quilting Community (Elementary School)
Carol Duehr and Christina Nugent   97

Snapshot: Disaster Relief
Patricia O'Brien   113

The Heroes Among Us: Building a Culture of Service
and Compassion (Middle School)
    Patricia B. Fisher, Sheila Sanders, and Carol Teague   115

Thoreau and Trigonometry: Designing a
City Park (High School)
    Katherine Stevens   127

Snapshot: Becoming Service-Minded
    Peggy Chessmore   139

Bay Ridge, Brooklyn: Painting A Community
Portrait (Middle School)
    Bayan Ebeid and Laura Kelly   141

Science

The Aquarium Architects (Middle School)
    Karen MacDonald and Christine Griffin   161

Listening to Robins (Primary School)
    Jeanne Anderson and Karen Wohlwend   181

"What's in the Water You Drink?" (Middle School)
    Cheryl Sims   203

Snapshot: What Is Service?   225

Putting Down Roots: Erosion Control on the
South Platte River (Middle School)
    Wendy Ward   227

Snapshot: When Service Counts   245

Stewards of the Elements (Elementary School)
    Chris Quigley, Bryan Street, and Chris Weaver   249

Appendix

About the Authors   285

Service Resources   288

Expeditionary Learning Design Principles   289

FOREWORD

Outward Bound is rooted in service. You might say service, rather than adventure, is the central idea in Outward Bound. Kurt Hahn, who founded Outward Bound, thought compassion the most important quality of all to keep alive in individuals and in the world at large.

He believed that training for rescue service stoked the fires of compassion. The point of the physical rigor of an Outward Bound course, the point of getting fit for it (or, in some cases, trying to get fit doing it) is to be in good enough shape that you can be ready to help someone when he or she needs it. Hahn also appreciated the more mundane aspects of service. One of the things he watched for and commented on in his students' behavior on expeditions was whether they cleaned up the pots and pans and voluntarily took on the little service-chores of expedition life.

Hahn understood the connection between character and service. "We are crew, not passengers," he wrote. "We are ennobled by consequential acts of service to others." The service at the center of Outward Bound is what makes it different and sets it apart from the other programs that take people into the wilderness. It involves more than adventures in wild and beautiful places. It offers a form of education that brings out the best in people, and the fact that there is selflessness in it gives it power and purpose.

Joshua Miner, the American teacher who brought Outward Bound to the United States, often reminded listeners that *Non Sibi*, "not for oneself," was the motto of Gordonstoun, Hahn's school in Scotland. Recently, when some Outward Bound board members asked Josh to clarify just what constituted authentic Outward Bound, he said it boiled down to two things. It was Outward Bound if people accomplished things they would not have believed they could do, and if they worried about others more than themselves.

Outward Bound began, in fact, as a program to train young men for service in the British merchant marine. It took only a fifty-year hop, skip, and jump from that to Expeditionary Learning Outward Bound, a framework and design for comprehensive school improvement that uses the pedagogy and philosophy and ethic of Outward Bound to "do school," kindergarten through twelfth grade, to make the learning of reading, writing, arithmetic, history, and science more hands-on, more project-based, more full of fun and adventure, and at the same time just as rigorous academically as Outward Bound is rigorous physically.

Both teachers and students in Expeditionary Learning schools learn by doing. And the schools themselves develop a culture not unlike that of a small expeditionary team, where all the members have to help each other, serve each other, or the group will not make it where they are trying to go. So a good Expeditionary Learning school has an internal service ethic that it practices and works on and transfers to the community around it.

It is no surprise that powerful learning is connected to acts of service. Paul Ylvisaker, the former dean of the Harvard Graduate School of Education, wrote, "There is no learning without challenge and emotion." Service, especially person-to-person service, is full of both.

Some Outward Bound instructors and Expeditionary Learning teachers have made the mistake of thinking service was a requirement they had to add on to their Outward Bound courses or learning expeditions. Service should not be a component to satisfy a requirement, but the spirit that pervades and animates. It is much easier to get to academic work of a high standard through projects and expeditions driven by a service imperative than it is to get to powerful service experiences through expeditions driven by the need to meet curricular requirements. More and more, teachers in Expeditionary Learning schools begin planning a learning expedition with the idea of serving others. The examples that Emily Cousins and Amy Mednick have gathered in this book provide evidence that starting with service, putting service at the center, enhances rather than sacrifices academic rigor, motivates both teachers and students to go beyond what they think they can do, connects learning to life, and provides the powerful learning experiences that teachers and students alike remember for the rest of their lives.

—Greg Farrell
President, Expeditionary Learning Outward Bound

$\mathcal{A}$CKNOWLEDGMENTS

$\mathcal{W}$e acknowledge the craft wisdom and courage of educators in our partner schools who practice a deep commitment to service every day.

We would like to thank the Learn & Serve America program of the Corporation for National Service, the Surdna Foundation, Inc., and The Pfizer Foundation for their generous support of this project and for their efforts to bring service and character development into the heart of schools.

We would also like to thank New American Schools for their continued leadership, guidance, and assistance.

Special thanks to our many supporters over the years, including the following foundations: A.L. Mailman Family Foundation; DeWitt Wallace Reader's Digest Fund; Grace, George, and Judith Silverberg Foundation, Inc.; The Abbot and Dorothy H. Stevens Foundation; The Benny Slome Charitable Foundation; The Dragon Foundation; The Edna McConnell Clark Foundation; The Emily Davie and Joseph S. Kornfeld Foundation; The Geraldine R. Dodge Foundation; The J.M. Kaplan Fund; Marcy Miller Lewis Family Supporting Foundation; Public Welfare Foundation; The Sperry Fund.

We would also like the thank the following individuals: Helen E. Ammen, John L. Anderson, Thomas C. Barry, David O. Beim and Mrs. Raymond N. Beim, Frederick W. Beinecke, Leslie and Barbara Buckland, George B. Clairmont, Mr. and Mrs. Robert L. Clark,

Neil S. Fox, Robert L. Gable, William O. Grabe, Kaye, Scholer, Fierman, Hays, & Handler, LLP, Lee P. Klingenstein, Herbert V. Kohler, Jr., James W. McLane, L. Thomas Melly, Alexandra Olmsted, Katharine Olmsted, William E. Phillips, John Roberts, Frances and Paul Rubacha, Jonathan D. Sackler, Andrew Safran, Suzanne K. Schwerin, Jaye and T. Joseph Semrod, Irwin W. Silverberg, Winthrop H. Smith, Jr., Douglas T. Tansill, Brooks Thomas, Robert L. Turner, Andrews R. Walker, Dean K. Webster, and Priscilla B. Woods.

Introduction

The deliberate and conscious introduction of service into academic studies is a recent phenomenon and one that raises skepticism on the part of many teachers and parents. Won't service, some ask, take away from scholarly study? In *Service at the Heart of Learning,* teachers persuasively make the case that service in fact deepens intellectual growth and can prove a powerful motivator for giving young people a purpose to learn. Teachers make their case based on their own experience in classrooms ranging from kindergarten through twelfth grade in places as different as Hickory, North Carolina, and New York City.

It is striking that this is the first collection of accounts by teachers on this subject. It is new territory for teachers to venture into, and the act of writing and reflecting upon their experiences is also a new development in teaching practice. These teachers generously and candidly share lessons, successes, and failures as they try to teach in a way far different from how most of them were taught. This book is their act of service to our profession.

Expeditionary Learning Outward Bound schools commit themselves to ten design principles. Significantly, one is Service and Compassion. "We are crew, not passengers, and are strengthened by consequential acts of service to others," the principle explains. "One of a school's primary functions is to prepare students with the attitudes and skills to learn from and be of service to others." This ideal becomes a daily reality in schools and classrooms where an ethic of service permeates the culture. Several teachers observe that what begins as a service project gradually begins to influence how students treat each other; they are kinder, more patient, more respectful with their young colleagues. Jeanne Anderson and Karen Wohlwend note in "Listening to Robins" that young children caring for animals unleashes a deeper caring for other students. Deb Fordice, in "Seasons of Life," observes her students' growing compassion toward one another as they get to know the nursing home residents they are interviewing. Lifting children's concerns beyond themselves has the salutary effect of making them more thoughtful in their dealings with each other. Surely, this is one of the best side effects of fostering a culture of service in a whole school: the students and the adults become more caring people.

Service at the Heart of Learning is divided into two sections, Science and Humanities. Science may seem an unlikely dance partner for service and yet several narratives chronicle this successful match. On the elementary level, learning expeditions include a study of birds and an investigation of how one school uses its natural resources, while secondary-level expeditions explore erosion and water quality. In one instance, students design architectural plans for a proposed aquarium in Portland, Maine. In every case, learning science has a purpose for these students and draws them as citizens into the community beyond their classroom. The humanities expedition projects range from biographies and portraits of senior citizens to in-depth investigations of busing. High school students in Dubuque, Iowa, conduct community surveys to find out what neighbors want in a student-designed park. Whether writing a business letter or a book, students perform at higher levels because the audience is a real one and they have an authentic reason to communicate.

Across the disciplines, three themes emerge. The first is that teachers provide a great deal of infrastructure in order to enhance learning by the students both in content and character. There is nothing random about these teachers' teaching. They have a profound respect for students' own responsibility for learning, but they support that with very concrete, explicit expectations and significant preparation. This kind of conscious scaffolding prevents service from becoming mushy or watered-down. The tools these teachers use include student portfolios, product descriptors, extensive critique and revision, and skill building in a range of research resources and oral presentation techniques. Whatever discipline students are studying, they learn the particular vocabulary of that discipline. So when King Middle School students in Portland, Maine design an aquarium, they become young architects themselves.

Within the classroom, teachers use important rituals such as daily community meetings and journal reflections to foster a culture of service. They help students develop the awareness they will need to perform authentic service on their own. In "Stewards of the Elements," Chris Quigley, Bryan Street, and Chris Weaver write, "One of the most important capacities beyond meaningful service is the ability to identify and act on one's own values. Yet how can students discover their own values in service projects that are chosen only by the teacher?" The teachers in these narratives ensure that students have the experience of making meaningful choices within the service project.

At the school level, there is a commitment to creating extended blocks of time in which teachers can teach learning expeditions. Additionally, the schedule is configured to create much-needed common planning time for teachers who are working together. The school structure of multiyear teaching, or looping, is another feature of Expeditionary Learning schools that fosters a closer relationship between teachers and students and their families. Closer relationships nurture an ethic of service. Finally, professional development offered by Expeditionary Learning models service and calls on teachers to perform service as well. What teachers are asked to do with their students, teachers are called upon to do in their own professional development. For many, reconnecting with service fosters personal as well as professional growth.

The second theme that emerges in these narratives is that the role of the teacher changes to one who is a facilitator and guide. An ambitious service project cannot be entirely scripted and the teacher must play the leadership role in modeling flexibility, ingenuity, and follow-through. The teacher provides direct instruction as it is needed, and holds students accountable for their work. Many teachers in this book comment on how high their expectations were for their students, and how proud they were when they met or exceeded them.

The final theme is the benefits of service, which include expanding the classroom to the entire community. Service cultivates strong work habits for the world of work. It gives students an opportunity to experience for themselves that they are making a positive difference. Cheryl Sims observes that service gives students a chance to create knowledge and to pursue questions which, to date, do not have answers. Students contribute knowledge to the field, as they do in John Adelmann's account of his high school students who hosted the Tuskegee Airmen at a seminar in their honor in Dubuque, Iowa.

There are many good reasons for a school community to commit to infusing service into curriculum and culture, but the most compelling is that service calls upon our better selves. It is the surest route to fostering character development. Service coaxes us from our own narrow preoccupations and firmly held opinions into the "unknown"— whether that unknown is testing water quality or testing reservoirs of patience. Service is the Grand Canyon of character development and to deny our students the opportunity to explore it in its many glorious dimensions is to cheat them of one of education's greatest rewards: the joy of making a difference by sharing one's talents, knowledge, skills, and time.

As educators and parents, we are eager to ensure that students master content in many disciplines. In Expeditionary Learning partner schools, we are equally concerned that students develop qualities of perseverance, kindness, respect, compassion, teamwork, and the ability to reflect in solitude. These traits need an arena for study and acquisition, and as the teachers in this volume testify, learning expeditions offer a rich opportunity for combining intellectual and character development. The strength of these narratives is the testimony that embedding service in learning expeditions enhances learning on both fronts.

In Hebrew, "mitzvah" means an act of service. "The reward of the mitzvah is the mitzvah itself," it is written in the Torah. There are many reasons for service, but it is also important to remember that the service itself is its own reward. We give our students the opportunity to experience that special joy that comes from the mitzvah itself. We hope it stays with them for the rest of their lives.

—Meg Campbell
Director, Expeditionary Learning Outward Bound
Lecturer, Harvard Graduate School of Education

HUMANITIES

Seasons of Life:
Biography as Service

Deb Fordice

*I*t was 8:30 a.m. on June 3, the celebration day for the sixth graders at Audubon Elementary, a school for at-risk prekindergarten through sixth-grade students in downtown Dubuque, Iowa. It was almost time for the graduation ceremony to begin, and as smiling students clustered in front of the camera, one student stood out. Instead of sporting a new summer dress or slacks outfit, she wore an oversized sweatshirt. I listened as a student asked her, "Why didn't you get a new dress for graduation?" She simply replied, "I didn't have enough money."

She did not tell why she could not afford the new dress. But I knew. All year long Erica had been saving and then spending her hard-earned babysitting money to buy gifts for her newest and dearest friend, Ethel, an elderly resident of Bethany Retirement Home. Just two days before the sixth-grade graduation, Erica and her partner had presented Ethel with a gift that money cannot buy: a written history of Ethel's life.

Erica and Hayley had started the book in September and finished it in June. Writing life histories of nursing home residents was the core of a learning expedition called "Cycles of Life." The main project focused on developing teamwork, writing, interviewing, and technology skills while providing a service by giving time, attention, and a final product of a written biography to residents of a nearby nursing home. It did not take too many interview visits to see that many of the arranged intergenerational relationships were blossoming into genuine human connections and taking on personal meaning for both the students and the elderly people. Erica is one student who, in addition to learning academic skills through the writing project, increasingly internalized the joy of serving.

In chapter one of Ethyl's life story, she talked about her favorite childhood toy, a porcelain doll, the head of which had been cracked during play with a cousin. Erica asked Ethel if she could see the doll, and so began the first of many visits to Ethel's room in Bethany Home. Upon returning to school that day, Erica wrote in her Bethany diary, "I am going to save my money to buy Ethel a new porcelain doll." She did, and it was the first of many gifts Erica gave to Ethel.

Did the Bethany biography expedition have a profound impact on the lives of students and elderly people? Did the process of writing these biographies result in higher student achievement? As I reflect upon these questions, so many vivid and touching memories come back to me. In my heart I know that the power of this expedition was a result of the intertwining of the elements of service and academics.

THE BIRTH OF THE EXPEDITION

When my teaching partner, Geri Maloy, and I set out to frame the expedition, we wanted to create a project that would develop character by encouraging the students to think about someone besides themselves. We also wanted to work with Bethany Home, a retirement/ nursing home just four blocks from school. Bethany Home was a neighborhood gold mine waiting to be excavated. It offered students the chance to build meaningful bonds with good role models and to experience intergenerational relationships. It was within walking distance. Students could visit whenever they wanted, and so the expedition could expand beyond the school day and school year. Furthermore, there were no entrance fees or transportation costs.

But how could we be assured that visits to the retirement home would improve student learning? We decided that, academically, a theme of "Cycles of Life" would tie in naturally with our studies of ecosystems, astronomy, and ancient civilizations. Many of our excellent grade-level novels focused on human interdependence and relationships. It was through this curricular webbing that we brainstormed a communication component that would center on a yearlong series of student/resident interviews culminating in written histories of the residents' lives. This would give a driving purpose to each visit as well as direct the classroom work between visits. As we finished writing the framework for the expedition, with the biography writing at its heart, we knew the expedition would be special. However, I did not foresee the potential this expedition would have to affect lives of people all over the world.

THE IMPACT OF THE SERVICE

On September 13, 1996, a letter arrived at Audubon School from Alexandria, Egypt addressed to the sixth grade. Excerpts from the letter affirm the impact the students were making in the lives of the residents and their families:

Dear Ms. Fordice,

Thank you for the letter and certificate for my father, Jim McKee, who was a participant in the Bethany biography project…

Dad died on September 3rd, 1996…we want you to know how much he enjoyed being part of this great educational and touching program. He wrote to us often about the visits with the schoolboys and was very proud to be able to share his wealth of information and memories with the school boys, Matt Roloff and Josh Martin.

At the funeral home and also at the service held at Bethel Presbyterian Church in Waterloo, Iowa, the book, "Lean on Me,"

*by Matt and Josh, was a favorite item of conversation. It brought
many smiles, tears, and happy memories to all of us.*

*We want to thank you and Matt and Josh for this wonderful
project. It brought joy and pleasure to Dad, as he looked forward
to their visits. It was also a special news item for us, as he wrote
to his children who are scattered too faraway for frequent visits.
He was also pleased to be asked about his life and to have an
audience for his many stories and wealth of information in his
mind. We were so thankful that he was so alert and up-to-date
at age ninety-five.*

*Our congratulations again to Audubon School ... and all the
students, Bethany Home, and the sponsors of this fine program.
It brought untold friendship, love, and reward to all who have
learned about it. We thank you for our Dad, Jim McKee.*

Sincerely,
Laura McKee Pattee

This is one of several contacts from families of residents who have
passed away since their biographies were written. Another letter of
appreciation came from the daughter of a resident, along with a picture
of her father with his daughter and granddaughter, and some money
for a pizza party for the class.

Some of the most emotional experiences for both the students, the
residents' families, and me were times when the students and I attended
the visitations of residents who had passed away either during or
after the process of the biography writing. The first year we did this
expedition, just one week before we planned to present the books to
the residents, ninety-three-year-old Helen Schumacher died. Of
course, after an entire year of personal interviews, and writing her life
story, the boys were saddened by her death. Her biography was finished: laminated, bound, and gift-wrapped, and they were not able to
give it to her. I called the Bethany Home activities director, Debi
Ambrosy, to ask if it would be appropriate for me to bring the boys to
the visitation and allow them to present the biography to the family.

Debi thought it would be a good idea, and notified the family that we would be coming.

On the Saturday morning of the visitation, I took Eric and Greg to the church. When we approached the receiving line, I said to them, "That must be Helen's daughter at the front. What's her name, again?" Of course, they remembered and proudly responded, "Jean." I realized that these two boys, though they had never seen any of the people in that room, probably knew some things about Helen that nobody else knew, and now those things were written down for others to learn. The boys knew about her first boyfriend, her favorite color, the things she always dreamed of, and the things she valued most. And they were about to share this with a room full of Helen's descendants.

When we reached the front of the line, Jean, now in her sixties, said to Greg and Eric, "Oh, I know who you are. Just a minute." She then gathered her three brothers, their children, and grandchildren. The boys explained the project to the family, read excerpts from the book, and showed the attentive listeners their illustrations and photographs. One granddaughter, with teary eyes and a feeble voice, asked, "Are we all going to get a copy?" I explained that we only had this one copy, but they certainly could feel free to make as many copies of it as they liked. Before leaving the church, as the boys were signing the guest book, one of the grandsons came up to the boys in tears, hugged them and said, "Thank you. You just don't know how much this means to our family. Thank you so much."

On the way back to school, the boys and I reflected on the experience, realizing that even though they were not going to be able to give the book away to Helen at the big celebration the following week, they were able to experience firsthand the gratitude of the family. They witnessed the impact their work made on a lot of peoples' lives. They knew that their time and energy invested in writing Helen's biography would live on for many generations to come.

Another resident developed a brain tumor in the second semester of the project. The sixth-grade students who were writing his biography had finished about two-thirds of his life story when Ken was moved to another nursing home that had a more intensive care program.

Suddenly the students were invited to visit during a brief time when Ken was relatively alert and healthy. Upon short notice, only Adam could arrange to attend. On the way over, I tried to prepare Adam for how Ken's mental and physical abilities might have changed.

After I said hello to Ken, Adam approached Ken's bedside as I faded into the background and watched. Adam took Ken's hand, and with an increased volume in his voice, said, "Hi there, Ken. How are ya' doin?" Ken responded with a groaning type of sound, giving clear and direct eye contact to Adam. Adam continued his pursuit.

"I see you have the picture I drew for you."

I looked at Ken's bulletin board, empty except for one small photo and one large childlike drawing—Adam's.

"Are they treating you good here, Ken? You look great, Ken."

Mumble. Eye contact.

"Do you remember who I am, Ken?"

Eye contact, mumble.

"Yes, I'm Adam. I've been coming to see you at Bethany to ask you stuff about your life."

I told Adam to plug in his tape recorder and try to ask his prepared questions—any questions—to try to get any last information he could.

Adam referred to his list, asking the questions he had planned. When he discovered Ken was not making any sense of those questions, Adam set the list down and came closer to Ken. I was fighting tears, grieving the loss of Ken's ability to communicate, and so proud of Adam's ability to understand Ken's needs.

"Do you want to go back to Bethany, Ken?"

Ken answered clearly, "I don't know. We'll see."

Quickly I jumped in, teacher that I am, trying to seize the opportunity and afraid we might lose it if we did not move fast. "Adam," I suggested, "Ask him if he has any advice for you."

"Ken, do you have any advice for me? Like, what do you think I should do so I have a good life and things like that?"

"Be calm," Ken replied. "Be calm."

It made sense. Adam knew it. In addition to being able to carry Ken's words with him, he was able to put something down for the

"Reflections on Life" chapter, something that Ken had said in his own words.

In April of 1997, Adam and Mike finished their book, "Seasons of Life." Instead of a "Winter" chapter, there was a chapter entitled "A Change of Seasons," in which they explained the decline in Ken's health, his hospitalization, and his change in care. They finished the book in time to bring it to Ken's visitation.

In September of 1997, when Adam and Mike had moved on to junior high school, I got a call from Ken's daughter.

"Hello, Mrs. Fordice? I'm Ken Ritenour's daughter. You are the teacher of the boys that wrote the book for Dad, right? I'm sorry I haven't gotten back to you 'til now, but it's been kind of hard since Dad died. In fact, we were just trying to listen to the tapes, but it was too hard. I'd like to do something special for the boys."

I gave her the information she needed to contact them, and a week later, she personally went to the boys' houses to deliver a $100 savings bond to each of them.

Not only were the residents and their families impacted by the service, but the students were as well. Excerpts from some of the Bethany diaries show how proud and touched the children were through the writing of the biographies and the relationships they built:

Every visit we go to is something very special, very great, and something to look forward to. Not many times do you get to make a difference in someone's life so I am very grateful that I have the chance. —Erica Ward

I'm very happy she liked the biography, but I'm sad I had to leave. I could tell our resident didn't want us to leave, because when we were on the elevator back down at the base-ment, instead of getting off, Irene went all the way up to the third floor and back down. It was hard saying good-bye, but I know I will see her again. I plan on going to see her during the summer. —Jennifer Meyer

And then me and Drew shook his hand and left. I felt sad because he was a cool person. And I felt bad because I got to

work with Al for the entire year. I was getting close to him
because he was a special man. I felt sad because we had to
leave. And then I almost started to cry when we were walking
back. He is so special that I would want another chance to
be with Al. I think Drew almost started to cry. I bet Drew was
almost going to cry. —Chris Wardle

I feel that it's not time to say good-bye. I feel it is time to say hi.
This year was the best my life has ever been. I still wish I could
see Darlene every day. —Mallory Munson

We left with a smile on our faces. I left Bethany Home feeling I
had accomplished something great. —Dan Kohnen

These words are from the students' hearts. They tell me that true relationships were built, and that these elderly people changed the students' lives just as much as the students affected the lives of the residents and their families. The words make known the depth of emotion, pride, and character that can occur when time and energy are expended toward a worthy cause.

LAYING THE GROUNDWORK

In order to create an optimal setting for the growth of relationships and the development of academic skills through service, a lot of planning is necessary. This particular expedition is easily replicable in the sense that there are nursing homes near many schools and costs are minimal, but it does require a high degree of effort on the part of those coordinating the project as well as the participants. Before the biography expedition can begin, for instance, the teachers must contact the activities director of the retirement home. The activities director has to seek out enough residents who are willing to work on a yearlong project meeting monthly with children, and who are able to hear, communicate, and remember. The activities director then becomes responsible for arranging the residents in the monthly interview locations and coordinating the residents' travel to school activities. The success of the expedition partially depends upon the passion that the activities direc-

Vanessa Stock, a sixth grader at the Audubon Elementary School in Dubuque, Iowa, drew this portrait to illustrate her biography of a resident at the Bethany Home for senior citizens.

tor brings to the project. Therefore, it is important to work as a team and keep close communication with the nursing home before the project begins and as it unfolds.

Another key player is the art teacher. Our art teacher works with us in our expeditions, always knowing our main projects and concepts.

Our biographies include portrait sketches of the residents as well as illustrations to highlight chapter events. She starts out the year teaching the students how to draw self-portraits. The students then transfer those skills to the drawing of their resident-partners, which they do on their first visit. Later in the year, the students revise their drawings. The quality of their portraits is very high, due partly to the high expectations of our art teacher and to the students' desire to create the best drawings they can for their residents' books.

The classroom teachers' jobs begin with setting up background knowledge for the expedition. We explore student opinions of elderly people. We read articles about positive contributions of older adults. We learn songs that focus on "old folks" and their feelings, as well as songs about seasons and changes. We connect the theme of cycles to other curricular areas. We go to the park and adopt trees, drawing, measuring, and writing poetry about our trees in each season. Children's literature is rich in books about trees, seasons, respect for the earth, and life changes.

All the while we are laying the groundwork, we "kidwatch." Who needs extra help in writing? Who would be a help to a student who has difficulty writing? Who needs a good role model? Who would be a good role model? Who is shy? Who is outspoken? Who is responsible? Who needs help with organization? From these observations (and with our fingers tightly crossed), we create our list of sixth-grade partners who will work together all year to write the biography of one resident. The list is given to Debi, Bethany's activities director, and she in turn places the residents with the sixth-grade pairs. There are about forty-five to fifty students each year in our sixth grade, and so putting two students with each resident allows us to write twenty-two to twenty-five biographies annually. We keep the partnerships intact all year unless there is a death or illness of a resident, a student or resident moves away, or a new student moves in and needs to join a group. If there is a personality conflict, we make an analogy to the real world, teaching the students that in an adult job there may be coworkers who are not necessarily your best friends, but you still need to work with them and do a good job.

Our special-needs teacher comes into our classrooms to accommodate the students who need extra help in the writing process. Since we pair more advanced writers with less able writers, students provide the assistance needed when the special-needs teacher is not available. The partnered process is designed to help the less able writers learn writing skills from the more advanced writers, while allowing the top writers to use their own rich vocabulary and sentence structures. **Often less able writers are better illustrators than their partners,** and so students grow to understand that everyone has strengths and weaknesses, and it is by working together that we learn from each other and create a quality product.

Other groundwork includes discussing the format of the book with the students. How do they want to organize it? Our first year the book was entitled "Lean On Me" and was separated into chapters by stages of life: childhood, teen years, early adulthood, middle adulthood, and older adulthood. They also included a final chapter called "Reflections on Life." In our second year the title of the book was "Seasons of Life," divided into spring, summer, autumn, winter of life, and a reflections chapter. As teachers we prefer the seasonal approach because it more closely ties into the cycles theme.

Finally, the day in late September comes when the students get to meet the faces of the names on Debi's paper. The first meeting is informal with no interview. The students and residents share photographs, and the students draw the residents' portraits as they chat. Looking at videotapes of previous first meetings and students' written reflections, I can see that students are very eager to meet their residents, but also a bit nervous. As the year progresses, videotapes and reflections reveal a greater level of comfort. Many diary entries show that the students wish school could be longer on Bethany visit days, because they do not want to leave their residents.

Once the first visit is over, the students are very motivated to prepare for their first formal interview. The next several steps are stages that we repeat for every chapter. Starting at this point, we spend one hour, every day, all year, "doing Bethany," and work to integrate the rest of the curriculum within the cycles theme. For the first chapter's process, much teacher guidance is required. Therefore more time is necessary to complete the first chapter than all remaining chapters. During our first year we panicked when it was November before the first chapter was done and we still had five chapters to do. However, the subsequent chapters are done more and more efficiently as the students get used to the routine. By the time they write the last chapter, they are pretty self-sufficient. In fact, by that time they have developed such a strong strategy for the writing process that they are able to easily apply it to other writing formats.

THE BUILDING BLOCKS OF EACH CHAPTER

Before students begin each chapter, they refer to the prewriting and interviewing rubric, which Geri and I developed. This assessment tool gives the students specific guidelines for quality work in the journalism skills of developing questions and interviewing their residents. The students see the rubric before the process begins so they are aware of the expectations and can strive to do excellent work.

The first strategy the students learn and the first step to each chapter is webbing. If the chapter title is "Spring of Life," then we need to brainstorm what life events occur from infancy through the teen years. Students learn to start with the chapter title, or the topic, as the center circle. They throw out ideas as a whole group for the first chapter, becoming more independent with each chapter. Subtopics such as "birth," "infancy," "childhood," and "school" become the outer circles, attached to the center by spokes. Then the subtopics are brainstormed for ideas that will be transformed into questions in the next stage.

Once the web is completed, the next step is to turn the subtopic's details into questions. Geri came up with a great format for this: fold a piece of notebook paper in half to make a crease, and then unfold it. Each pair writes their questions on the left side of the paper, and leaves the right side of the paper blank. (In a later step of the process, the students fill in the right side.) What was listed as "date," a subspoke of "birth" on the web, now becomes "Eleanor, what was the date of your birth?" (We emphasize writing the resident's name at the start of each question to learn proper interview etiquette.) In this web-to-question step the students are becoming better prepared for the interview.

Before we go to Bethany to interview the residents, we practice in class. We interview each other, working on eye contact, saying the person's name first, and using clear diction and increased volume. Then a retired teacher comes to school so we can practice interviewing her. She is very good about saying things like, "I couldn't hear your question. Could you please speak a little louder?" (It helps to have outside people affirm what the teacher preaches.) We also practice listening skills, emphasizing the need to follow the person's answers to get more information, especially when the answer strays from the written list of questions. Some of the best information the students receive about the residents comes from times when the students set their lists aside and just really listen and converse. The students need to know that their list of questions is like a foundation. Those are the necessary questions. But as one builds the chapter, just as when building a house, one sometimes does things differently than planned.

The second meeting date is the first time students go to Bethany with tape recorders, cassette tapes, and interview questions. The big day has arrived when all of the prewriting and interview skills practiced at school will be needed in order to have a successful interview. Debi already has the room arranged so the students can go to their resident's tables, set up by electrical outlets, one book team per table. The sixth graders are responsible for checking to make sure their tape recorders are recording the interview. Once they are assured of that, they begin with their first question, reading it from their creased paper and listening intently to their resident. Students do not write the answers, but let the tape recorder get the information. The students spend about an hour and a half with their residents. Often the students finish their interviews before we need to go back to school and spend the remaining time visiting the residents in their rooms. Both parties enjoy this special time. This is also a convenient way for the students to get pictures of precious mementos from the residents' pasts to include in the biographies.

Upon returning to school, the students reflect and assess. They write in their "Bethany Diary" before and after each visit, as well as any

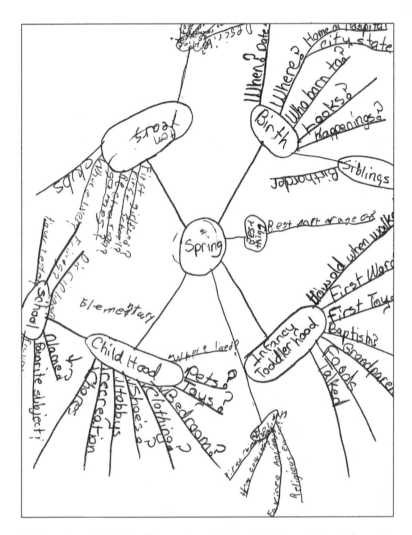

Sixth-grade students Adam Schumacher and Corey Adams used this web format to start generating questions for their interview with a senior citizen as part of a learning expedition on biographies at Audubon Elementary School in Dubuque, Iowa.

other desired time. We share as a whole group some of our experiences during the interviews: what we learned from our questioning, and how well we used the speaking and listening skills needed for good communication. We refer to the prewriting and interviewing rubric as a guide

BIRTH	
1. Martin, when were you born? (date & year)	March 16, 1925
2. Martin, where were you born?	Zwingal Iowa
3. Martin, who are your parents?	Ruth & Denlinger
4. Martin, do you remember what you look like?	Doesn't remember
5. Martin, what happened when you were born?	Doesn't remember
6. Martin, what order were you born in between you and your brothers and sisters?	2 older sisters, 2 younger brothers
7. Martin, why did you get the name you got?	Named after his great grandfather & grandfather

After completing the web, Adam Schumacher and Corey Adams generated a list of questions to guide their interview with a senior citizen.

for seeing where we are now and how we can improve the next time. Then the students meet with their sixth-grade Bethany partners to talk over their individual progress in more detail. Partners mark the rubrics according to the level of achievement for the interview just completed.

The next step is to transcribe the tape-recorded interviews into notes, writing the answers to the questions on the right side of the creased papers. Student partners listen to the tape, pausing it when they hear something they need to write down. We make sure to tell the students that any important information that was not directly an answer to a question should also be written down. These notes will eventually turn into sentences, paragraphs, and chapters.

After the notes are taken, students write their first draft of the chapter. This is a tricky step, because they need to organize their notes into paragraphs as well as construct well-written sentences. We use a specific process to ensure that both students contribute and improve their writing skills. Partners compose sentences together verbally and then take turns writing every other sentence. While they write, they discuss things like, "Make sure you put a capital there," or "Let's use a different word than *said*," or "How could we say that so it sounds more interesting?"

When they have finished writing their first draft, they self edit and peer edit their work. For quality guidelines they refer to the writing rubric addressing chapter form, mechanics, and language usage. The next step is for partners to confer with the teacher about their draft. The students read through their chapter, alternately by paragraph, without interruption. Then, using the rubric, we go back to the beginning and assess what was good and what needs improvement. Usually, there are several "back to the drawing board" stages, including revision and further conferences, before the chapter is stamped for computer approval. The written rubric is filed (as are all the Bethany rubrics) for documentation in the portfolio.

Once the students are ready for their first computer draft, they take their stamped written draft and sit side by side at a computer. One student types while the other person watches and edits. We require students to save their chapters on both students' disks so there is a backup. The Expeditionary Learning design principle of Success and Failure arises many times in this stage. Of course, the computers take a lot of the blame, but it is really important that the students learn *through experience* the need to save frequently while they are word processing.

When students lose entire chapters, they become very frustrated, yet they learn a lesson.

> *During the school year of having Bethany there were good times, great times, and very, very bad times ... When getting all that stress it makes you mad, but getting mad helps you learn how to deal with your problems, and that helped me a lot this year.* —Eric Daughetee

After the computer copy of the chapter is perfected, the student partners assess their computer skills using the technology rubric. The rubric addresses keyboard and organizational skills and, later in the year, the ability to use additional technology such as a digital camera and a scanner. The class members celebrate as they share their chapter with the large group. The hard copy of their chapter, along with illustrations that have been informally critiqued and revised, is filed for compiling into their book at the end of the year. An optional step is to add borders around the text that reflect the chapter.

The process then begins again for the next chapter, and the next, until the book is finished. Our learning atmosphere is a hub of activity, with partners sprinkled across all areas of the room. Webbing, question writing, and writing of rough drafts can happen anywhere in the classroom. Elderly voices emerge from tape recorders, followed by a squeak of a pause button and the verbal interplay between sixth-grade partners as the notes are spoken before being written down. Headphone sets are put on, then removed as students speak to each other about what was heard. A conference sign-up adorns the chalkboard as the teachers buzz from student pair to student pair, then back to the conference table to hear and see another pair's draft.

After the last chapter is finished our students add scanned photos and documents to the biographies. We invite the residents to school to preview them. They bring photographs and important documents with them and use the scanner with the students. The residents are amazed at the technology and the students' ability to use it. The final technology rubric helps the students assess their skills in the use of the digital camera and the scanner.

In May the students create a personalized cover and a dedication page for the biography. Then the books are ready for photocopying and lamination. Each student gets a black and white copy, but the resident gets the beautiful color copy. It adds to the service aspect when the students give the best copy away to their resident.

MEANINGFUL SERVICE AND HIGH ACADEMIC ACHIEVEMENT

Student-to-student relationships affect learning as significantly as the intergenerational friendships do. When two students work together so closely all year long, they become like siblings. It is very interesting to watch their relationships grow. They learn how to solve problems. They know when to back off, and when to take over. In the end, they probably know their partners better than most of the other students do.

One relationship that stands out in my mind is of Eric D. and Eric S., two boys for whom I really had to cross my fingers when I decided to pair them as Bethany partners. All year long they fought like cats and dogs. Eric D. would complain that Eric S. was driving him crazy because he would not do anything right, while Eric S. retaliated, crying, "Well, he won't *let* me do anything!" When Meg Campbell, executive director of Expeditionary Learning Outward Bound, came to visit, she asked the students what they were learning about working together. Both Erics had something to tell her about how it can be very hard to work together all the time, but they know it can be like that in "the real world."

When it was time for our district writing assessment in the spring, the students were told to write an essay about something they had lost. After a few quiet minutes, sobbing arose from the front corner of the room. It was Eric S. He was thinking about his grandfather who had passed away. Nobody said anything or did anything—except for his partner. Eric D. got up, went in front of Eric S.'s desk, knelt down, and patted him on the hand, asking, "Are you gonna be O.K., buddy?" Eric D. was willing to be compassionate to his "cats and dogs partner" in front of the whole class. It was as if he knew that he had the highest right to that privilege. And he felt safe enough around twenty-five other

Spring of Life

A cry was heard in the home of James and Elizabeth McDermott as the life of Cecelia McDermott began on March 9, 1912, in the state of Iowa.

Cecelia was born on the ninth of March in the year 1912 in Pleasant Grove, Iowa. She was the child of James and Elizabeth McDermott and one of eight children. There was nothing really happening as the light of the house of McDermott was burning. She was chubby with curls of red hair glistening in the sunshine. She had the middle name Elizabeth after her wonderful mother.

As a child, Cecelia lived on a farm in Pleasant Grove. She was baptized with her loving godparents Joe Connolly and Mary McDermott. Cecelia stood up on her chubby legs as she walked about the house at a year old. Her first words, "Let me in!," were spoken at a year old....

The final draft of the opening of a biography of a resident at the Bethany Home for senior citizens, by Audubon Elementary sixth-grade students Kayla Blocklinger and Ben Root, is accomplished after many revisions.

sixth graders to show compassion toward someone who usually went unbefriended. This incident was an example of the freedom of expression and willingness to share that filled the classroom that year. Intimacy and caring were part of the classroom culture. When there is this type of acceptance, children are free to take risks in their learning as well.

That writing assessment was a revelation to me not only because of what happened between those two boys. There was another Expeditionary Learning-related belief that came alive for me as well: "less is more." My fears about digging so deeply into this writing process rather than writing a wide variety of things over the course of the year were dispelled the very day of the benchmark writing test. When I gave the students the district writing assessment topic, "Something I Have Lost," we verbally brainstormed several possibilities together. But then I realized they were ready to fly on their own. They independently began webbing their own ideas, transferred them into well-constructed paragraphs, and topped the essays off with exemplary introductions and conclusions.

Why was I so amazed at the ease with which they tackled the task? After all, this process is exactly what they had done six times already this year in an effort to create something of quality for someone they cared about: brainstorm, web, and form organized paragraphs into meaningful "essays" called chapters, each of which had a catchy introduction and conclusion. The students had internalized a writing process which they had learned through a meaningful context. They were so prepared for this assignment that the random sampling of sixth graders from Audubon scored nearly twice as high as the district's sixth-grade average. To me, "less is more" means that if students deeply understand a concept or process, they will be able to apply their knowledge to other similar situations, pulling from their experiences and making connections in order to construct meaning. When they are asked to do a piece of persuasive writing or any other kind of writing we did not get to because we were busy with Bethany, they will be able to take what they know so well and apply it with a new twist. The basic tools of writing will be there.

As I reflect back upon what elements make this expedition so powerful, I believe it is primarily the students' concern for their residents that focus their learning and make them want to do such quality work. The more we talk about their residents, the more the students get excited about making great books for them. The process is rooted in revision, and the revision is inspired by their relationships with their residents. Students choose to revise text and redo illustrations. During Meg Campbell's visit, the students told her that "the work has to be good, because it is the story about someone's life." Their academics are grounded in meaningful service. Their residents are special people, for whom they want to make a special gift.

These special relationships instill in the children a joy of service, which becomes a chief motivator for the production of quality work. I had never in previous years seen students take such care in the writing process. The writing is more purposeful and important than any of my former students' writing assignments. The students show me that they care about their work by taking on a high level of ownership in the writing process. During each chapter's initial stage of developing inter-view questions, students collaborate with their own partners and among other partnerships to be absolutely sure they are asking good questions and not leaving out any important life events. Student pairs take it upon themselves to ask other groups, "Is there anything we're forgetting?" I do not have to go around to everyone and suggest that they expand upon their ideas because they are too busy going around and double checking for themselves. After interviews, when it is time to write the chapters, students put a lot of time and thought into how each sentence could most interestingly be phrased. I hear, "How about …" and "Or, maybe we could say…" and "Yeah, that sounds good, but instead of using the word 'happy,' let's say…"

Even at the end of the last Bethany year, when I thought we were ready to laminate the books, students were still making revisions voluntarily. I remember how Erica kept coming back to me at the last minute saying, "Mrs. Fordice, if it's not too late, let's take the other cover out of our file and put this one in for Ethel's book instead." The students work hard, collaborate, and go back to the drawing board after self-editing and peer- and teacher-student critique sessions. They understand the need to use time wisely, to learn from past mistakes, and to improve by using suggestions from others. At the beginning of the year, they get a lot of guidance in terms of self-assessment, peer critique, and the writing process. But as the year progresses, so does their level of independence in writing and their ability to assess their own progress.

I feel happy because I know the biography took a long time, and now, when it is finished, you see the final copy and you know it is the best that you can do. —Jennifer Meyer

I feel so relieved that the biography is done. Not that I didn't like the project but because we can look back at all the progress we made. —Jolene Thomas

Today was one of the best days for me. I overcame my fear of the biography being wrong and was very happy when there was only one mistake. On this very special day, I got to see some of Darlene's friends. Darlene gave us a kiss on the cheek and great big hugs for a job well done. —Mallory Munson

I think I have made a lot of progress throughout the year. I had a lot of fun. I wish that when I get older I will be able to do that and I will be able to tell the kids how I did the Bethany project. —Jolene Thomas

These reflections are a wonderful culminating assessment of the students' viewpoints about the importance and the quality of their work. The students knew they had done something very meaningful while they were learning.

The district writing benchmark test, coupled with the ongoing assessments throughout the year, provide evidence of successful learning. The multiple drafts show revision from draft to draft and increasing independence from chapter to chapter. The rubrics keep the students aware of expectations, and provide an opportunity to see growth over time. The students' reflections reveal a pride and an emotional engagement in their work.

SERVICE STRENGTHENS OUR CLASSROOM CULTURE

The atmosphere during a Bethany interview is very soft and caring. When the focus is on someone besides oneself, there is less of a need to put on false appearances. Often a sixth grader performs all sorts of acts to be accepted by his or her peers. At Bethany the only "images" the students need to present are kindness, gentleness, selflessness, and concern. The residents accept the students as they are, and the students respond to this with respect and appreciation. These qualities carry

This portrait, by sixth grader Kristi Morrison of Audubon Elementary School in Dubuque, Iowa, illustrated her biography of a senior citizen.

over to the classroom whenever we talk about Bethany Home and the residents. The students speak very tenderly as they share the progress of the biographies and what they experience at each interview. Parents tell us that their children's conversations about their Bethany partners are respectful and enthusiastic. The warmth of the student-resident encounters sifts into the classroom more and more as the year goes on.

The difference the service made in the community of our classroom became very clear to me during the year when we adapted the expedition and did not include the biography project. After doing the Bethany biography expedition for two years, Debi, the activities director at Bethany, thought it would be difficult to find enough willing and able residents to continue for another year. We agreed to take a break for a year, but keep our working relationship intact for the future.

Because we had so much success with the interviews and the book writing, we kept some parts of the expedition, but we changed much of it for the 1997–98 school year. Instead of interviewing retirement home residents and writing biographies, we interviewed long-time Dubuque residents about the impact of key twentieth century events on Dubuque's people and businesses. The final product was a beautiful decade-by-decade collection of vignettes and scanned photographs and artifacts from the interviewed Dubuque citizens. Each interviewed person received an impressive, laminated color copy of the book, and a copy was given to the public library.

However, the adaptation had less of an impact educationally and emotionally than the original biography expedition. Students did not have as much individual responsibility for quality work since the whole class was creating one collection. The vignettes did not provide the opportunity for quality writing, since they were only one to three paragraphs each. The time allowed in a trimester was not long enough to establish the depth of relationships found in the biography project. Although the students were well-mannered and appreciative, there was not as much substance to the expedition in terms of mutual sacrifice of time and energy. Though the adapted project had less of a long-term impact on the students, it did serve the purpose of bringing information from textbooks to life through people from our home town, and for this reason it was very worthwhile.

After "doing Bethany" for two years, the year without it was also different in terms of emotional depth. I missed the warmth that used to permeate class discussions as curricular concepts often pointed back to Bethany. During the non-Bethany year, when we talked about how our "adopted" trees at the neighborhood park were changing through their seasons of life, I found myself getting teary while my students looked at me with blank faces. Without the common experience of an ongoing significant relationship with an elderly person, our expedition was diluted, and so was the bond between students within the classroom. There was something about giving themselves to these elderly people that softened the students like putty and molded them into a caring community of learners. The service of being the only ones to preserve someone's life in written form was an awesome task that the students tackled with pride and passion.

Another key difference in the non-Bethany year was that our classroom community was not as wonderfully unified as during the Bethany expeditions. During Bethany we had common conversational topics, songs to sing, and rigorous (sometimes stressful) work that *lasted an entire year*. When the end of the year came during Bethany years, it was the climax rather than the relief. We were involved right to the end, and spent our last days wrapping gifts and practicing poetry and songs in anticipation of the final celebration. The students were comrades on a long voyage and could not wait for the end of the year—not to finally leave elementary school and get on to junior high, but to give away the biographies and celebrate their accomplishments.

Our biography presentation celebration of the 1997 Bethany project year was three days before the end of school. The second to the last day was "fun day" spent at a nearby park in organized competitive activities. Our class had a great feeling of unity that year, and when we won first place for sportsmanship, it seemed to be a final symbol of the spirit of oneness within our classroom community. Upon our return to school, Adam shouted, "This is the best way to end sixth grade! First Bethany, and then this! What an awesome year!"

The next day was the big graduation day. I had a hard time facing my students with dry eyes that morning, because the year had become so increasingly emotional and had just culminated in our Bethany celebration. Across the front of the gym stood rows and rows of folding

The Spring of Life

Alfred Koopman began life not knowing what challenges he would encounter, and what life would hold for him. He took life one day at a time and watched his story become authored.

Alfred Koopman's life began on a farm on Nov. 24, 1914. He was number four of eleven born to Albin and Lena Koopman. Alfred is a little brother to Edmund, Herbert, and Cletus and is a big brother to Elvina, Raymond, Helen, Gildagard, Mary, and Margaret. He was also a big brother to "Little" Rose who died at two months old.

Alfred had many celebrations in his life. One of the most important ceremonies was the sacrament of baptism. He was baptized into the Catholic faith as a baby.

Steve Leifker, a sixth-grade student at Audubon Elementary School in Dubuque, Iowa, completed this final draft of his biography of a resident at the Bethany Home for senior citizens.

chairs with a big string of reserved signs crossing the front row. About a half an hour before the ceremony, the guests of honor arrived. It took them a while to get from the curb outside to their seats, since many of them have wheelchairs, walkers, or canes, and those that still can manage without aids walk slowly and deliberately. But they came to see their young friends on their big day. They came to hear the students sing "Turn, Turn, Turn" one last time, and to see them get their certificate of promotion to junior high school. Every child being honored in the ceremony had written the life story of someone sitting in the front row or someone who could not attend but was there in spirit.

It was incredibly hard to say good-bye to my students that day. After the assembly and reception, one teacher came up to me and remarked, "What a huggy group!" It was obvious how close the students had become.

WHAT LIES AHEAD?

I cannot teach another year without deep service in an expedition. The difference in quality work, classroom unity, and emotional growth is so apparent to me. As Geri and I were closing down our classroom after the last day of school in 1998, we took time to reflect upon what was missing during this year without Bethany. We, as teachers, have been changed by the Bethany expedition. When we read a book about a relationship between a younger person and an older person, it affects us very deeply. We have begun to share reflections on what is really important in life. We buy each other books about growing older and elderly advice for happy living.

We struggle with the need to "take the time to smell the flowers" versus spending the extra time and great deal of energy it takes to do the Bethany project. However, we know that the substance, the depth, and the richness of the Bethany experience is something that we cannot let slip by when it is right there at our fingertips.

There will be some changes as we venture back into the biography expedition. In our first year of the Bethany project, we managed to complete the expedition on a shoestring budget. We borrowed tape recorders from other classrooms and used four old computers for fifty students. In 1996, however, the Bethany biography expedition was awarded first place in a national "Educators Unsung Heroes Awards" program, receiving $27,000 to enhance the project. Northern Life Insurance, the company which sponsors the grant program, awarded Audubon $2,000 for a semifinal placement, and the grand prize of $25,000 for winning first place. The grant has allowed us to greatly improve the quality of the books, decrease our student/computer ratio, and expand the project to include other intergenerational activities.

Some of the ideas we have for the future will be supported by the grant, but many do not require additional resources. For instance, we are looking at the possibility of working with other nursing or retirement homes in order to ease Debi's burden and to avoid repeating the project with the same residents. Geri and I need to better schedule the use of computer time. Reading exemplary biographies would deepen the literacy work and set professional standards and expectations. Sharing copies of the novels which the students read with the residents would also open up new possibilities. The students could use E-mail, letter-writing, and conversations to talk about the novels with the residents. As an extension of this, we plan to deepen students' technology skills by allowing them to teach the residents how to use software and E-mail. We will also encourage residents' families to submit pictures and memories through E-mail or letters to add to the biographies. The tasks are a bit overwhelming, but the possibilities are endless and exciting.

As we prepare for another year of the biography expedition, I anticipate a lot of hard work and difficult challenges, but I know that the fruits of our labors will be the growth of rich relationships as we cultivate our academic skills. Teaching and learning become even more special when the focus is on a rigorous project that deeply benefits others. Service provides an authentic reason and desire to improve, to care, to give, and to connect. These are the qualities that educators desire to instill in their students. These are the qualities that we as a society need to find in ourselves and give to our children.

"What Can We Do About It?"
Busing Ends in Denver

Sally Carey

It was the end of January when I asked my seventh-grade students to raise their hands if they rode the bus to school. More than a third of the class responded. When I told them that this, Hill Middle School, would not be their school next year, they were shocked.

"What do you mean?" they demanded. I asked if they had heard or read that the Denver court order on busing for integration had been recently lifted. Most of the students, along with their brothers and sisters, have been going to the same schools their parents, aunts, and uncles had attended. They did not know those schools were determined by their address, race, and a long-standing order of the court. The pandemonium that followed was fueled by rapid-fire questions:

"How could they do that?"

"Why did they do that?"

"Who decided that?"

"Can they make us?" As this reality began to take shape in their minds, impassioned responses flew around the room.

"That's the stupidest thing I've ever heard, busing kids because of their skin color!"

"It's unfair!" It was clear there was a whole lot we needed to find out about this court order and the impending change. The students knew their future depended on it.

Our team of seventh-grade teachers recognized that this was a once-in-a-lifetime learning opportunity. Our school district was facing the end of twenty-one years of court-ordered busing. This change was a rich and deep topic to explore. However, as the two core team teachers and I began developing the service learning expedition for the year, we realized it did not fit into the planned curriculum. At the same time, we believed this sweeping change was too compelling to ignore. So we changed our tack. We began to look for ways we could address district standards through a learning expedition that centered on this historic transition. The standards turned out to be the foundation for the academic integrity of the unit. As we posed possible guiding questions, identified learning and service goals, and came up with specific activities, the list of relevant standards and disciplines grew. Our excitement and enthusiasm grew as well.

As staff members planning this expedition, we felt it was important for the students to have ownership of the service to be done. I knew from past service learning projects that the more students are involved in the decision-making steps of identifying real needs and selecting options for action, the more students invest themselves in the work and learning needed to accomplish their goals. We had selected the topic not only for its historic relevance but also for its appeal to students, knowing they would be compelled to act on their own behalf. Had this not been the case, their involvement in identifying an issue to take on would have been more crucial. In spite of our motivations, we still worried that allowing the students to identify and develop their own projects would be chaotic and out of control. Because this open-ended approach felt impossible to plan for, we decided students would have to develop written plans for what they wanted to do. Each team would be very clear about the nature of its project, the reasoning behind it, and its action plan. This became part of our security blanket, along with several core curricular products that satisfied the academic needs of the unit and allayed most of our fears.

As teachers our share of the initial groundwork included finding opportunities for students to assist in the transition back to neighborhood schools. We contacted the school district's planning and secondary school departments to ask how they planned to facilitate the transition. We discovered they were going to mail an information packet to parents in February that included new boundary maps, explanations of options and deadlines, and school assignments. We knew there was plenty of room for other things to be done.

Almost two-thirds of the students at Hill Middle School, located in East Central Denver, are bused in from several satellite neighborhoods in East Denver, including the majority of the Latino students in the bilingual program. Hearing-impaired students from around the city are also bused in to a magnet program housed at Hill. The school itself is organized into "houses" or teams, each of which has a distinct philosophy and shares a core team of teachers. Although Hill is not officially an Expeditionary Learning school, our team, Team Quest, participates in Expeditionary Learning professional development and implements many of the core practices and design principles. The thirty students in each of the two Team Quest seventh-grade classes reflected the ethnic mix of the school, one-third each Latino, African American, and Anglo. They also reflected the academic mix of abilities and included several hearing-impaired students. We had no idea how many students rode the bus to school, but we knew the number would be significant.

Armed with an expedition plan that included students doing a research paper (one of the requirements for the year), conducting a survey, and developing service projects based on the results, we set a course. We had carefully planned the expedition so that it would meet six language arts, three math, two history, and two geography standards. Brimming with excitement and trepidation, we sailed into the maelstrom of student-driven learning.

After our initial conversation when the students discovered that they would be profoundly affected by the end of busing, they were ready to dig in. In the following two weeks, the two classes learned research skills, including taking notes from texts and oral presentations. They began researching busing on the Internet, through the city's computerized data base, and at the school's library. They read and discussed Brown versus the Board of Education. The staff found sets of new and old school boundary maps and copies of a booklet published by the League of Women Voters of Denver explaining the court-ordered desegregation of Denver Public Schools. The students read and discussed parts of the booklet together in class and finished reading it on their own.

The booklet's principal author happened to be a current school board member. We invited her to meet with the class to discuss the booklet and talk about busing in Denver. This was a great opportunity for the students to ask questions about desegregation based on their own findings and reflections. One question in particular stands out for me. With all the innocence that only a fresh look at the data could express, Tamika wanted to know, "Why, after all this busing for equal opportunity, did the African American students not do any better with their test scores?"

For homework during this time, students interviewed community members, family, and neighbors for information, recollections, and feelings about the court order, its effects, and now its reversal. They decided whom they wanted to interview, but they were required to take notes from at least three interviews. The object was to gather and share a variety of points of view on court-ordered busing. Every day, it seemed, someone would rush into class excitedly waving some document or story regarding desegregation. As the discoverers summarized and shared their findings with the class, the students would discuss how each new piece fit in their puzzle. When Ronald, usually a quiet nonparticipator, came in shouting, "Look what I got! Look what I got!" while waving a copy of the original court order for Denver, we knew these students saw themselves as the leaders.

We spent several days guiding brainstorming sessions to explore the changes that might come with the return of students to their neighborhood schools. This challenged the students to make predictions based on their diverse array of information and perspectives. Asking them,

"How will this affect you, your family, your school, the whole community?" added several dimensions for consideration. As possibilities emerged, the personal implications focused their thinking. They looked around the classroom and realized that they would not be seeing each other next year. These two classes had formed a team in the sixth grade and continued together into the seventh. They were not just any random group, they were Team Quest.

"What about our teachers? They won't know us or what we can do, like they do here."

"What about the kind of work we do? Do any of these other schools have teams like ours?"

"I was planning on taking a computer elective next year. What if my new school doesn't offer it? What if they don't have a computer lab? Is that fair?"

"Will Hill still have shop classes?"

"How will I see my friends when we only can see each other here at school?" Suddenly, changes in demographics had translated into changes in staffing, resources, programs, electives, after-school activities, and friendships.

We began to create a list of issues that concerned them. That was easy. When I asked them, "Now, what do you want to do about it?" the class became suddenly quiet.

"What do you mean, Ms. Carey? What *can* we do about it?" a few students ventured.

The policies, procedures and personnel involved in district and school governance sprang to life as we discussed how these decisions get made. Although there is a student position on each of the middle schools' site-governance committees, these positions remain largely unfilled.

"Can we represent what kids want without being elected? Can we do that?" they wanted to know.

"Why not?" I asked. This was clearly new territory for them.

"Do you have to be elected or asked for your opinion before you can offer it?" This was beginning to sound more possible.

"Maybe we can't vote," Hisam volunteered, "but we can go and tell them what we want."

"Yeah, let's do that!" a swell of voices concurred. They definitely wanted to help shape their futures.

"Okay," I said, navigating this rising wave of excitement. "Is there anyone besides our school who should know what electives and after-school activities you want?" Silence. "What about the schools you may be going to? Does that matter?" The scope of this change hit them again in a very concrete way. We listed the six other middle schools they would be reassigned to. Additionally, I pointed out, students will now be able to choose to attend any of the district's twenty middle schools. Everyone agreed that it would take too much time to get around to all of those, but perhaps they could inform the district's school board in order to reach a bigger audience. Considering this, they were able to focus the scope of their input.

Next we helped the students conduct a survey. This was a critical piece we hoped would deepen and broaden the curricular content. A few selected questions worked their magic. I asked them who they would want to speak for. As a class, they numbered thirty. As a team, there were sixty of them. "How many sixth and seventh graders are there in the school?" I asked.

"About six hundred," someone guessed.

"That's right. So who would have the biggest impact, sixty students or six hundred?" The need for a survey became clear.

We continued into week three designing, testing, and making plans to conduct a one-page survey. In order to construct a survey, we relied on the K.I.S.S.—Keep It Short and Simple—formula. Generating the survey questions involved narrowing the scope of information the students thought was pertinent. We started with their list of concerns created from our brainstorming sessions. The survey gradually narrowed its focus (to keep it to one page) to what students would want to know about their new schools and questions regarding students' preferences for a variety of electives and after-school activities. We worked on finding the right phrasing to elicit that information consistently. This crafting process also involved a discussion on the kinds of questions we wanted to use and how to respond—yes/no, circle a choice, or fill in a response.

Through this process, students continued to refine their thinking about what they wanted to know and why. The class persisted in this task because they realized how their choices of words and questions would influence the results. They also knew that these results would be used to make their wishes known with school administrators who would be making decisions regarding *their* future. The stakes were very real and personal. It took several days of discussion and group work to come up with a first draft.

The students "field-tested" the survey on a small group of students who had been absent earlier. The testing was an important step, because it revealed some ambiguity in the phrasing of a few questions and a couple of misspellings not previously caught. After minor revisions, the survey was ready to go. Several students translated the survey into Spanish so that the bilingual classes could be represented. Some students who were ahead in their work typed and retyped the survey as it went through revisions, then made all the necessary copies.

For the surveying itself, the students constructed a schedule of classes, times, and teams involved. The Quest teachers had already circulated a memo to the other staff explaining the project and asking their permission for Quest students to come in and conduct their survey. This important courtesy helped pave the way for students' actions. Only the classes in which teachers responded positively— about 90 percent—were surveyed.

The students' energy and attention began to build daily as we brainstormed possible projects to assist in the transition to neighborhood schools. These ideas ranged from the ambitious—filming a video for prospective students—to the practical—presenting student preferences for electives and after-school activities to school administrators. Each day we increasingly felt the need for the survey data to guide us.

Students formed project teams, including those who would meet with the twenty-two sixth- and seventh-grade classes who agreed to be surveyed. The surveying itself began to present a challenge.

"What are we gonna say?" Peter wanted to know. "How do we explain this survey and make sure they fill it out right?" It was a good thing they had just finished a drama unit that included script writing.

Putting those skills to work, they crafted scripts and rehearsed. Once they had a polished presentation, they were ready to begin the survey.

We packed a lot into the two forty-five-minute periods each Quest Team class had blocked together every day. At times it seemed chaotic with six groups going in different directions, but they all were focused on planning what they needed to get done. By the end of the week, over five hundred students had filled out surveys, and the next challenge presented itself.

At this point, a new long-term substitute, Amy Parker, joined us as the math/science team member for this two-person core team. As she recalls, "I walked into the class for the first time and was immediately besieged by students begging for help in compiling their surveys and using percentages and graphs to represent their results!" Right away, math classes got busy with the calculations and discussions necessary to analyze survey data. This also allowed for an additional block of time, the ninety-minute math/science period, for students to work on the busing project.

"Can you believe this?" an astonished Courtney exclaimed waving a paper filled with computations. "Most of the kids in over half the classes we surveyed don't know what school is their home school for next year!"

"Somebody should tell them," a classmate replied.

"Hey, we could do that!" piped in a voice suddenly filled with inspiration. Another service learning project sprang to life.

Week five brought a blizzard of activity. During language arts/social studies, students worked with their self-selected teams developing detailed plans for one of the class projects. Some teams worked on understanding the new boundary maps and application process for selecting a school of choice in order to inform other students of their options. Seven teams contacted the schools Hill students would be attending next year and set up after-school meetings with the principals or assistant principals. Hill staff provided the transportation, but the sessions, which were planned and rehearsed ahead of time, were conducted entirely by the students. In these meetings students presented the survey results regarding the electives and after-school activities

A Framework to Organize Your Project
Taking Action

1. What action are you now going to take?

I will call the assistant principal at Gove Middle School to make an appointment and share the needs and concerns of Hill students going to Gove.

I will also present the graphs and surveys to the school board and Collaborative Decision-Making Committee.

2. Why is it important for *you* to take this action?

It is important for me to meet the assistant principal because Gove may be able to help with the concerns and needs for new students, and knowing about their schools will make them more comfortable.

Presenting to the school board and CDM will show how changing school boundaries will affect many students and their families.

3. What satisfaction do *you* hope to get from doing this?

I'm concerned about the concerns of students and I want to make them feel more comfortable about going to another school. I'm also hoping to get a good grade.

4. Describe your action plan.

—call assistant principal and ask for appointment
—think up questions and concerns of students
—bring our graphs, surveys, and brochures
—go to the school
—talk with assistant principal
—share the information we have with Hill students
—finish graphs
—review all the information we will be presenting
—know my parts.

Xi Wang, a seventh grader at Hill Middle School in Denver, wrote this action plan to focus her efforts to help students make the transition from busing to neighborhood schools.

students wanted, broken down by grade level and type of class (bilingual or not). The results also included requests for information students wanted to know ahead of time about their new school, such as schedules, rules, dress codes, class teams, etc. Other teams were working on a video tour of the school and an informational brochure from the students' point of view. Another team decided to tackle transportation concerns. School choice was an option for those who could provide their own transportation to and from school. The Quest students realized that this in itself raised equity issues and wanted to discuss bus fees, schedules, and routes with the Regional Transportation District officials.

In math students translated raw data into percentages, then fractions and back again. They discussed statistical significance, analyzed survey results, and plotted charts and graphs representing the data on the computer.

During this time students had multiple opportunities to receive feedback on their work. They turned in their notes, plans, phone contacts, reflections, scripts, etc. on a weekly basis. This helped keep them accountable for their progress and offered a vehicle for focused feedback from teachers. They wrote reflections about what they planned to do and the specific steps involved, and also why this action was important to them. There were verbal check-ins daily and lots of ongoing troubleshooting, but in a hectic atmosphere it was helpful to structure the more concrete feedback sessions as well. Students also received immediate feedback from staff and classmates who observed rehearsals or read over plans. The groups who were making presentations to other schools found great comfort in having a rehearsed script to help them with their nervousness, and the feedback from others helped them to anticipate and prepare for any questions that might be asked.

"Boy, that was harder than I thought it would be," Nick exclaimed, returning from another class where he and a partner tried to explain the new boundary maps. "We had to actually go kid by kid through the whole class to help them find on the map where they live and what their new school is."

"Yeah, and the kids wouldn't listen at the same time so I had to repeat the directions for the survey over and over again!" an incredu-

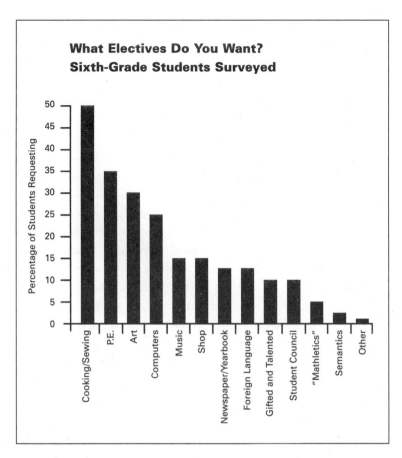

What Electives Do You Want?
Sixth-Grade Students Surveyed

This graph, prepared by seventh graders Stacy Allen, Hisam Derani, Charles Silverman, and Xi Wang, illustrates the electives sixth graders at Hill Middle School hope to have in their new schools once busing ends and students are assigned to neighborhood schools.

lous teammate added. It was exciting to hear the feedback of the groups as they reported on the success of their missions. Other groups listened and made adjustments in their plans.

José, a very quiet student, was visibly nervous on the ride over to the middle school where he and a partner were meeting with the assistant principal. But on the way back he kept repeating, "Did you hear what she said? She said it was important information and we explained it very well! Did I do good, Ms. Carey? I think I did great! I can't believe I did it!"

At the beginning of March a Quest team selected by the teacher made their presentation of survey results to the Denver Board of Education. This was the best way, the students reasoned, they could have input to other schools, the superintendent, and board without going through multiple meetings. They had a lot of rehearsal and practice, having just met with Hill's governance body, the Collaborative Decision-Making Committee, which would make decisions about what electives to keep, staffing, and other programming issues. But the level of nervousness rose in relation to the importance of the audience.

The night of the presentation students passed out packets of survey data to each board member. The four students took their turns at the podium. Charlie explained the reasons for doing the survey. Xi gave the background information on court-ordered busing that they had researched. Hisam and Stacy presented the data that had been organized by grade level and graphed using the computer. After answering questions, the students were thanked by board members for their excellent presentation. One board member exclaimed how useful the students' work would be because the data they had gathered was exactly what the Mayor's City Schools Coordinating Commission was looking for.

"We'd like it if you could present this to them at their next meeting in early April," the board member requested. There was no doubt about the success and importance of the students' work. We all basked in the glow of recognition for work well done.

With spring break beginning in two weeks, it was time to wrap up the projects. The video group learned that although they persisted, their goal of a polished piece was unrealistic within the time available. The brochure group had also floundered, with complications of their own doing. While others were basking in the glow of their successes, the members of the video and brochure groups were uncharacteristically quiet. All students evaluated their own work and accomplishments and were also graded by the teacher. Charlie's final reflection seemed to sum up the impact and feeling of the whole group. "Nothing [in the project] would be eliminated, if it were up to me. I think that we got some administrators to listen to us and take our suggestions seriously. It [the transition] will now be easier for all us students."

We, the staff, had learned a few things also. When students are inspired, they will go the distance to learn what they need to know to get the job done. The more real the work is to them, and the more important the outcome, the more they will do to ensure it is done right. The groups who made presentations to others—administrators or fellow students—were especially successful in the quality and completion of their projects.

As the focus of school work shifted to writing research papers about busing and desegregation, the students turned to the gold mine of skills and information they had accumulated through the expedition. Court-ordered desegregation and its reversal and impact were now deeply personal. All that these students, team members, and citizens learned would be lessons for a lifetime.

DO A GREATER DEED

Michelle Brantley

At Middle College High School in Memphis, Tennessee, students are charged to "do a greater deed" with what they have learned. Although important, it is not enough for students to simply master a subject or concept. Students are given a more empowering challenge through their expeditions; they try to find ways to positively change and affect the lives of others with what they know.

Students in Florence Roach's personal-computing classes set out on a journey exploring the myriad personal and professional uses of computers. The students learned functions ranging from word processing and spreadsheets to the basic navigation of hardware. Through portions of their research conducted by survey, these students found that many people in their communities and families were not computer literate. Taking on the challenge of "doing a greater deed" with what they had learned, students at Middle College turned their classroom into an after-school computer learning lab.

Every Monday evening for a month, parents and other friends of the community gathered after work from 6 to 8 p.m. to learn basic computing skills. The students took full responsibility in organizing, publicizing, and staffing the sessions each week. At the end of the sessions, the participants were given certificates for their hard work and participation. Both parents and students were proud of their accomplishments.

In another act of service, students in a performing arts class at Middle College used their talents to offer young girls in a local Girl Scout troop messages of hope and self-esteem. Using the dramatic arts, students cowrote and directed three skits which primarily focused on resisting peer pressure and learning to love and accept one's self. The students created multiple drafts of their skits and their peers critiqued them to ensure that the performances would be interesting as well as relevant. After the performances, the audience was given the opportunity to talk candidly about the issues during a structured debriefing that was also organized and facilitated by the performing arts students.

Whether through the practical skills gained from computers or the valuable lessons learned by sharing stories, students are proactive in passing on the knowledge they have gained in hopes of benefiting the lives of others. These are just a few examples of how students are taking responsibility, not only for what they are learning, but for what others learn as well.

Tuskegee Airmen
Touch Down in Dubuque

John Adelmann

I will always remember the day when Drew, a high school sopho-
more, gave a noontime address to the Rotary Club in Dubuque, Iowa.
There he stood at the podium, resplendent in his black hobnailed boots
and jeans, a black *Rage Against the Machine* T-shirt, with a lock of
blonde hair dyed green sneaking out from under his cap worn backwards with the word "Rancid" sewn on it. Drew was there to answer
questions posed to him by the local Rotarians about the Tuskegee
Airmen research project his class was working on, and to raise civic and
financial support for the effort. The Rotary president phoned me the
very next day and brushed aside my attempted apology for the featured
speaker's sartorial splendor by saying, "John, it was good for some of
our members to see Drew, just like that, and hear the knowledge he was
able to present. Sometimes you just have to look past the outer appearance and understand that these kids want to be a part of the community as well. We were all very impressed with your presentation, and we
want the students to come back when this project is over to tell us how
things went."

What follows is an account of how an academically oriented service project accomplished far more than most people ever would have thought possible. What follows is a chronicle of how a class of at-risk high school students and a group of aging veterans of World War II came together in the spring of 1998 to celebrate the Airmen's accomplishments, and made some history of their own in the process. What follows is a true story of how an audacious dream became a thrilling reality.

This expedition began with a personal phone call in June, 1997. Having visited the United States Air Force Museum in Dayton, Ohio several years ago, I thought it the appropriate place to continue my research of the famous all-Black Air Force pilots of World War II, the Tuskegee Airmen. Until now, this inspiring story of men who overcame institutional prejudice and established a remarkable war combat record has been woefully underreported; our school district's history textbook mentions nothing about the U. S. Army Air Corps cadets of World War II. From my own learning, I knew the Airmen persevered in an era when Blacks were deemed incapable of operating front-line aircraft. Their determination to learn how to fly and to fight for their country during World War II, if only to prove they had the capacity and the willingness to do so, has become the stuff of legend.

In 1944, when the all-Black 332nd Fighter Group finally was assigned escort duty to protect the 15th Air Force bomber crews who flew the deadly skies of Europe and the Mediterranean, they knew they had "arrived." In reading the stirring accounts of bomber crews who were escorted by the men of the 332nd, I learned that the Tuskegee Airmen quickly developed a respected reputation in the U. S. Army Air Corps for always being on time and in the best flying position to protect the bombers. In over 15,000 individual combat missions, the Airmen never lost one American bomber to enemy aircraft. That combat record stands to this day. Several Airmen even sank a German destroyer using only their wing-mounted machine guns, an unprecedented wartime feat. In addition, 450 Airmen earned over 850 air medals and other citations for combat bravery and leadership. These men and the contribution they made to the war effort certainly deserved more attention.

Through my own research and long-time interest in military aviation, I learned that the organization known as the Confederate Air Force (CAF) worked to preserve the nation's military aviation history by salvaging famous aircraft. I also learned that the CAF's Southern Minnesota Wing was in the process of restoring a rare North American P-51C Mustang, the kind of plane the Tuskegee Airmen flew during the war. There were only four of these aircraft left in existence. The CAF's Red Tail Project had set a goal of restoring the Mustang and getting it into operational status; the project would take several years and cost nearly $450,000. When complete, *Skipper's Darlin'* would take its place with the other Confederate Air Force aircraft and become a flying tribute to the brave men of the 332nd Fighter Group who fought for democracy and freedom at home and abroad.

The deeper I got into the material, and the more contacts I made, I began to recognize the incredible potential for developing a class research project with a service opportunity directly connected to the topic they would be studying. Students could conduct research and compile it into a book, and with their new-found knowledge they could enlighten the public and garner support to raise money for the Red Tail Project. Maybe, just maybe, I thought, we could actually invite some Airmen to come to Dubuque. The fact that no one had ever done anything like this was all the more reason to try it.

I have always been a firm believer in having our at-risk population work with and learn from local citizens, and then give something back to the community in the form of a book, a presentation, or a performance-based project. I know that once the students realize their audience would be someone other than myself, they will most likely become motivated to do their best work. Already my students of years past had published their findings and given presentations to local college and traditional high school history classes. With this experience under my belt, I *knew* that we could pull off this Tuskegee research project, too. All I had to do now was convince the latest crop of at-risk youth that *they* could do it.

From an English teacher's standpoint, this project would open up several opportunities for the students to "go public" with their work, a powerful motivator in its own right. Eventually, students would write, critique, and revise speeches. They would write business letters soliciting corporate support that would be judged by their ability to get the point across effectively. They would generate historical-research papers that would be refined, edited, and submitted for publication. And of course, thank-you letters would be required as a matter of courtesy and propriety. In short, every single piece of historical research and writing required by this class would have a real audience and a real purpose. This was no longer a sterile English course, where grammar lessons are taught in a vacuum. Nor was it a stultifying American history class, where countless names and dates are learned by rote. This was American history and English coming together for a real-world assignment: to learn about the Tuskegee Airmen and tell their story to the world.

THE IOWA CONNECTION

When school began at Central Alternative High in August, 1997, the class was scheduled to meet for a two-period block for nine weeks. Called the "Tuskegee Airmen Research Project," it was offered for one history credit. Students could stay with the group for the second quarter, or move on. I realized that the project would extend into the third quarter as well, to coincide with a nebulous idea of staging a public seminar in February, the culmination of the entire project. Without trying to pin me down for all the particulars at this stage, the Central staff gave me the latitude I needed to get the job done.

The HBO movie, *The Tuskegee Airmen,* proved to be an effective tool to help the students begin to learn about the obstacles these men overcame, but it paled in comparison to the personal contacts I had made doing my own research and speaking with Tuskegee Airmen over the phone. The film was based on a true story, but the characters were composites with fictitious names; I had to find a way to make these individuals come alive for the class. When Colonel Wofford, a former Airman I had met the past summer, sent us a list of twenty-five names and phone numbers, we were on our way. The one problem we faced, however, was that none of the names on the list were local folks. At least that is what I thought. But the Colonel had done his homework. "Work for the Iowa connection," he had told me over the summer. I smiled and nodded, even though I did not really understand what he meant—until I got his letter.

The list had names, phone numbers, and a brief description of each Airman. Colonel Wofford added that he had already called and written to everyone on this list, encouraging them to help us in any way possible. The students now saw that these were actual men who were still very much alive and well, and were only too happy to help us. The students recognized that they would soon be learning about history from the men who had made it.

Almost as soon as I announced the arrival of Colonel Wofford's letter, Tony, a senior, set himself to correspond with everyone on the list. He had no prior knowledge of the Airmen, but he instantly saw the wisdom in contacting each Airman personally, to get their individual perspectives. As a class we discussed questions that might be included in a good questionnaire. Before long, Tony got the idea. He proceeded to create a standardized, detailed questionnaire and a personal cover letter for each Airman. Eventually, he would quickly stick his head in the room for attendance, and then disappear. He typically spent the entire two-period classes in the learning center, hunched over the computer, typing away, crafting his questionnaire.

When I asked the students what they thought about inviting a few Airmen to town, no one said it was a *bad* idea, but everyone had at least one question and were not shy about asking it. Would they even want to come? After all, most of these veterans were in their seventies. What would they do when they got here? What if Dubuque weather in February was bad? While they did not say anything at the time, several students later confided that they thought I was nuts, that this would never happen. "So where are these guys going to stay?" "How much is all this going to cost?" "How are we going to raise money?" For a small school such as ours, fund-raising was always a challenge. I translated student questions into project assignments. Since everyone was suddenly concerned with where the Airmen might stay, and how much that would cost, the first assignment was to research lodging and accommodations.

Christina said she would be willing to write letters to local motels, but she did not know how to construct a business letter, nor did she know all the names and addresses of the local establishments. But now there was a reason to learn how to create a persuasive letter, and to make it look just right. After all, she reasoned, the motel operators would not think much of us unless we followed the right format and had all the words spelled correctly.

After considerable thought, I assigned myself the task of calling some Airmen and inviting them to Dubuque. At this stage, I felt I had the best overview of the project, and did not want to have the Airmen decline to participate simply because a student could not answer all their questions over the phone. At the top of the list was Airman Lee Archer, who unofficially was credited with shooting down five enemy aircraft in the Mediterranean Theater of Operations. He had earned the coveted title of "Ace," along with the Distinguished Flying Cross and sixteen Oak Clusters, and had flown 169 combat missions. (Fifty was the average number for White pilots, after which they would be reassigned to less hazardous duty.) The official record reads only four and one-half enemy kills, perhaps a nagging reminder of the 1925 pseudoscientific War College Report that erroneously concluded that Blacks did not have what it took to become an "Ace," let alone operate or maintain complicated frontline military aircraft.

When I finally reached Lee in New Rochelle, New York, I hemmed and hawed, and then finally asked the big question: if we paid his expenses, would he be willing to join us for a seminar in Dubuque in February? Through the receiver I heard Lee thumb through his calendar as we talked about the Yankees, and then he said enthusiastically, "Yes, the 23rd of February is open. I'll pencil you in right now." When I hung up the phone I sat down and cried. There was no other way to express my emotions. Not only did I just talk to one of the men about whom I had read so much in doing my own research on the Airmen, but he had just agreed to be a part of our project, whatever it was going to be! The next phone call held an even bigger surprise. Alongside the name of Tuskegee Airman Robert Martin of Chicago, Colonel Wofford had typed the three-word phrase, "Dubuque school system." I did not think much about it. Over the years, the city's ethnic mix had not included many African Americans; I simply could not imagine a Tuskegee Airman connection to Dubuque, directly or indirectly.

When Bob Martin came on the line, he exclaimed, "Oh, yes, John, Ken told me all about your project. I think it's just wonderful. How can I help?" I asked him what the cryptic "Dubuque school system" meant. "Why, I attended Lincoln Elementary, Washington Junior High, and I graduated from Dubuque Senior High School in 1936," he replied. I almost dropped the phone. "I was born in Dubuque, and my father was a podiatrist." Here was our Dubuque connection to the Tuskegee Airmen and to American history. Bob said he would be only too happy to join us.

Another name on the Wofford list was Airman Joe Gomer, who grew up in Iowa Falls, Iowa and was now living in Duluth. He agreed to join us, too, and cracked, "As long as you have something for me to do. I don't want to be sitting in my hotel room all day!" Airman Luther Smith, whose mother was a native Dubuquer(!), resided in Des Moines when the war broke out; these days he lived not far away in Pennsylvania. When I told him the local chapter of the Experimental Aircraft Association may afford him the opportunity to take a ride in a restored AT-6 trainer like the Airmen trained in, he responded, "Well, you won't have to ask me twice!" The genius of Colonel Wofford's "Iowa connection" had become apparent. For good measure, we also invited Red Tail Project director Colonel John Schuck and his wife, Diane. Everyone was eager to join us, even if no one knew in September what in the world we would be doing in less than six months. *But they were coming!*

When I told the class that four Airmen had agreed to be with us in February, their initial response was inversely proportional to my personal enthusiasm. Maybe because in September, February seemed so far away. Maybe because it was all too good to be true. But, I thought, so what? We can still get going on other things. Once the students got their heads into this research, invariably they would run across the names of Archer, Martin, Smith, and Gomer. *Then* the fun would begin.

After watching *The Tuskegee Airmen* movie and discussing its significance, the classroom became a beehive of activity. Students were beginning to make surprising connections between the Airmen and what they already knew about the World War II era.

"Weren't we fighting against Hitler because of his racist policies towards the Jews?" asked Russ.

"Yes," I responded. "The belief that some individuals were inferior led to the creation of Nazi extermination camps."

"But we were being racist against Black people in America at the same time," Russ shot back. "I think we need to write about that, too. You know, compare Hitler's views and ours. Maybe we were just as guilty."

"Good idea," I responded. "We will turn that research paper into a chapter in our book." Comments and questions generated more comments and questions.

C. J. groused, "Why did they call themselves 'Tuskegee Airmen'?" I pointed him to some reference material in the learning center on Booker T. Washington and Tuskegee Institute, and suggested he begin his research there.

"I think we need to know about what the Airmen thought about being discriminated against, and why they would want to fight for a country that didn't support them," Joey piped up. I told him that he should confer with his research buddy Tony right away and make sure those kinds of questions were included in the questionnaire that soon would be mailed out.

"Were there any women pilots in those days?" asked Emily. My personal study had revealed that Bessie Coleman was a dynamic Black aviator in the 1920s. Even though Bessie had no direct relation to the Airmen, Emily "found" her topic and never looked back. When I challenged her to see if a connection could be made to the Airmen, she concluded that Bessie could have been a role model for the Black youth of that day and for the future cadets of Tuskegee. Therefore, she should be in our book. Go for it, I told her.

SOMETHING TO PROVE

One day during class I passed around the photos I took of the P-51C Mustang being restored in Minneapolis. I also "introduced" the students to Colonel Wofford and John Schuck. "What's the Confederate Air Force?" sniffed Kenny. "How do they get the money to do this stuff? Who gets to fly the planes when they're completed? How much does it cost to fly these planes they restore? Where do they get spare parts from? Where do they keep the planes? Who owns them when they're restored?" I didn't exactly know those answers, I told him, but if he would write down all the questions he could think of and send them off to the Confederate Air Force Headquarters in Midland, Texas, they might just respond. He did and they did. The information Kenny received and interpreted became the basis of a chapter of the research book on the Confederate Air Force. More connections were being made. The momentum was building.

As soon as Christina sent her business letters, the issue of how to pay for airfares and accommodations temporarily fell by the wayside. But still there was activity aplenty. By now, some students were carefully studying several video tapes on the Airmen, including *Wings for This Man,* the U. S. Army Air Corps' official account of the Tuskegee story, narrated by Ronald Reagan. Others were reading and learning from the Airmen's responses to Tony's survey. And still others were developing their own historical sketches on topics such as race relations in the United States before World War II, or writing reflective pieces on what it was like to give a speech in front of a large audience. In order for them to raise funds, I figured, the students would really have to know what they were talking about first. Study now. Raise money later.

The Dubuque chapter of the Experimental Aircraft Association (EAA) is comprised of commercial and military flying enthusiasts. Many chapters, including Dubuque's, sponsor a special activity called "The Young Eagles Program." They strive to provide free opportunities for two million young people to experience the exhilaration of flight by the year 2000. The "no cost" part of the deal particularly appealed to me. I made a few inquiries in mid-November, and announced one day in class that whenever weekend atmospheric conditions were right, there would be an opportunity for any and all takers to ride in a real plane, courtesy of the Dubuque EAA. Four brave souls stepped forward, and soon became the Weather Channel's biggest fans.

By this time, most of the students were taking the research project very seriously, and could carry on a pretty sophisticated conversation about what they had learned and internalized: who the Tuskegee Airmen were; what they had to face; what this project was all about. But you really cannot learn about flying by reading a book, or even by watching vintage World War II gun camera footage. You have to strap yourself into a plane, taxi down the runway, and let aerodynamics do the rest.

On a cold, crisp, and spectacularly clear December Sunday afternoon, the students gathered at the airport to wait for their flight. A local newspaper reporter and photographer arrived to learn their story. We all sat down, and after the reporter posed her first question, I excused myself and left her with the students. When I returned, the researchers/budding conversationalists were still at it, occasionally glancing out the window to see if the plane they would be flying had returned yet. The reporter was writing furiously. This story would not suffer from lack of information, I thought.

When the Monday morning edition of the Dubuque *Telegraph Herald* arrived, there—on the front page, no less—was a color photo of a Central student, Jamaica, and her buddies in the cockpit of a Cessna 150 with their headsets on, looking like they owned the airport. The headline read, "Central students identify with Airmen." The students were now telling the story on their own, and the article was replete with great quotations. An interesting parallel between the military's perceptions of the Airmen fifty years ago and the public's impression of alternative students today was not lost on Drew: "These guys had something to prove. The world didn't believe that Black men could fly planes, let alone protect bombers. Sometimes it feels like we have something to prove, too, just because we go to Central. Some people think we're lazy and won't ever make anything of ourselves." (Being an alternative high school for "at-risk" students, the public's misconceptions of our hallowed institution were considerable.) Anthony added, "Yeah, these men had to fight to fight. They were fighting to stop oppression over there, but they were still oppressed over here."

It was obvious that the students were now personally identifying with the Airmen, but equally interesting was the fact that American history was finally coming to life for them. Copilot Jamaica expanded the scope of the conversation with the reporter and said, "When you're up there in the plane, you're going 150 mph, but it feels like 10. The pilots in the P-51s went about 375 mph. I have so many things I want to ask the Airmen." Sarah put the whole day in perspective: "When you think of history, you think of dead people. This project is really helping history come alive for us. We're actually going to meet some of these men and talk with them. That's really exciting for something that's school-related." I couldn't have said it better myself.

Unless their names appear in the police beat or their faces grace the sports pages, the opportunities for traditional high school students to get recognized in local newspapers are pretty slim; academic endeavors are rarely reported. For students who have not experienced much academic success and attend alternative schools, where organized sports teams typically do not even exist, the chances of making the papers are virtually nil. However, in one Sunday afternoon, weeks of study and building excitement crystallized in an in-depth article that took seriously what the students had to say. Members of the famous Tuskegee Airmen indeed would be coming to Dubuque in a few months, and the students of Central Alternative High School were making it happen. This was the big time. It was now official.

After Eddie Nicholson, manager of Dubuque's landmark hotel, the Julien Inn, read the Central/Tuskegee story in the paper that day, and then opened his business letter from Christina, he called the school to say he would be honored to have the Airmen stay at the Julien—at no cost to us! We were stunned. "What do I say to the other motel people I wrote to when they call us back?" Christina inquired. I answered her question with a question: What do *you* think you should say? "That we got a better deal from someone else?" she ventured. Yes, I laughed, but try to break it to them gently. The young correspondent smiled, and got busy crafting another business letter. This time she did not need any help.

In the meantime, Tony and fellow senior Chris volunteered to give a speech to the members of the local EAA to raise money for our expenses. On the way to the meeting one rainy December evening, these intrepid researchers ignored my repeated suggestions to write a few things down to help organize their thoughts before they addressed the group. Neither presentation was very good. On the way home, their front-to-back-seat conversation focused exclusively on how they should have done a better job preparing and giving their speeches. I kept quiet and drove, listening to their impromptu critique session.

Evidently, the EAA audience saw past the halting addresses because they contributed $500 to the cause. Now there was some *real* money on the table; the article in the paper and the research were beginning to pay dividends. We determined that the total cost to fly all our guests to Dubuque would be a hair under $2,000, and with just one contribution, we were already a quarter of the way there. In the students' eyes, that seemingly insurmountable expense figure was getting cut down to size. They were doing it. And it was just December. With the research continuing and the students' confidence growing daily, the next step would be to get into some serious fundraising to completely cover our expenses, pay for printing our research book, and contribute to the Red Tail Project.

DOING ORIGINAL HISTORICAL RESEARCH

At the start of the second quarter, my teaching colleague Tim Ebeling joined me, bringing with him five students with behavior disorders, teaching associate Carol Cross, and student teacher Ron Vest, who was cutting his professional teeth in Tim's English classes. In order to help the students develop their public-speaking skills, Tim set up a series of practice runs for students brave enough to venture into the community.

"What makes for a successful and effective public speech?" Tim queried.

"Well, you have to make good eye contact," said Amanda.

"You need to have a good introduction," added Chris. I stared at him intently, hoping to telepathically prod him into remembering and repeating some of those how-to-give-a-speech pearls of wisdom he voiced in the car.

"You have to give people the idea that you know what you're talking about," quipped Sara. The students' responses became a rubric of sorts, and it served us well as they evaluated and critiqued each other's speeches before other volunteers ventured into the community.

After the Christmas break, Tim and I established a public speaking schedule for the fundraising presentations to local organizations. Some were more interested in getting up early to mingle with the Dubuque Morning Optimists, while others wanted to speak only after they (and their audience?) were fully awake. In most cases, students were allotted a minimum of ten minutes to talk by the organizations.

"Ten minutes? How are we going to fill ten minutes?" they moaned.

"Well," Tim and I usually responded, "look around you and check out the different topics currently under investigation by your fellow researchers. Why not sit down with them and find out what they have discovered? Talking about the Red Tail Project alone could take five minutes. How about creating something to hand out to share with your audience, something they could read and take with them?"

That was a great idea. Drew quickly was becoming the class's Red Tail Project information guru, and he put together a Tuskegee Airmen research information packet explaining the various topics of student research and the need for financial backing that would serve him and his speech-giving colleagues well when they spoke in public: "If you will now turn to page six in the packet we have placed at your table, you will notice the itemized breakdown of the cost to restore the P-51C Mustang we received from the Southern Minnesota Wing of the Confederate Air Force. On page seven, we have listed the airfare costs to bring the Airmen to Dubuque." Most speeches did not exceed the imposed time limit. However, so many questions were generated from the audience that usually we had no problem sopping up the remaining minutes.

Lucius "Buddy" Johnson

How were race relations during this time period? "Racism in the country was well known in the South, but not so much in the North." If you were facing such racism, what made you decide to go to war? "To prove I was the best. The love of the country also let my people know I cared. Fighting and flying for the United States was important to me because it was my country and I loved her. All my family was here."

What was it like during your first solo flight? "I was flying free as a bird. I had made it! I can do it all, and having a sense of self pride all ran through my mind. The thing that motivated me during training was to prove to the officers that I was good and better than they could imagine. I also wanted to prove that Colored flyers were just as good as our counterparts. There was a morale problem at the base. You had to be strong or turn a deaf ear to the problem— me, being from the North, I just turned my thoughts and lessons to the business at hand. You could tell the problems with the reactions of some of the White officers. There was very little to do to get away. Only if you had the desire to find it. You could go to church or visit the college."

"I think it took so long for the Tuskegee Airmen to get recognition because the newspapers and radio stations never let the public know what we did."

After sending a survey to Tuskegee Airmen, Tony Culpepper, a senior at Central Alternative High School in Dubuque, Iowa, compiled their reflections into an extensive report. Here is an excerpt about Lucius "Buddy" Johnson.

The efforts of our public speakers were paying off handsomely, so we had more time to focus on the progress of the research book through the month of January. By now, the airfare expenses were totally covered. So were our projected research-book printing costs. Anything collected now would go to the Red Tail Project. Drew learned from his research that the Minnesota State Legislature had agreed to match Red Tail Project contributions from outside the state up to $100,000. So one dollar instantly became two. The students' public speaking refrain became, "Help us get the Airmen to Dubuque, and we'll do the rest."

In the world of an alternative education student, a book may not necessarily be judged by its cover, but the number of its pages always receives solemn consideration. On our first go-round, we tallied up 139 pages! No one said anything, but I knew everyone was thinking: how big will this be when we're done?

"Remember," Tim said, "this total does not include a page reflection from each of you, complete with your photograph; responses from Airmen yet to be received; and perhaps observations from some of you on what it was like to fly with Bill Fitch or give a speech to the Kiwanis Club." We no longer used the diminutive word "booklet" to describe the compiled research. This here document was going to be a book.

Tony was now getting several letters a week from the Airmen, so Tim and I had him pick out a few choice responses to read to the entire class. He would go on to get a 50 percent response to his original mailing, a phenomenal accomplishment. Several respondents even made duplicates of Tony's questionnaire and sent them to other Airmen—a testimony to the willingness of Airmen nationwide to contribute to our body of knowledge.

As Tony leafed through his bursting notebook, everyone sat rapt with attention. "Why would you want to fight for a country that didn't support you?" was one of many insightful questions Tony asked after talking with Joey Burns. "This Airman, a Mr. Watson, he writes that it was *his* country, and the letters in 'my country' are all capitalized," Tony told his mates, shaking the letter in front of him. "He really wanted to prove himself by learning how to fly." Laughing with anticipation, Tony sifted through several pages of the questionnaire and then continued, "Oh yeah, here it is. I asked him what went through his mind when he first soloed at Tuskegee. Mr. Watson says here, 'My only thought was, how in the hell am I going to land this thing in one piece?'" Students who flew with the EAA laughed the loudest on that one. Tony continued, "He said that he is very glad we are doing this research." Here was an actual letter, written by an actual Airman, with actual answers to our questions. No longer depending on secondary sources of information for their study, now the students were making personal connections with the men who made history. Then Tony dropped a bombshell on all of us. "And Mr. Watson says here in his personal letter to me that he wants to buy a copy of the research when it's done." We had just made our first sale of a book that was not even in its final form yet.

Reading the Airmen's responses to the class was one thing, but Tony needed to organize the questions and answers to make for interesting reading for a larger audience. At first, he had no clue how to interpret the data, so I took one of the answer sheets (most of the Airmen wrote out their responses on the lines Tony provided), and composed a written interview for his consideration. I explained how he could creatively have the Airmen "speak" as if they were sitting across the table from him. That sole example was all Tony needed; once again, we saw him fleetingly for morning attendance, and then he was off. When the 230-page book was printed, Tony's individual contribution came in at over sixty pages. I made a contact with William Holton, the historian of the Tuskegee Airmen Oral History Documentation Project at Howard University in Washington, D. C. He was very impressed with the sample of work Tony sent him. As a result of Tony's diligence and attention to accuracy and detail, Bill Holton entered all the Airmen's interviews compiled by Tony, as well as our research book, into the national database.

After Christmas break, a sense of quiet determination permeated the class. No one was coming in late anymore, and students grew increasingly impatient for Tim or me to get on with the morning announcements. After all, they had things to do! And everyone was now sensing that our "Tuskegee thing" was going to be big.

As the third quarter got underway in mid-January, Shirley Deppe, Central's art teacher, joined our team. She specifically tailored one of her art classes to focus on creating decorations for the seminar. (Throughout, the Central staff's flexibility and willingness to contribute to the project was a real strength.) According to Shirley, the students who signed up for this class really wanted to be there. "They already knew about the Tuskegee project because of the publicity and excitement it was generating throughout the school, and this gave students who otherwise would not have been able to join the research class the chance to become participants and contributors," she told me. "This was something the students were really interested in. They knew early on that they would be in charge, and would be given the responsibility to decorate the ballroom where the seminar would take place. The timing was perfect because we had just enough days to get these projects done. When we were down to about a week to go, the tension was pretty obvious, but I channeled it to step up the production. It all worked out very well."

Shirley and her students visited the seminar site and came back brimming with ideas. They acted right away and developed an expense budget. At one point, her class came to our room and made a formal proposal for a little funding. To be honest, Tim and I had not included decorations in our original expense projections. However, the addresses delivered by members of our seasoned "Tuskegee Airmen Speakers' Bureau" by now had generated well over $3,500 in contributions; the research students had no problem approving a new $200 art budget account. After a brief discussion, the vote was unanimous. "Hey, no problem! We'll make that up by selling a few books," cracked Drew. We all laughed, but not because it was beyond the realm of possibility any more.

Shirley's students decided to make large cardboard silhouettes of Red-Tailed P-51C Mustangs which they hung like mobiles from the ballroom ceiling. These works of art became genuine historic souvenirs for attendants who asked permission to take them down at the end of the evening for the Airmen to autograph. The art class also designed the placards that helped identify the student work that was going to be displayed on tables, and the ballroom walls were draped with 450 soldier silhouettes and 850 medals to graphically represent what the Airmen had accomplished as a group. The students' coordinated artistic contribution made an impressive, unified statement for the entire evening. The ballroom looked absolutely wonderful.

As the students delved deeper into the Tuskegee Airmen story, the research book steadily evolved into something more than just a recitation of the Airmen's wartime exploits. The students wanted to tell the *whole* Tuskegee story, including what race relations in America were like before and during the war; what Hitler's racial policies were, and how disturbingly similar they were to what was being practiced in the States; what the Confederate Air Force is; and what it was like to fly with the EAA, to list just a few topics. But writing is easier said than done.

Tim deserves the credit for being tenaciously committed to the "joy of drafts and revision." Not everyone in the class possessed what you would call outstanding composition skills, and for some students, the specter of red-ink comments on their drafts was downright discouraging. On some days, a few students wanted Tim's head on a pole, but he was able to convince one and all that we were not writing this research book for ourselves; it was being written to tell the story of the Tuskegee Airmen, and everyone wanted to get it right.

As Tim saw it, "It is my job as a teacher of writing to assist the students in discovering their 'voice' and then give them an audience to whom they can speak. The Tuskegee Airmen Research Project enabled me to do both. As the students uncovered information about these little-known war heroes, they developed a desire to let others know what they were finding. The students wanted to be sure that their written words were precise and accurate. Because they had made personal connections with the Airmen, their writing was rich with emotion. To get students to write, they must believe they have something to say; there was plenty to say about the Tuskegee Airmen."

When the time came to decide what the research book cover would look like, the class discussion was spirited and lengthy. Everyone seemed to have a point of view, and Tim and I were determined to hear one and all. Once we settled on a title and the layout, Tim's teaching associate, Carol, took the prototype; with her technology skills and three brand-new ink cartridges, she printed three hundred covers that depicted a Red-Tailed Mustang flying "high cover," protecting American B-24 bombers as they made their way to the oil fields of Ploesti in 1944. With considerable enthusiasm, aviation artist Troy White of De

Reflections

I really didn't know anything about the Tuskegee Airmen until I was put into this history class. I thought that our mission would be almost impossible to accomplish. I had my doubts as to whether or not we could pull this whole thing off. As the work began to be accomplished, and the donations began to roll in, I began to believe that we were going to reach our goals. I believe that our class did a great job with this project.

The message that I learned from the Tuskegee Airmen is that you can't let people intimidate you. You must do your best and work hard. If you do that, you will succeed. You have to put your mind to it. Just don't ever give up!

These reflections written by Tamelia Harris at Central Alternative High School show her sense of pride in accomplishing the seemingly impossible tasks of writing a research book and hosting Tuskegee Airmen in Dubuque, Iowa.

Land, Florida gave us permission to reproduce his copyrighted image. He also made two limited edition art prints available for us to raffle off during the seminar. We studied the titles of other books written about the Airmen, and came up with *The Tuskegee Airmen: Victory at Home and Abroad.* It had a special ring to it. And *it was ours.*

With just under a month to go, our Tuskegee account had mushroomed to a whopping $4,800. Chris and Tony once again teamed up, this time to do a live interview on local radio. A video crew from Iowa Public Television was returning to continue working on a feature story for the weekly show called "Living in Iowa." At this point in the year, the sight of TV cameras and reporters at school hardly raised an eyebrow any more.

The *Telegraph Herald's* weekly teen page, called "The Alt," published an article by Central's Amanda Greve and Tiffiny Green who wrote about the Airmen on the Thursday before the seminar. Titling their story "Beating the Odds," Amanda and Tiffiny gave their readers a synopsis of their research project, a preview of what the Monday night seminar would be, and set forth the invitation to attend: "Our Central family would like to invite you to attend this unprecedented event. In the Tuskegee Airmen Research Project, we are not only reliving history, we are making history. Come to the seminar. You might be surprised at what the Airmen and the Central students have accomplished."

Everything that seemed so impossibly out of reach just a few short months ago now was within our grasp: the Airmen were coming. The Julien was ready. The public was behind us. Three hundred research books were printed, collated, and bound. We had enough money to stuff a Mustang cockpit. Just like the Airmen, the students overcame the obstacles, and indeed had "arrived." We were feeling pretty good.

TUSKEGEE AIRMEN TOUCH DOWN IN DUBUQUE

Airman Joe Gomer's flight from Minneapolis arrived on Friday, February 20th, at about 4 p.m. Russ, Chris, Tom, and Drew were at the airport to meet him, as were the local media, plus a reporter and photographer for the *Des Moines Sunday Register*. "I'm so excited about this project," gushed Chris to the FOX-40 reporter. "I'm going to be the master of ceremonies for our Tuskegee Airmen public seminar which will be at Loras College on Monday night from 6 to 9:30 p.m. I've never been so enthusiastic about anything in school like this." He did not miss a beat, and got in a free plug for the seminar to boot. He had come a long way since that inexperienced speech he gave to the EAA in November. His enthusiasm stemmed from the fact that he had worked very hard, maintained his focus, and learned from his mistakes. And he saw all of it paying off, big time.

Speaking about the Airmen to *Register* reporter Charles Bullard, Tom said, "They've definitely become my role model." (Tom had been in the class during the first quarter, and graduated at the end of the third quarter. He was leaving for the Marines the day after the seminar.) He continued, "When I feel down in boot camp, I'm just going to start thinking of them and I'm going to try to persevere just like they did."

The rest of the Airmen arrived on Saturday afternoon, and many of the students were on hand to welcome them at the airport, as were several Central teachers, and more than a few local citizens who had been following our exploits from the get-go. By now, the students had pictures of all the Airmen and knew them on sight. While they and their guests mingled in the airport lobby, I went away by myself in a corner and wept. In my wildest imaginings just five months ago, never could I have expected that all of this would be coming together so perfectly. All the Airmen were here. The research book was done, and it was impressive. All the expenses were covered. The Red Tail Project account continued to grow. The students were, to say the least, engaged. The public was behind us. It was simply overpowering. Loras College had planned a few weekend activities for the Airmen, so all that was left was to get ready for the seminar. But first, the Airmen would be the honored guests at Central Alternative High School on Monday morning.

Besides being a history teacher at Central, I am also the student government advisor. In this capacity, I did not want to appear to be railroading the school's student leaders into planning something for the Airmen, so I purposely left the room when the Tuskegee project came up for discussion two weeks before the seminar. However, when I returned, the students were already deciding which school board members and other guests they would be inviting to their Tuskegee Airmen brunch that was going to be held in the staff workroom on Monday morning at 10 a.m. "We have it all covered, John," said Ann, student government president and Drew's older sister. "We already talked to David (the principal), and found out how much we have in our account. We're going to make breakfast for the whole class, the Airmen, and our guests." Talk about democracy in action.

After the brunch, the four Airmen, along with Red Tail Project director John Schuck and his wife Diane, spent time with the students in the very classroom where so much had taken place to get us to this day. I think the reality of it all stunned the students into silence: Lee Archer,

Luther Smith, Bob Martin, and Joe Gomer are really here, sitting in our seats! I looked around and commented wistfully, "Gee, the room hasn't been this quiet since the last snow day." The room erupted in laughter, and that broke the ice. Our district superintendent, Dr. Joel Morris, stood behind my desk in the corner, shaking his head and smiling as he rifled through his own new research book. The dazzled school board members strategically sat between students and Airmen to get both ends of the conversation.

We sat in our customary circle, and all the Airmen expressed their sincere thanks to the students for the terrific work accomplished on their behalf. Lee Archer said, "For these young people who want to know something about what I went through, it's important to me that they get the real picture." Soon, pens were whirling, bodies were weaving, and research books were darting about the room, as the students scooped up autographs from the men they now called heroes, while the Airmen got signatures from the young people who had become *their* heroes. However, little did we know that this animated classroom commotion was just a preview of what we would experience later that afternoon and evening.

After the brunch at Central, the faculty, staff, and students of Bob Martin's alma mater, Washington Junior High School, held a schoolwide assembly in his honor. Principal Art Roling presented Bob Martin with a plaque honoring his achievements as a Tuskegee Airman while Lee Archer, Luther Smith, and Joe Gomer looked on with pride. Then two student government leaders went on stage with a huge cardboard "check." After we had made a Tuskegee presentation to their student government group in October, the members immediately took charge of their own fundraising project and gave brief speeches to their schoolmates during the school's lunch hours. They told everyone that Tuskegee Airman Robert Martin was a "Wash" graduate, and that there would be an opportunity for all current "Wash" students to honor him and his fellow Airmen by contributing to The Red Tail Project plane restoration. During November and December, the students sold Washington Junior High School baseball pennants.

Today, their hard work was made manifest in the check that now took center stage.

Drew and Chris, representing Central, also took their places on the stage. After delivering a few brief speeches about the Airmen to their classmates, the junior high students proudly presented to the students of Central a check for $450 for The Red Tail Project, bringing the audience to its feet. Never before had two schools in Dubuque worked like this for a common goal.

CLIMAX OF THE FINAL PRESENTATION

No one had any idea how many folks would show up at the Graber Ballroom at Loras College. Our Iowa winter had been unseasonably warm; storm clouds threatened rain. And Monday night seemed a bit odd to stage an event such as this, but it was what we were offered back in September, so we took it. While Chris, Drew, and I were with the Airmen at Washington Junior High, Shirley and Tim transported the rest of the class to Loras College. In the newly built, spacious ballroom, the students set up their display tables, complete with drafts, charts, scale aircraft models, correspondence, photographs, and of course, copies of the research book available for cash. Above them, P-51 mobiles responded slowly to the air conditioner's whispers. Additional Mustang aircraft were taped to the walls; when the mini-spotlights were turned on, every cardboard cut-out was strikingly highlighted.

The doors opened promptly at 6 p.m., and the crowd began to file in. Display tables throughout the ballroom allowed students to discuss their research in an informal setting with the general public for about an hour before the actual seminar began. While everyone was nervous about facing the public, no one backed away from the task. These students *knew* what they were talking about. Now *they* were the experts. Folks were coming to hear *them*.

Before long, most of the seats were taken, but folks kept arriving. In one corner of the ballroom sat James, a quiet young man who decided to tackle a rather challenging, technical study of the different types of aircraft flown by the Allies and the Nazis during the war. Never one to initiate a conversation in class, James nevertheless would respond thoughtfully to anything you asked of him. As the crowd grew ever larger, he appeared a little forlorn, alone in a sea of humanity, sitting behind his table with the sign that advertised, "Combat Aircraft of World War II." I decided to move in his direction. Someone intercepted me to ask where the electrical outlets were, and by the time I resumed my route to James, he had an audience of several people beginning to gather around his display. I just stood and watched. When he rose from his chair, flashed a smile, and began gesturing pilot-style with his hands, I knew he would not need any help from me.

The students who entered the research class at the beginning of the third quarter knew they would not be able to contribute to the research book, but there was still much for them to do. Tim, Shirley, and I were determined to have students be responsible for as much of this public event as possible. So we called for five students to step forward to introduce our esteemed guests to the audience.

Sheleece was not the most confident young woman in the class, but she had volunteered to introduce one of the Airmen. Earlier in the day, Tim took Sheleece and the other students into the principal's office for a little peace and quiet, and worked with each of them on their speeches. They also critiqued each other. When they arrived at the Ballroom that night, they were all dressed up and ready to roll.

The television lights and the din of the crowd gave the place an expectant, rally atmosphere. Present in the crowd were long-time residents of Dubuque who came to say hello to the hometown boy-made-good, Bob Martin; bomber crew veterans who came to say thank you to the men who escorted their planes to the targets and back; students from the University of Wisconsin, Platteville; students from most of Dubuque' high schools and colleges; proud family members who marveled at what their Central students had accomplished; and former GIs and aviation buffs who wanted to shake the hands of the men who flew P-51s across Europe.

As the time approached to gavel the assembly to order, every seat was filled. Five hundred chairs had been set up; at least two hundred more were brought in from other areas of the building. By the time the formal program finally began, the standing portion of the crowd was ten deep. Loras College officials later estimated the audience at nearly nine hundred people. That was more than four times the number of students in our *entire school!*

At precisely 7 p.m., Chris, as master of ceremonies, made his way to the podium to open the formal portion of the proceedings; the crowd noise ended abruptly. This time, his speech was written down, and well-rehearsed: "Ladies and gentlemen, we welcome you this evening to Central Alternative High School's Tuskegee Airmen seminar," he began proudly. "We have done a lot of hard work, and we are ready to tell you what we have learned."

After a few welcoming comments by our principal and other Loras College representatives, the students, reading from well-thought out and profoundly moving speeches, introduced the Airmen and the Red Tail Project director. Each guest received a standing ovation as he took the podium and after concluding his remarks. Lee Archer, Luther Smith, Bob Martin, Joe Gomer, and John Schuck all praised the students for their tremendous effort in researching and presenting the Tuskegee Airmen story to the public. Each Airman shared personal wartime experiences of discrimination and combat success, and then declared that they were not bitter, but became stronger individuals for having gone through the experience. An animated John Schuck predicted, "With a little bit of luck and God's will, the Red Tailed Mustang will visit Dubuque sometime during 1999." Everyone cheered.

After she introduced Airman Robert Martin, and all the Airmen addressed the audience, Sheleece told me, "One lady actually thought I was a Loras College student, because she said I did such a good job with my speech. She said we had done a terrific job, and she was real glad she made it."

During the question and answer period after the formal presentation, James Bowman, retired assistant superintendent of the Des Moines, Iowa public school system, rose from his seat in the audience and addressed the citizens of Dubuque. Luther Smith had given me James Bowman's name; we tracked him down and invited him to

Christina Hinkel, a student at Central Alternative High School in Dubuque, Iowa, wrote these reflections on the importance of bringing the accomplishments of the Tuskegee Airmen to public attention.

attend the seminar. He, too, was a Tuskegee Airman, class of 1945A, who flew P-40s and P-47s.

"I am amazed by what I have seen here tonight," he said to the assembled throng. "Living in Des Moines, you hear stories about Dubuque, how this town is not very supportive of minority people, and that there isn't much to be expected here." Indeed, our city had experienced some racial strife in the 1980s which actually made the front page of the *New York Times;* despite the fact that the town's minority population was just about 4 percent of the total, some folks just could not get along. "But what you have done here tonight is very important," Bowman continued. "You have made it your task to correct an historical wrong." He told me later, "What is even more significant is that you and most of your students are *not* African Americans. You made it a responsibility for the students to portray history accurately. The integrity with which you approached this project has been one of the best lessons I have ever seen as an educator, and it was a service and a valuable lesson for all the people of Dubuque."

In one corner of the ballroom, Drew once again was being interviewed for another soon-to-be front page article that would run the next morning. By now this seasoned veteran of the local lecture circuit could spout Red Tail Project facts and figures in his sleep. "I've been studying these guys for so long, now that I've met them I feel like I've known them all my life," he told the reporter. "It's an experience I'm never going to forget." Almost nine hundred other folks agreed with Drew.

The next thing anyone knew, it was 9:30 p.m. We had sold nearly two hundred research books, and the plastic aquariums Sarah brought to handle the free-will offering at the doors were filled to overflowing. The raffle tickets for the four donated, limited-edition aviation art prints depicting Tuskegee Airmen exploits were almost sold out. And even after the winners were announced, many people remained just to talk with the students and the Airmen, to get autographs and pose for pictures. Bob Martin chatted with John Owens, who was now living in Cedar Rapids. The two men had grown up next door to each other in Dubuque. A color photo of this reunion accompanied the Tuesday morning article.

The final figure for Monday night's take was close to $3,000. As the huge crowd slowly melted away, several students helped return the many chairs people had carted into the ballroom from other areas in the building. Anthony stayed behind to make sure everything was ship-shape. He and I finally left the Loras College Alumni Center at 11:45 p.m. Tim told us later that Loras College called our school office and said they had never witnessed such a complete clean-up operation like that from any other outside organization who used their facilities.

The next morning, we all rode out to the airport to see the Airmen off. "John, you know what? Lee Archer told me that he would never forget this weekend," crowed J. C. "To see a part of history, and be a part of history, feels really good." That certainly was the understatement of the year.

AFTERMATH

The final class activity called for the students to collectively write thank-you notes to the many people and organizations who helped make the Tuskegee Airmen project and seminar a success. When a few moans and complaints percolated to the surface, Tim smoothly reminded the class of how pleasant this would have been if we had had to raise the money all by ourselves. The griping subsided. Recipients of those thank-you notes were deeply impressed, and many called the school just to say thank you for the thank-you.

In one section of the research book, students shared their personal observations about the class and their part in it. The insights and assessments made by these at-risk youth were as profound as they were enlightening. Some outside observers might have suspected that since the research was rather compartmentalized, most students never really gained an overall perspective of the project. But Tony had already thought about that dynamic when he wrote, "If someone was to say to me that I didn't know the whole story, I would respond by letting them know how wrong they were. The whole class would report back to the others one by one every few days. When I would come back up to class from the library, I would have to tell the rest of the class what I was doing while I was gone and I told them what new information it was that I received. Everyone else did the same thing. That's how the class kept updated with everyone's research and we got the whole story on the Tuskegee Airmen."

John Schuck, the Red Tail Project director, wrote the students to express his appreciation for their research work and the financial contribution to the P-51 restoration. In part he said, "We are still so overwhelmed by your selfless efforts on behalf of the Red Tail Project that our words pale in comparison. Your story, like that of the Tuskegee

Airmen themselves, deserves telling and retelling." Speaking on his wife's behalf, he concluded, "To have been included in this magnificent program was one of the most memorable times of our lives."

Benjamin O. Davis, Jr. was the commanding officer of the 332nd Fighter Group. We made sure he received a copy of the research book and a special video tape with all the local news coverage, plus the segment from Iowa Public Television. Now living in Alexandria, Virginia, General Davis wrote to say, "Your students, in my opinion, did indeed capture the essential traits of [the Tuskegee Airmen] that made them the greatest flying unit that it has been my privilege to command. Additionally, it gives me much pleasure to see the legacy of the Tuskegee Airmen reflected in the determination of the students as they strive to apply what they learned from this research about overcoming obstacles and adversities to bring greater substance and meaning to their own lives. I salute you in bringing this about."

No other high school class had ever made the Dubuque *Telegraph Herald's* "Alt" page twice in one year. When their second feature article was published in late March, the writing team of Greve and Green broke precedent. This time, the headline read, "Central Savors Tuskegee Day." These graduating seniors did not mince any words, and reminded me of the truism that says, "It sure ain't braggin' if you can back it up."

"One could say that the seminar didn't go exactly as planned," Amanda and Tiffiny began. "More people showed up than expected. The students sold more books than anticipated, and they raised more than $3,000 for the Red Tail Project. We believe the Central students and the Tuskegee Airmen have this in common: They both exceeded the expectations others had set for them. Seeing the Airmen smiling from ear to ear… made the students feel good. It was great knowing that we were finally giving the Airmen the ovation that should have happened fifty years ago."

In May, just a few days before Central's graduation, the final installment of the on-going Tuskegee Airmen research project made the newspaper. The students proudly announced that with subsequent sales of their book, plus the contributions generated the night of the seminar, and after $2,500 in expenses were covered, they proudly raised a grand total of $5,252 for The Red Tail Project! A check for that amount soon would be making its way to the Confederate Air Force headquarters in Midland, Texas. And they reminded the reporter that the State of Minnesota would be matching their dollar amount. By now, Drew could sense when a reporter was in or near the building, and he managed to get in a few parting comments: "In the beginning, I figured we'd raise a couple hundred bucks. The final revenues shocked me."

In addition, a portion of the proceeds from each book had been earmarked for a Central High School scholarship fund; the amount stood at $450. Graduating senior Tony was presented with that award during Central's Commencement. So in a sense, the grand total generated by the entire project was more like $13,000.

When asked what we would do differently if we had to do it again, my first reaction is to say "nothing." But after thinking about things for a while, and consulting with Tim and Shirley, a few considerations emerge.

By the time the Airmen arrived in Dubuque, our war chest was brimming, so Tim and I decided to throw a dinner party Saturday night at the Julien, just for the Airmen and the students. Now you have to understand what kind of reputation the Julien has in Dubuque: it is where many of the town's civic organizations hold their meetings and banquets; where visiting dignitaries cool their heels; where some high schools have their proms. If you are an at-risk student, the thought of entering this revered landmark wearing anything less than a suit, tuxedo, or an evening gown is just something too scary to ponder. We had a list of students who said they were going to attend, but for some reason, we wound up with less than half the class. We never really explored the reason(s) why more students did not appear, and we regret that this teenage angst was not better anticipated and addressed, and that more students were not able to enjoy a fine dinner and intimate conversation with the Airmen.

While at the podium during the time I presided over the question and answer period in the seminar, I had a singularly golden chance to call all the students up on stage to receive what I am certain would have been a stupendous standing ovation from the overflow crowd. There

Reflections

The part of the research that I did was on personal views and observations. I was assigned a few questions at the beginning of the year and I couldn't find the information that I needed in books. That's when I decided to go to John with the idea of writing letters to the Airmen and having them answer questions. This way I could have firsthand accounts of what really went on. The thing that motivated me to do this was the work itself. The further along I got in my work, the more interested I became in the information I was receiving and processing....

I think that the Tuskegee Airmen are a very important chapter in the United States history. Meek Stalling, a former Tuskegee Airman, told me, "...we are America's best-kept secret." I agree with this. I think that what I learned from the Airmen is that no matter what you want, you can achieve it through hard work and perseverance.

Tony Culpepper, a senior at Central Alternative High School in Dubuque, Iowa, wrote these reflections on his experience doing primary research on the Tuskegee Airmen.

was plenty of time to do it. It certainly was appropriate. It did not happen. What a powerful experience that would have been for the students. That lost opportunity haunts me to this day.

Letters of congratulations continue to arrive at school. They are mostly written in long-hand by the Airmen who responded to the survey, by their wives, or by other family members. But because most of the students in the class were graduating seniors who have since gone on to the next phase of their lives, they probably will not read many of these letters. At first I felt badly about this, because the comments written to the students are so poignant and heartfelt. "You have told our story," is the common refrain. "I am telling everyone I meet about the students in Iowa who wrote this book." But as I look back on the whole endeavor, I see student smiles when our goals were reached or surpassed; I sense the pride and workmanship that made the research book the impressive document it is; and I bear witness to the lives of students changed forever because of the incredible interaction they had with men nearly four times their age, but with whom they really had so much in common. The letters are just icing on the cake.

In August, 1998, I was invited to address the 27th Annual Tuskegee Airmen Convention in Washington, D. C. My speech covered only the basics, but the Air Force audio-visual wizards who were on the scene helped me show Iowa Public Television's *Living in Iowa* segment on the Tuskegee project called, "Earning Their Wings," to the enthusiastic and appreciative group. I met several men whose names would be familiar to anyone who read our book. Lee Archer was there too, and told me of a letter he received from a young man just after our February seminar. He beamed, "He told me in his letter that I had inspired him to stay in school. He wrote, 'If you could make it, then I can, too,' and he's invited me to his graduation! I told him if I'm still around then, I'll be there."

A few days after I got back from D. C., I got a letter from Luther Smith. He said in part, "The videotape [of local news coverage] was very effective in showing who the Dubuque students are, and what they accomplished in their own words. You and your students created a remarkable chapter for the Tuskegee Airmen story. I am glad that you were able to see how the Tuskegee Airmen felt about your accomplishments."

Soon after the school year came to an end, friends and even teachers from other schools came up to me and asked, "What are you going to do to top this?" I can only say this project was a once-in-a-lifetime experience. However, given our philosophy of teaching that insists on having students assume responsibility for their own learning; challenges them to overcome seemingly impossible obstacles; provides an opportunity for students to tell their story to a larger audience; and builds an attitude of service into the curriculum, whatever the topic is, we are in for some life-changing excitement.

"WE HAVE NO HEROES"

PAOLA RUOCCO

"We have no heroes. We have no one to look up to," Hana, a sixth grader said in the midst of our class discussion on role models. I had hoped that our conversation about heroic figures might inspire the students, but Hana's comment seemed to capture the general feeling in the class.

When I pressed the students to identify people they admired, some remarked that sports figures and celebrities were their only role models. Yet even these figures were not ideal. Many students felt that these supposedly heroic athletes did not give enough back to their own communities. They believed that when some of them performed community service, they did it as a public relations move or because their contract stipulated it. Just giving money or a little time was not enough to make a hero. The people who were in the public eye, the students believed, had an obligation to be role models and leaders in the truest sense of the word, especially since so many youths looked up to them. It was clear that the students felt that even though the public considered sports figures heroes and role models, they themselves did not. The discussion left me with a deep sadness. It was clear that my students felt that their public figures were not true heroes. I could feel their cynicism; it was palpable.

This conversation stayed with me for some time. Our school, School for the Physical City, draws a diverse group of students from across New York City. Yet all these students could agree that they had no one to look up to. I decided to plan a learning expedition on heroes. In addition to challenging students with explorations of conflicts in Egypt and India, I wanted to challenge them on a moral level as well. I wanted my students to know that leaders do exist all around them, and many of them are not in the public eye. I wanted them to realize that they themselves could be leaders and heroes that others could look to for inspiration and guidance.

The sixth-grade social studies curriculum requires students to study world cultures. For our expedition, "Conflict and Heroism," we examined Egypt and India at different points in history. To study the many-faceted sides of conflict, we focused our study of Egypt on the Suez Canal, including the region during British and Egyptian rule, the building and construction of the canal, the Six-Day War, and finally the future of the Suez Canal. To study heroism, we looked at India during Mohandas Gandhi's independence movement. Each of these historical examinations gave the students opportunities to analyze, question, and wonder about the nature of conflict and heroism. As a companion project to their study of India, each student developed a service project related to an issue that concerned him or her. The following chapter will highlight three segments of the expedition: the literature book groups, our study of India, and the service projects.

DOES CONFLICT ALWAYS CREATE HEROISM?

I always ask my students to analyze the guiding questions for an expedition. I do not give them any background or research time; I want them to consider and wonder about the questions I generate and then develop their own. Both my questions and theirs can be used as reference points throughout the expedition. My guiding questions for this expedition were:

- Does conflict create heroism?
- How can we be heroic even if we do not win the conflict?
- When does conflict create heroism?
- What elements need to exist in order for conflict to arise?

After looking at these, students generated their own questions and comments. Their reactions were, as always, varied and interesting.

"Is the reason we have so much heroism because we have so much conflict or the other way around?" —Sofia Frank

"Do you believe that there are more heroic people now than ten or twenty years ago?" —Rachel Shearhouse

"Is a good deed heroism?" —Omar Soliman

"Why are there so many racial conflicts?" —Luis Germosen

"You are a hero when you have done your best." —Amy Kuntz

The students' responses and reactions were thoughtful and thought-provoking. We now had to create a paradigm to examine conflict and criteria for heroism. The students read articles from the *New York Times* "Friends in Need" series. These articles highlighted people throughout the New York area who were helping a community or a cause about which they cared. From these articles, the students created the following paradigm to look at conflict:

- What is the conflict/issue?
- Who is involved in the conflict/issue?
- Where is it taking place?
- Why did it happen?
- What was its resolution, if any?

They also developed their criteria for heroism:

- Helpful
- Caring
- Selfless

~ Brave

~ Intelligent

The articles in the *Times* helped students generate these models, but they also served another purpose. As the students read, they became aware of and immersed in issues affecting their city and local communities. Some noted that the person they read about had an office near their houses. One student read about someone helping single mothers—like her own mother. The students had their first glimmer of knowing that there were everyday people doing good works. They noted that the people highlighted in these articles were not on television or famous. They pointed out that these people did their work because they cared about their communities and wanted to help their fellow human beings.

EXPLORING CONFLICT AND HEROISM THROUGH LITERATURE

While the students studied Egypt, they took part in book groups. The books, while not directly related to Egypt, connected to the expedition through the themes of conflict and heroism. The book groups consisted of two or three students, and each group chose from a list of books that centered on characters facing difficult conflicts: *The Giver*, L. Lowry; *Nilda*, N. Mohr; *House on Mango Street*, S. Cisneros; *Rumble Fish*, S.E. Hinton; *The Outsiders*, S.E. Hinton; *Alan and Naomi*, M. Leroy; and *The Friends*, R. Guy.

Once they began to read these books, I asked them to focus their group discussion on specific ideas or concepts. Having different things to look for in the books gave the groups focus. One day I asked them to reread a section of their book and find examples of conflict. When we shared these with the whole class, it was fascinating to hear the many different examples.

"Those who walk in our neighborhood are afraid of us and think we are dangerous," one student said about the *House on Mango Street*.

"No one is allowed to lie in Jonas's community," said another about

The Giver. "But since he is being trained by the Giver, he is allowed to lie, which also separates him from his community."

"In *The Friends,* Phyllisia doesn't want to hang out with Edith because she is Black."

As we presented these conflicts to one another, students began to see that conflict can generate from any number of reasons. They realized that conflict is complicated and often has many sides and perspectives.

During the book group sessions, I would meander from table to table and listen in, offering an idea or impression. I tried to be as unobtrusive as possible. Before the end of class time, students would write brief reflections on both the content and the process of the group's discussion. They also developed their own homework (with my approval). Many assignments were quite creative. Some developed advertisements that would be seen in *The Giver's* futuristic world. Some created imaginary dialogues between themselves and the character. Still others wrote text and made drawings of pivotal scenes.

To examine and think about the role of heroism in these different novels, I asked students to write a persuasive essay answering the question: "Is my character a hero or not?" We had been working on the persuasive essay standard all year, and this assignment gave them another opportunity to work toward the standard set by the state. Also, when writing about books, we had been working very hard on getting away from only summarizing the books in their writing. When reading both class books and independent books, the students responded in the humanities journals in various forms: notes and quotes, five habits of mind, questions about plot or character or both. This groundwork helped immensely when they wrote more formally; they knew they had already formed opinions about these books in their weekly literature responses. Further, they knew that they could find examples in the text itself which "proved" or supported their opinions. Finally, the essay gave the students another forum in which to think about, examine, and articulate the nature of heroism. This challenged them. Some began to see that, like conflict, heroism can be defined in many different ways.

Bridget wrote about Steve, a character in *Rumble Fish.* She struggled with the basic question, Is he a hero or not? She had to reconcile the fact that he sometimes is but circumstances lead him away from being heroic.

Many had different ideas about Nilda from Mohr's novel by the same name. The main character, a poor Latina girl living during World War II, does not have conflict until she is told her mother will die. Some felt she did not do anything to make herself a heroine, others believed that her survival through adolescent struggles and her mother's death make her heroic.

Alan and Naomi is a story set in Brooklyn during World War II. It tells of a the friendship between Alan and Naomi, a Jewish refugee from France. In this heart-wrenching story, Naomi cannot overcome her brutal and horrific past, even though Alan helps her through love and friendship. Naomi is eventually sent to a sanitarium. Many struggled a long time in deciding Alan's heroism despite the fact that Naomi is not cured. Some felt that he could have done more, others thought he was truly heroic for having simply tried.

Those who wrote about Lowry's *The Giver* also struggled. They felt that the main character, Jonas, is in some ways heroic. But Amy, for example, felt that he was not completely heroic because he betrays and leaves his family.

I was impressed by the range and depth of thought in the students' comments. They began to see how very complicated it is to be brave or selfless in the face of hard choices. By looking at different kinds of conflict and the actions taken by these characters, students engaged in rich and thoughtful conversations on the nature of heroism.

LEARNING ABOUT GANDHI INSPIRES SERVICE

In this part of the expedition, students studied India under the British Raj and Gandhi's independence movement. At the same time, students had to design and complete a service project around an issue that concerned them. This parallel structure served the students well. They were inspired by Gandhi's resolve and calm in the face of injustice; they learned that his humble beginnings did not minimize the strength of his convictions and the passion behind his ideas. His very simple background made many

Amy Kuntz, a sixth grader at School for the Physical City in New York City, listed
her criteria, and those of her classmates, for service in this journal entry.

students realize how desire for change and improvement in one's world
can happen even if one is not famous. It made firm connections to our
conversation about role models that had inspired the expedition.

We began to read background information on India and started to
read an autobiography of Gandhi, *The Power of Pacifism*. As we read
Gandhi's story, I asked the students to consider the following question:
"What would you be willing to fight for?"

The question fit very well with our study of Gandhi and what he
sacrificed for the cause he believed in. Students' own interests came to
the fore. We charted all of the issues they would be willing to fight for,
or against: homelessness, AIDS, animal rights, domestic violence, youth

violence, gay and lesbian rights, civil rights, pollution and litter, recycling, ovarian cancer, and children's rights.

The students then wrote brief reflections on why the issue was important to them. Olivia said she was interested in knowing how to help the homeless because she saw so many on her way to school. Leonard and Luis wanted to know how to help young people who are drawn into gangs, because they saw many of their friends going into gangs. Another student already did volunteer work at an animal shelter and wanted to get others involved. Still another student grew interested in the subject of domestic violence after meeting a family friend who worked with survivors of domestic abuse. The reasons were as varied as the issues. All of them, though, shared a common theme: the students cared deeply about the issues. They wanted to do something to change what they saw as an injustice—much like Gandhi espoused.

Once the students had zeroed in on an issue, they had to locate an organization that supported their cause. We spent a day or so charting these organizations. We then discussed how we defined "service." The students looked at three different examples of service: a teacher stays after school to help a student, someone gives money to charity, and someone volunteers her time. Once they had decided whether or not they considered the examples service, they had to justify their decisions. This sparked an interesting and often heated discussion. Many, for instance, felt that a teacher staying late to help a student was not service because it was part of her job. Some felt that volunteering was service, but it had to be continuous. Most agreed that there needed to be a commitment to doing the service. Finally, many agreed that giving money was not service. Service meant giving up your time and, perhaps, sacrificing something for the good of something else.

After we had established a common definition of service, the students focused on designing a project that would help their issue. Once I approved their proposals, they launched into their service work. In the end, they wrote reflections on the design and implementation of their action.

Most of the students chose to inform others about their issue either by creating posters and putting them up in their neighborhood, or giving oral presentations to their classmates. Danielle, whose project revolved around AIDS, marched in the annual AIDS march along with other classmates (and me). She informed us about the march and the purpose of getting sponsors. Tama, whose subject was ovarian cancer, felt strongly that women be informed as early as possible. She knew that this information had saved her mother's life and thought that the best way for her to help her "cause" was to inform women about ovarian cancer and the importance of early detection. Barret, whose project was on conflict mediation, chose to interview our peer mediator trainer and then make pamphlets to inform other students throughout School for the Physical City about the value and importance of peer mediation. Paul, whose project centered on civil rights, spent a day shadowing a woman at the American Civil Liberties Union and then reported back to the class.

When students reflected on how it felt to do their service action, many expressed a little embarrassment along with pride. Those who put up posters in their neighborhoods were self-conscious, but also recognized that the poster could help someone. Those who did volunteer work were more apt to feel proud of giving their time to the cause that concerned them. In general, the students felt empowered by implementing the service project they designed. Many felt they were doing something positive towards an issue that concerned them deeply.

In retrospect, I wish I had given the students more help in developing and carrying out their service projects. It would have been useful to look at and research what other community service projects students had done at School for the Physical City. We could have also looked at sources describing kinds of community services or volunteer works. These would have given the students more ideas and choices when developing their service projects.

I felt it was important that each class experience the work of service as a group, so each class voted on performing a service action for the community. One group went to Prospect Park in Brooklyn to clean up the trash. We set out early in the morning with large plastic bags and gloves. Once we arrived, little clusters of students fanned out through the park, armed with trash bags and eagle eyes (though one did not

Problems, Anyone?

Are you having a problem?
If you or anyone you know is having a problem or conflict, I suggest you try conflict mediation or self-conflict mediation.

What is conflict mediation and self-conflict mediation?
Conflict mediation is when two or more people have a conflict, they go to a teacher, mediator or just a person who is skilled in conflict mediation and state the conflict.... Self-conflict mediation is something I've created. The difference between it and normal conflict mediation is that self-conflict mediation requires you to be the mediator. You have to mediate the conflict between yourself and your peers. For self-conflict mediation you go though the same process as conflict mediation except you must be more of a listener

and ask questions like "Why do you think that?"...

Can every person do self-conflict mediation?
Yes, but it is not magic.... There are skills to develop on the way like being agreeable, calm, positive, and a good listener. You should not be mean or point out all the reasons you do not like the other person.

Steps of self-conflict mediation

1. Do your peers who are having the conflict with you want self-conflict mediation?

2. Try to get them to state the problem. Why are they mad at you? Why are you mad at them?

3. Try to get them to say what they really feel about you.

4. Come to a solution to the problem and stick with it.

This is excerpted from a brochure written by sixth grader Barret Wall as part of his service project on peer mediation at School for the Physical City.

have to strain to see all the trash strewn throughout the park). We picked up a tremendous amount of trash in four hours. Many students were amazed and horrified that people could be so careless and leave so much trash on the grass. Some students who lived in the neighborhood vowed to keep their park clean from now on.

While we worked, I noticed acts of kindness between students — picking up trash the other did not want to, or helping carry the heavier bags. At then end of the long day, we all shared some ice cream and played in a nearby neighborhood. Though some had complained earlier, most of the students said they were glad they came, glad to have done something positive, to have done their part. The day's efforts were worth it simply to hear those words.

The other class chose to volunteer at the Lower East Side Recycling Center. The students and I expected to be separating bottles and cans. Instead, we spent the day beautifying the center. We raked and weeded to create a huge compost pile, and we planted new trees and bushes. It was an exceedingly hot day, but the students persevered. Again, I saw many acts of kindness. Matt offered his hat to another student who was clearly suffering under the heat. Students helped each other pull weeds, dig holes, and take away dead leaves. We were joined by a group of older volunteers, and we worked well together. When we broke for lunch, we sat by the river and a sense of calm and pleasure permeated our group. The students were happy with themselves and each other. The bus ride back was filled with laughter and the satisfaction of a job well done.

With both groups, the service actions helped seal the bonds of our community. Through the giving of a hand, the sharing of lunch, or the loaning of a hat, these students demonstrated that they had developed a sense of friendship and responsibility toward one another. This year, I have seen these same students helping each other in times of crisis, eating lunch together, being together in the morning before school.

Though students may have balked at first, both of these experiences brought out the true nature of our community and a sense of importance of service. The students recognized they were doing good works like those mentioned in the *New York Times* articles, or like the Indians who fought with Gandhi. Many said that doing something positive for the community, both in a group and individually, was an empowering and heroic act. They realized that they did have a voice they could use to fight injustice by joining marches, volunteering their time, and informing others.

EXPEDITION PORTFOLIOS

As students were completing their service projects, I assigned a year-end portfolio project. In addition to a collection of their guiding questions and research interests, the portfolio included essays on leadership, the relevance of Gandhi's message today, and their definition of heroism; and reflections on the meaning of service, the reason they chose their service project, and what it was like to complete it. I had a twofold rationale for giving them this hefty assignment. I wanted the students to leave my classroom with a document that attested to the ideas, creativity, warmth, and dignity they had demonstrated during the semester. I also wanted them to see the breadth of their learning throughout the expedition. For instance, it was a powerful experience for one student, Tana, to compare our first disillusioned conversation about heroes to her final reflections: "I used to think heroism was just someone who did something risky and unusual. That theory isn't half of it. Heroism could be anything from picking up a piece of trash to changing the world."

The portfolios also illustrated that performing any kind of service inevitably enlightens and empowers. Many of my students continue to do community work. Recently, a group of students went on a march protesting the use of child labor by American companies abroad. One of the students who went was Hana, who just last year had so potently expressed her cynicism toward the concept of heroes, leaders, and role models. As she spoke to the class about the march she said: "It's important to know that we (kids) have a voice and can act on the things we see are wrong in our world. We can do something about it."

QUILTING COMMUNITY

CAROL DUEHR AND
CHRISTINA NUGENT

*T*he students' voices rose into a crescendo of excitement as they entered the doors of CyCare Plaza. Not only would they be viewing the entries from Dubuque businesses for the Festival of Trees but they would also see their entry—a quilt, on official display for the very first time. The students scurried ahead and eagerly sought out our quilt display, and their cries of discovery quickly drew the rest of the class like a magnet. As we gathered around the quilt, a hush of awe fell over our group. We watched the play of emotions on our students' faces as they stood mesmerized by the quilt they had crafted for their learning expedition, "Communities Past and Present." With undeniable pride they pointed out their own squares to classmates and anyone else who came to see what had captivated the interest of so many children. We smiled as we listened to students explain the process of making the quilt to those who gathered around. During our long walk back to school, students continued to discuss the quilt. We had hoped that all the hard work they had put into the quilt would benefit someone, but we were just beginning to realize the impact this project had made on our students.

We teach at Fulton Intermediate Center in Dubuque, Iowa. About 75 percent of our students receive reduced-cost or free lunches and about 55 percent have been identified for special needs. To meet the needs of our diverse population, our class sizes range from twenty to twenty-five students. As a team of four teachers, we develop long-range plans for our expeditions and then work more closely in teams of two. Our first expedition in fifth grade, "Communities Past and Present," is based on the study of United States history from the 1400s through the Civil War. Guiding questions are "What skills do we need to become successful community members?" and "What are the similarities and differences between our community and communities of the past?" This is the second time we have completed this expedition, and throughout this chapter we refer to both years. Each year is a learning experience for us as well as our students. Since we continually ask our students to revise and improve their work, we expect the same from ourselves.

At the start of this expedition we were not thinking of the impact that service would have on our students but rather on the community we needed to build. Since the beginning of the fifth grade is also the start of a multiyear teaching cycle, we spent a lot of time building a classroom community with the knowledge that all initial community building would benefit us throughout the two years. In the beginning, we did a number of team-building initiatives and participated daily in a community circle. During community circle we developed classroom rules, problem solved, role played, and shared bits and pieces of ourselves with the classroom community. Discussion centered on our classroom as a community, on our school, city, and state as communities, and on our responsibilities as community members.

To emphasize the diversity of communities, even one as small as our classroom, we invited guest speakers to heighten our awareness of the many unique learners in our school. The learning disabilities teacher explained what it was like to have a learning disability and the nurse provided insights into particular medical conditions affecting individuals in our classroom such as diabetes and Prader-Willi. Next we developed a working vocabulary of the skills necessary to become a responsible community member, such as collaboration, cooperation, respect, tolerance, service, trust, honesty, and dependability.

This flowed naturally into a study of "Communities Past and Present" during which we applied the knowledge we had learned about what makes an exemplary community member to the different periods in the history of the United States. The first communities we studied were the Native Americans. We focused on the cooperation and collaboration necessary for the Iroquois nation to thrive as they built their longhouses and formed the Iroquois confederation. Groups of students built longhouses much like the Iroquois did, practicing the skills we had discussed. The next communities we studied were the early colonists. We used our textbook as a resource to learn about the different ethnic groups that were the first settlers in the New World. Since storytelling is an essential part of community history, we read folk tales from different cultures to aid us in understanding how different communities functioned. Novels such as *Morning Girl, The Witch of Blackbird Pond, A Lion to Guard Us, Pedro's Journey, The First Thanksgiving, Sarah Morton's Day,* and *A Journey to the New World* helped students understand the perspectives represented by each ethnic group.

LEARNING TO ASK FOR STUDENT INPUT

Meanwhile the Festival of Trees was fast approaching. The Festival of Trees is an annual event sponsored by Mercy Health Center, a local hospital, as the primary fund-raiser for their rural outreach program, which supplements costs incurred by rural families who cannot afford insurance. Local businesses and organizations donate decorated trees, wall hangings, pictures, and holiday decorations to be auctioned. This program had special significance to us because Carol's niece had directly benefited from this fund-raiser during a time of critical need.

We had participated in the past when a class decorated a tree for the auction. That year it had been more of a teacher-generated project; we had come up with the idea of decorating a tree and the type of ornaments to make. We wanted the decorations to connect with the curriculum, studying our heritage and explorers, so one class made flags from other countries, two other classes made Swedish dolls and ornaments from other countries, and the fourth class made a tree skirt representing the world. We provided the materials and directed the activity. Inevitably, this made the activity a service project rather than service learning.

In retrospect, we were glad we had participated because, even though our process was not linked to the Expeditionary Learning principles, the students enjoyed being part of a worthy project. Yet we realized that it could have been a much more powerful learning experience if it were more student centered and rooted into our curriculum. We knew the students would learn more about their role in the community if they could take greater ownership of the project. Ideally, all the ideas and problem solving would come from the students. Our role would change from director to facilitator. We vowed that next time we did this expedition, we would turn to our students for help.

By means of introduction, we started with the premise that a good community member gives back to his or her community through service. The students discussed different types of services we receive from our community, such as fire and police protection, water supply, and garbage pickup. Then we talked about how we could give back to our community. We explained to our students the purpose of the Festival of Trees and its special meaning to us. We displayed pictures of the project from the previous year, and the students expressed enthusiasm about continuing the tradition. They thought it was a great way to give back to their community. Since we wanted our project to be service learning and not an isolated service project, we threw the ball into the students' hands. During community circles we brainstormed ideas of possible projects that would meet the festival's criteria, yet also showcase what the students had been learning. We asked if they had ever been to the Festival of Trees. A few had, so we were able to discuss the different types of entries they saw there, such as trees, wreaths, paintings, wall hangings, ceramics, crafts, and quilted items. The classes rejected many of the ideas because they were too small to involve everyone or could not adequately show what they had learned. Some liked the tree idea but the majority of students were most excited about the quilt idea.

The next question was, what aspect of our learning would be best displayed on a quilt? Up to this point, the focus of the expedition had been on explorers and early colonists. In class discussions we talked about how the colonists and explorers relied on oral storytelling to keep their culture alive, to entertain, and to teach their children. Students studied folk tales as cultural artifacts of different communities. While some students wanted the quilt to depict different explorers or the colonists' daily life, most wanted to illustrate the folk tales they were reading. Quilts and folk tales seemed like a natural fit. We looked at a number of quilts and discovered that many quilts tell a story. Students decided they could each make their own quilt squares that illustrated different folk tales. This gave each student ownership and a chance to showcase their learning. It was a wonderful idea just waiting to come to life.

"How do we decide who gets to do which folk tale?" was the next question everyone asked. Some students had a favorite folk tale, but many students wanted to do the same popular folk tales. After a lengthy problem-solving session, we decided that students would choose a folk tale from their ethnic background. The ensuing discussion about ancestors tied in well with our expedition. We could have gone to the public library and found genealogical information or had students interview their grandparents searching for family trees. However, in the interest of time we had students ask their parents. Interestingly, the students connected their diverse backgrounds to the diverse heritage of the colonists. Fortunately, there were only a few students who chose the same folk tale, so it was decided that, since our quilt was going to be very large and each picture would be unique, several duplicate choices would not be a problem.

THE QUILT HELPS BUILD WRITING SKILLS

The students did many language arts activities with the folk tales as a base. First, they did a story map of their folk tale. The story map included main character(s), setting, problem, five main events, and solution, all of which helped students complete the next activity, a summary or retelling of the story. In order to make this a more interesting task, students wrote a letter to a friend summarizing their folk tales as well as the reasons they chose that particular folk tale. This presented an excellent way of practicing summarizing or retelling, a comprehensive strategy that is a school-district outcome. Because the students had chosen the folk tales themselves, the activities had meaning for them. The skill also seemed easier to master because they needed it for the quilt. Each quilt square had to tell the story of their folk tale. Without the summarizing skill, students could not draw the picture. The folk tales students chose became *their* folk tales.

As we plan our expeditions, we look at how we can meaningfully integrate district outcomes into our expeditions. Since we were studying folk tales, we thought that this would be the perfect place to teach the writing skill of compare and contrast. First, we listened to several different versions of *Cinderella* such as *The Rough Face Girl,* an Algonquin Cinderella, and *Yeh Shen,* a Chinese Cinderella. Because we were studying folk tales, the students had a purpose for comparison. It was much more meaningful than if we had taught the skill in isolation, such as comparing/contrasting a chair and a stool. Since everything we studied throughout the day was so interrelated, the students viewed this writing project as another step toward the successful completion of the quilt.

To produce quality comparison essays, we delved into the writing process. After reading the different versions, students brainstormed in chart form the similarities and differences of the two stories. After we modeled the writing of a rough draft from the brainstorm list, students wrote their own rough drafts. Teacher and students created a revision checklist that included components such as topic and closing sentences, varied sentence beginnings, and sequence. After the students checked their own essays against the checklist, they rewrote them. Then students helped each other revise. This was accomplished in several ways. Students chose to meet with one other student, a small group of students, or the whole class to critique their essays and check them against the revision checklist. They then rewrote their essays again. Next, students had conferences with the teacher. This entire critiquing process helped students work toward a final draft.

STUDENTS TAKE CHARGE

While we were working on all these language arts skills, we were still very concerned with how to pay for the quilt project. Since our funds were nonexistent, our initial step was to procure money for the necessary materials. The first time we taught this expedition, a student suggested writing letters to Dubuque businesses asking them to sponsor our project. This became an appropriate time for a lesson on how to write a business letter. Students anxiously awaited a response and were delighted when the first donation came. We were able to totally fund the quilt in this manner.

The second time we went through the expedition, we were waiting for students to come up with this suggestion because it was fairly simple and it met our needs. But instead, the students suggested a garage sale. This was the last thing we wanted to do especially since parent-teacher conferences were the next week. However, it was a student-generated idea and we wanted the students to feel ownership and to know we appreciated and supported their ideas. So we started to make plans. After some debate, we decided to hold a white elephant sale in the school gym during conference days. Students brought items for the sale as well as baked goods. They recruited parents to supervise the operation and volunteered to help themselves. Students really took responsibility for the sale, and it was not as much work as we thought it would be. As the items started arriving, we expected our revenue from the sale would not be that substantial. Imagine our surprise when the final count showed that we had netted $116.

Remembering our previous blunders, we approached the making of the quilt with a different mindset. The first time, in our eagerness to get the project rolling, teachers hurried out to buy the materials so we could get started. The next day we excitedly shared what we had bought, but were disappointed when the students did not seem as excited as we were. Belatedly we realized the mistake we had made when a student remarked, "Oh, is that what *you* picked?" in a not so favorable tone. Much to our chagrin, we had inadvertently taken over their project. In our enthusiasm we had taken the responsibility for learning away from the students. Fortunately, we had learned from our mistake and this time our objective was to give the students more choices, responsibility, and ownership. The teachers met at the store late Saturday night to gather material samples. On Monday, students voted for the favorites and a choice was made.

Next, students had to design a pattern for the quilt. For the first quilt we gave the material to experienced quilters who decided on the pattern. But now we realized that designing the quilt provided a variety of interesting math learning opportunities. We started with a book about quilts by Patricia Polacco called *The Keeping Quilt,* which provided an excellent literature connection. We then used colored cubes to lay out the pattern. Groups of four students were given eighty white cubes and a handful of contrasting color cubes to arrange into a rectangular pattern. After the group had decided on one pattern, they took paper squares of their pattern and glued them onto white paper. When they were finished, each group had a paper quilt. From this diagram they had to figure out how much material was needed to make the quilt and estimate the cost. This is very difficult to do. Many adult quilters have a hard time figuring out the amount of material they need. If this activity were a problem in a textbook or on a worksheet, the students would have immediately given up, but because they needed this information to complete the quilt, they were willing to persevere. This task also met—in a meaningful way—our school district outcome for problem solving with a picture or diagram. When they were done, the classes voted on which pattern to use.

Each time we do this project, we think of more activities we could do next time. One idea would be to keep a tally of deposits and expenditures on a giant checkbook register, but taking the time to do these activities can be scary. We have to cover a lot of curriculum. Yet since students benefit from an in-depth approach to a topic, rather than a superficial touching of the surface, these activities are well worth the time. We would also like time to deepen the connections between the quilt and the community they were serving. People who have benefited from the program as well as directors of the program could visit the classroom and explain the program's importance. This would help the students to empathize and see the urgency of this need.

A PUBLIC AUDIENCE SETS HIGH STANDARDS

To ensure a quality product, we knew we had to set standards for the quilt square. We brainstormed with our students, and decided to divide the standards into two parts: content and appearance. Since a quilt tells a story, students decided that it was imperative for our quilt squares to tell a story. The content of each quilt square needed to include a major scene and/or character indicative of the story. Because the quilt would be on display next to products created by Dubuque's finest artisans, the appearance of our quilt had to meet that standard. We brought in several quilts as examples. Students decided that appearance involved neatness, details, composition, and color.

Using these standards as their goal, the students launched into the first draft of their squares. The art teacher became involved in the expedition and used art classes to work with students on their drafts. Then we held a critiquing session similar to those for writing. The students used the standards to give positive comments about their classmates' drawings as well as to suggest ways to improve the drawings. A wide range of artistic ability required some students to make numerous changes while others were able to proceed after only one draft. Students learned valuable lessons during this draft session, including using rulers, sketching lightly in pencil, and erasing carefully. Once students completed their revisions, they started working on cardstock using fabric crayons. Final drafts were completed when the class agreed that the standards had been met, and it was the student's personal best effort.

Doing multiple drafts, critiquing, and redoing work, ensures a quality product. Students were very concerned about the appearance of the finished quilt. Because it was to go on public display, their level of concern was raised and they strived for their very best. One student had had a very difficult time producing quality work since the beginning of the school year. His attitude was, "I did it, that's all that is important." But the "hook" of service and public display really had him convinced of the importance of quality work. Since this process, he has been working very hard in all areas. Before the quilt, he had felt that one draft was sufficient. After, he saw the merits of multiple drafts and became willing to do things more than once. He also learned how to follow a rubric and to

Sean Kramer, a fifth-grade student at Fulton Intermediate Center in Dubuque, Iowa, drew this first draft of his quilt square which would be added to a whole-class quilt. The squares illustrated folk tales from different cultures. Sean's depicts the story of "Stone Soup."

create a quality product based on criteria. For example, in the past he hurriedly finished writing notes in his learning journal without care to detail. Now, he checks the rubric while working, making sure that he uses straight lines, does not doodle, and writes neatly.

This is the final, more detailed draft of the quilt square by Sean Kramer, a fifth grader at Fulton Intermediate Center in Dubuque, Iowa.

After completing the squares, the next step was to transfer the drawings to the fabric. Our ineptitude with the fabric crayons turned out to be rather humorous. We spent a whole period trying to iron the drawings onto the fabric only to discover that we were ironing the wrong side. Finally one of the students suggested what we had thought was illogical. We needed to iron on the paper not the fabric.

PUTTING THE PIECES TOGETHER

In the meantime, we needed to find quilters. We were starting to panic because the deadline was near. The first year we did this expedition, our original plan had been to have the teachers stitch the quilt together. Instead we decided to pull back and let the students solve the problem. We encouraged them to start by searching the phone book for possible quilting sources. Unfortunately, this led to little success in the quilting department, but it did lead to a lesson on how to use the phone book, as well as a lesson in persistence. During another problem-solving session, some students suggested asking grandmothers who had quilting experience, and one student suggested his church group. Although the church group was already busy working on a quilt, two women, Helen Schlung and Ruth Hudson, were willing to take on the project at no cost. One of the women suffered from Alzheimer's disease and quilting was a means of keeping herself busy and focused. She was the one who pieced the quilt together and did the bulk of the quilting. The entire process was completed in less than two weeks. She even quilted around the towers in Rapunzel's block and around each brick of the Three Little Pigs' house.

This time we wanted the students to do more of the quilting. But the quilt had to be sewn together first. We brainstormed with the students different ways the quilt could be sewn. Students suggested sewing it themselves, having the teachers sew it, and having parents sew it. We discussed the pros and cons of these options. Students were still working on the final drafts of their squares and our deadline was drawing near, so having them sew it was not a good use of time. Since asking the teachers to do it would have made it our project, that idea was nixed. The children decided to find a parent who could sew it over the weekend. Students were a little disappointed they would not sew the squares together, but they were relieved they would be able to quilt it themselves.

Once the whole quilt was sewn together, the quality of the students' work began to shine through. We set up a full-size quilt rack, borrowed from a teacher, in the learning center. After having practiced stitching on fabric in the classroom so our stitches would be neat and even, students were ready to quilt. Each class went down to the learning center. Some students quilted while others did their school work on the floor around the quilt rack. Amazingly we had plenty of help around the quilt rack. Teachers' and students' family members, mentors, and college students came in to help thread and tie off needles. It was wonderful to teach a lesson around the quilt rack, whether it was division, a lesson on the colonists, or spelling. We would ask a question of the class, and students on the floor would raise their hands as well as students at the quilt rack. We could almost imagine that we were in an old log school house, the smell of a fire in an old iron stove permeating the air.

There were virtually no discipline problems. Students were on task, both on the floor and at the rack. Positive comments such as, "Wow, your stitches are really neat!" and "I can't believe how fast you can do that!" and "You are really good at this!" floated around the room. We had tried all year to get students to give put-ups rather than put-downs and now they were being successful at it. Students could see the positive contributions of their peers in the class. It was not necessarily the smartest students or the neatest workers who were good quilters. One student who struggles academically really took on a leadership role, because he was one of the only ones that could tie knots. It was so gratifying to hear other students, whom he normally relied on for support, asking him for help. The process helped nurture the "intimacy and caring" we strived to create in our room. After the quilt was finished and the students were having a particularly difficult time getting along, we would remind students of the quilt and talk about how we worked together as a team, and that would always get us back on track toward being a productive community.

The whole quilting process took about one day per class. We could see the students' sense of pride increase as the quilt progressed. They thought their paper squares were well done. Once they saw their square ironed on the quilt, they were impressed. But we could really see the pride glowing on their faces as they finished quilting their own square. The year Helen and Ruth did the quilting, the final project was good, but having the students do the quilting themselves was much better. Students had more pride in the final product because they did more of the work. They learned to recognize that every student was a valuable contributor to the project.

The students also learned a great lesson on deadlines. Many students hand in homework late. Their philosophy is "Better late than never!" However the quilt *had* to be done on time. As the deadline approached and a lot of work remained ahead, one student asked, "Why can't we just hang this a couple of days late?" We discussed the fact that the quilt would not bring in as much money if it were not displayed as long as the other items. Displaying the quilt late would also be a poor reflection on our school.

On Friday afternoon the quilt was finally ready to be taken off the rack. We had just enough time to have a parent slip-stitch the edges before it needed to be hung on Monday. Teachers and students alike anxiously awaited taking the quilt to be put on display, as well as visiting CyCare to see it displayed. As part of the Festival of Trees festivities, Mercy Center sponsored a reception for the people who had sponsored an entry or had bid on entries in previous years. As teachers, we wanted the opportunity to represent the students at the opening celebration. We donned our holiday finery for a night of good food, drink, and hobnobbing. After we had filled our plates with goodies, we went to stand unobtrusively admiring our quilt. Although it was an outstanding entry in our eyes, we were unprepared for the comments of viewers. "Wow! Isn't this beautiful!" "What a lot of work!" "The colors are beautiful!"

The quilt was such a hit that the local newspaper asked to do a story about it. Because our school is located in a lower socioeconomic neighborhood, we often receive negative publicity. The newspaper article was a chance for positive press for our school. It boosted our students' self-esteem to see a picture of their quilt in the paper and Fulton represented in a positive manner. Many students came to school with the article carefully cut out of the paper. The laminating machine was steaming as it worked overtime.

CyCare, where the Festival of Trees was held, houses our business partner, HBO & Co. They offered to treat teachers and students to holiday cookies and give us a chance to view our quilt along with the rest of the displays. Since we can always be enticed by food and we were not sure all of our students would have a chance to view the quilt on display on their own, we decided it was worth the twenty-block walk in unpredictable November weather. As we walked in the door several students were ahead of the rest of the group. In a matter of seconds one of these students had rushed back to literally drag us to see the quilt. He chattered excitedly as he pulled us along, "Look at how much money has been bid!" and "Do you see my square, huh, do you see it?" The other students, though no less enthusiastic, waited patiently to have their picture taken with the quilt. Two adult chaperones stood next to the quilt to keep people from walking in front of it while pictures were being taken. The smiles on their faces showed their pride as they told anyone who would listen, "These are the students from Fulton who made this quilt." Not only were the students thrilled by the sight of our quilt, they were also duly impressed by the bids. The final bid on the first quilt brought $400 to the Festival of Trees fund. Our quilt was one of the biggest money makers for the Rural Outreach program.

Realizing that our project would not have been a success without the enormous help of many people, we felt the need to express our gratitude. The first year we made a quilt it was the quilters, Helen and Ruth, to whom we knew we had to show our appreciation, and students came up with the wonderful suggestion of compiling a book that would describe the process. Since we had used the digital camera to record each step, it was easy for students to write about their experience. It probably would have been better if we had reflected on each step in a journal. This would have helped students realize the amount of work that went into the quilt and the many things they learned from the project.

In addition to the books, students sent invitations to Helen, Ruth, and the winner of the quilt asking them to visit Fulton. Helen was the only one able to come, but her visit was a great success. Again our students made us very proud as they conducted themselves as model eleven-year-olds. They acted as perfect hosts, asked appropriate questions, and officiated as tour guides. Helen was visibly moved by the students' delight in meeting her and with their presentation of the book and a check from leftover funds. The students did a wonderful job expressing their gratitude for all the hard work she did on the quilt. After all, she was the one that helped make their quilt squares come to life. Individually, each square was good, but once all of the squares were sewn together the end product was amazing.

The service learning component of the expedition was a very powerful learning experience for all of us. This really came to light when, at the end of the school year, we put together showcase portfolios based on the ten Expeditionary Learning design principles. Again and again, students chose aspects of the quilt experience as examples of the different principles. The quilt showed many wonderful ideas, such as the beautiful squares' designs and the fundraising rummage sale. The students nurtured intimacy and caring by helping each other to quilt. Students took on the responsibility for their own learning when they came up with the idea of the quilt, planned its layout, selected the material, raised the money, and quilted the squares. Students solved problems that they never thought they could and created squares more beautiful than they thought possible.

The students collaborated in many ways. Without the help of every student, the quilt would not have been a success. They demonstrated the power of diversity and inclusivity. It would have been easier to create a quilt with just those students we thought were readily capable. However, everyone was included, from the brightest student to the educationally challenged. The many successes and failures the students encountered in writing, drawing, and problem solving helped the students to challenge themselves and strive for their best. At the end of the expedition, when we took time for solitude and reflection, students could see the many skills they had learned and the things they had accomplished.

The common goal we had strived to achieve, the teamwork and caring that students showed toward each other during the seeking of that goal, and the collective pride we shared at the end of the experience united us. That bond carried through to the next year and was an important part of our success as a community. We teachers will carry the power of this experience with us throughout our lives, and we hope the students will too.

DISASTER RELIEF

Patricia O'Brien

Midway through the 1998–1999 school year the worst flooding in recorded history inundated parts of San Antonio. Hours of media coverage alerted everyone to the magnitude of the disaster. Our school community, Bonham Elementary, later learned that ten families at Gates Elementary, a sister Expeditionary Learning Outward Bound school, had suffered a devastating loss in the flooding.

"I was shocked when I saw the streets flooded and some places were just full of water," Matthew wrote, "but what really hurt me inside was when my teacher told us that ten families [at another Expeditionary Learning school] had been flooded. All of their stuff was just gone."

Originally, the second-grade teachers had planned to incorporate a disaster relief collection for one of the national relief organizations as the service for

our expedition on land forms. But we realized we had the opportunity to address a real community need that the students could relate to. The disaster relief would no longer focus on a national organization, but instead on those flood victims from Gates Elementary School. What a relevant way for our students to learn how the earth's land forms affect the daily lives of people just like themselves. After a brainstorming session, we decided to collect various toiletries and school supplies. The collection would run for eight school days.

Bonham Elementary School serves two homeless shelters and most of our students are from low-income families. Our students always come through to help others in need. This project proved to be no exception.

One second-grade class designed banners and posters to publicize the project. Students in another second grade drew and compiled bilingual Spanish and

English coloring books on land forms. Bonham teachers and staff provided each of the twenty flood victims with two complete school uniforms. The entire school community had become involved in the important endeavor.

Finally, we completed the collection and it was time for the second graders to determine how the items would be divided. The students decided to make a bag for toiletries and a bag for school supplies for each of the flood victims. When our students read the flood victims' names on each bag, it seemed they took over personal ownership of that bag.

"I felt sorry for them," Sarah remarked. "They lost all their stuff and did not have a home. I was so happy to buy things for them."

Not all of our students showed such enthusiasm for this project, as Kia wrote in her daily journal. "Some of the people got things that I don't have like shampoo, conditioner, cologne,

and towels. I thought this stuff was for us. I felt angry that we were giving it to other people, but then I was kind of happy that I helped."

Three second graders accompanied the teachers and social worker to make the delivery to the flood victims. Students loaded the boxes into the truck and off we went. On arrival at Gates, we learned that the principal had arranged for our students to distribute the items to each flood victim. This made a lasting impression on our students.

Andrew reported on returning to Bonham, "When I went to Gates Elementary School and those kids were there, I felt great because I was giving them that stuff. I also felt grateful because they said thank you and they wanted to visit our school. When I gave a little boy a bag with colors and pencils he was hugging the bag. He said that he had never had pencils like that. He even said that those pencils were beautiful."

THE HEROES AMONG US:
BUILDING A CULTURE
OF SERVICE AND COMPASSION

PATRICIA B. FISHER,

SHEILA SANDERS,

AND CAROL TEAGUE

The entrance to the sixth-grade wing at College Park Middle School looks like many schools across the country, except for one addition. The wall just to the right of the main hallway is covered with an expansive mosaic made of multicolored, student-created tiles. In bright blues, reds, purples, and yellows, each tile depicts a heroic quality, such as bravery, imagination, hope, and strength. At the center rests a large panel that reads, "A Hero's Journey." Students made this wall as a culminating project of a learning expedition on everyday heroes. Instead of asking students to make paintings on paper or canvas, we wanted them to make a permanent contribution to the school. A monument to the students' hard work, this wall reminds the whole school that College Park Middle School expects and fosters heroic qualities in all its students.

"A Hero's Journey" is a sixth-grade learning expedition that helps students develop responsibility, compassion, cooperation, and service, as well as strong academic skills. The expedition takes our sixth graders through the process of looking at heroes in literature and everyday life to develop their own definition of a hero. Once students have an understanding of heroic qualities, they explore the possibility that everyone can become a hero by the way they meet the challenges and circumstances in their lives.

Although our school, located in the small city of Hickory, North Carolina, is not officially an Expeditionary Learning school, we have worked extensively with the North Carolina Outward Bound School, attended Expeditionary Learning professional development opportunities, and adopted many Expeditionary Learning practices. Like Expeditionary Learning, our school places a strong focus on service. Each year, the sixth grade explores service to self, the seventh grade addresses service to school, and the eighth grade concentrates on service to community. Over time, the students learn the skills they need to be active members of the community, and together the school builds a culture in which service, compassion, and respect for others are the norm.

It takes time to foster this kind of community, and we start in the sixth grade with the heroes expedition to introduce students to examples of how people face adversity, stand for their own ideals, and become compassionate toward those around them. Five guiding questions lead the students through this seven-week expedition. Each of the three sixth-grade teams participates in the main activities that help them explore the guiding questions. Each content-area teacher chooses other activities that demonstrate their individual creativity and fit the standards in math, language arts, social studies, and science.

Throughout the expedition, students keep a hero portfolio according to a list of criteria that meet the North Carolina competency requirements. The portfolios include samples of work from math, social studies, art, science, reading, and language arts. Rubrics help students understand the expectations we have for their assignments and for their portfolios as a whole. Not only do the portfolios provide students with a record of their learning, they also give parents an entry point into the expedition and the students' work.

We have done this expedition a number of times, and we are always looking for ways to improve it. We ask students to evaluate the expedition, and we encourage them to plan lessons with the classroom teachers. We also ask the parents to give their opinions, and we ask them to be very candid when we ask, "What has your child learned about him- or herself? What heroic qualities surfaced? Did you feel that this expedition was successful? Why or why not?" These reflections help us measure our success and plan improvements. Each year, the expedition evolves slightly differently. Below, we share an account of our first year.

OFFERING A HELPING HAND

We began the expedition by asking, "What is a hero?"

"Michael Jordan," many students called out.

"Brad Pitt," called a few.

"Dennis Rodman."

"George Washington," one student remembered.

"Buffy the Vampire Slayer!" shouted another.

"What makes these people heroes?" we asked. "Is there a difference between heroes and famous stars?"

This led to a discussion about the relationship between heroism and celebrity. Each student brainstormed deeper meanings to the word "hero." Small groups compared their ideas and recorded them on word maps before sharing them with the class. The students began to see a different meaning of the word. Their earliest concept of a "true hero" continued to evolve throughout the expedition through exposure to stories, discussions, and community resource people.

Given the diversity of languages and cultures within our student body, we decided that sign language would give us all a new, shared way of communicating. As one of the launching events of our expedition, we invited deaf students from a local college to visit our classrooms. During their presentation, they signed the song "Hero" by Mariah

Carey. Our students were impressed and excited by seeing a song performed this way, and they were curious about what the song meant for our guests. The song became a theme for our classes, uniting us in our common focus on heroes. It also gave our students a reason to learn sign language, because they knew signing the song would be a major part of our culminating activity of celebrating heroes with the school, parents, and community members.

One student, usually reluctant to join the class in academic activities, was quickly hooked on signing. After mastering the signs himself, he became the official tutor in his homeroom. As word spread that Sam knew the signs, he traveled to other classes to help practice the signing. Agreeing to finish all his work, he would beg for the class to practice the song during the last few minutes of each class. He had found a chance to shine and to help others.

Another student wrote of her experience learning to sign:

I think it is really neat that we are learning the signs for a song. It looks very pretty with signs. The phrase in the song that means the most to me is "that a hero lies in you." I think that is important because it expresses that there is a hero in everyone. This is important for people to understand so they will believe in themselves. A word that means a lot to me in the song is "strong." I think a hero needs to be strong. Strong at heart, strong at will, and strong in mind.

We knew from our own experience that Outward Bound adventure activities would help us build a larger, cooperative school community. College Park is fortunate to have a ropes course with high and low elements nearby, and so in the first week of the heroes expedition, we asked students to do the ropes course in groups of ten. To be successful in each element (high or low), students had to demonstrate cooperation, compassion, and responsibility. The high elements forced each child to stretch from his or her comfort zone and take a risk. Looking up from the ground to the heights to which they must climb could be a frightening experience. One student described the experience from her point of view:

Our group did the high elements first. After what seemed like hours we finally harnessed everybody up. Then we went into a team cheer. Being pumped up we went down through the woods to our first high element called the "pamper pole." We had to harness to a rope, climb up a ladder about twenty-five pegs till we reached a platform. Looking down, people were about an inch big. The ground swayed. Out in front of me were several thick ropes and a trapeze bar. I saw the faces and heard the cheers from my group. Our leader said we would learn a lot today about compassion and trust while helping each other and I realized how important my team was to me....

Everybody had their fears, but they achieved going a little farther up the ladder and jumping off the platform. People who got on the "screamer" were brave enough to let out a little shout without being embarrassed. After that trip people felt good about themselves.

The feeling of going one step further than they thought they could was overwhelming. Throughout the day, students realized that each person had a quality that could be contributed to a group effort. Teachers and course leaders saw some students demonstrating leadership abilities, others suggesting ideas to the group, and all cooperating to accomplish a task. By the end of the day, every child felt like a "hero." They internalized this experience and realized that if they could meet and overcome these obstacles, they could meet obstacles in other areas of their lives.

When all the students completed the ropes courses, we asked them to reflect in their journals about the day. We encouraged them to make connections between their experiences on the course and our conversations about heroes. One student wrote:

Teamwork. What is teamwork? At the ropes course we learned exactly what this means. We learned that even though you want to be a leader, a true leader has to work with a team. You can't climb a ten-foot wall without a helping hand. We learned that not only do you use teamwork in physical help, but also to

accomplish self-achievements. You need teamwork for encour-
agement. Cooperation was another group achievement. At the
ropes course, we accomplished many goals. We wouldn't have
said we accomplished many goals if everyone had not accepted
the challenge. On that day, every student faced a challenge
and every student beat a challenge. When we failed, we learned
that you are successful when you learn from failure.

EVERYDAY HEROES

With a stronger sense of community in place, students launched into
the second week and the next guiding question: "How does a hero look,
feel, and sound?" Students started the expedition with the idea that
heroes are famous and glamorous. We invited a number of speakers to
illustrate that heroes can look like everyday people and that heroic
events happen in everyday life. Our first speaker was a parent who told
a story from her youth. She explained that her sister, with whom she
had often competed, once stayed up most of the night to help her avoid
an embarrassing situation and win a contest.

"Through this I learned a very important lesson," she told the students. "Because of our normal sibling rivalries, I had never considered
my sister a hero. Through her understanding of the situation and her
compassion for me, she unselfishly gave of her time and talent to help
me be a winner. On that day, I learned the true meaning of the word
hero."

During this week, students read the biography of Captain Scott
O'Grady in *Basher Five-Two* and became fascinated with his adventures
and survival techniques to avoid capture in Bosnia. Bravery, patriotism,
and determination are among the heroic qualities our students identified, discussed, and related to their own lives.

Students realized that heroes are not always perfect in body when
they read an article in *Life* entitled "Will of Steel," by Allison Adato.
It told about Aimee Mullins who was born without fibulas and had
both legs amputated below the knee at age one. She now runs for the
Georgetown University track team as a serious competitor. Students

were shocked to see pictures of tennis shoes attached to pieces of steel that take the place of her feet.

In week three, students heard about the heroics of everyday life from members of our own school community. An administrator in our school's central office shared his story of being a product of a single-parent family in a heavy gang neighborhood. Without any focus in his life, he told the students, he joined the armed forces. While a soldier in Vietnam, he determined to make something of himself when he returned home. First he completed a college degree to teach, then to be a principal, and now he has a doctorate degree in education. His desire to achieve truly impressed the students.

Justin, a seventh-grade student, came into our classes and told the students how, in the end of his sixth-grade year, he learned he had a form of cancer that required the amputation of his leg below the knee. Spellbound, students watched as he took off his prosthetic leg and bravely explained how it felt to lose your leg to save your life.

After each speaker, students had quiet time to reflect on the qualities they saw in each of the visitors. A deeper meaning of the word "hero" began to emerge after each presentation. One student wrote after Justin's visit:

Justin is a seventh grader at College Park. Last year he had his leg amputated. I think he was chosen to speak to us because of how he has overcome this. He talked to us about how it felt and what kind of things he had to go through. Justin now has a fake leg. He said that at first it was very hard to walk with. But now Justin has mastered walking and has begun to learn to run. He is a hero because he has accepted what has happened to him and made the best of it."

Students used these reflections as preparation for more polished essays. For instance, in the sixth grade, the North Carolina writing requirements include clarification and descriptive essays. Our students used the prompt, "A person I consider a hero is…" They identified three characteristics to express the significance of their chosen person. One of the students chose her grandfather in Ohio as her hero, hoping she could present the essay and a hand-drawn picture to him as a gift. Regretfully, her grandfather died as the expedition was drawing to an end. Realizing the significance of this special tribute, the mother requested the essay to share with the family and friends.

We encouraged students to start looking within themselves for the heroic qualities they saw in others. To help them make these connections, we asked them to create life maps. Students illustrated these maps with important moments from birth to the present, including the "hills and valleys" or the "highs and lows" of their lives. As they filled in the details, stories emerged that related to the heroic stories we were hearing from our speakers. Students began looking at events in their lives in a new light.

A GLOBAL VIEW

After seeing heroes in everyday life, we began to explore the role ordinary people play in the quest for world peace. Our guiding question for the next phase of the expedition was "What is a world without peace?" Social studies classes incorporated current events of the past few years in Eastern Europe. Searching for an answer to the guiding question, students studied heroic figures who have sacrificed in order to provide a higher quality of life for all. They read about the history of the Berlin Wall and focused on two brothers, Karl and Kurt, who found themselves on opposite sides. In a seminar, students empathized with Karl and Kurt, brothers who were separated at birth and whose paths crossed in a bizarre and tragic way.

Students also read *Zlata's Diary*. In her journal, Zlata Filipovic, a child from Sarajevo, chronicles the horrors of her city under Serb attack. Comparing herself to Anne Frank, she relates her despair of being robbed of her childhood. Excellent lessons flowed from this book into all areas of the curriculum. Students wrote detailed letters to Zlata, created their own journals, and used Venn diagrams and charts to compare her to Anne Frank. One student wrote:

> *Zlata was a courageous, brave, and important hero for Sarajevo. Zlata, a small girl in a large war...Who would have thought*

that she could have been a hero? It is amazing all the close
escapes she had ... almost losing her mother, almost getting hit
by a shell. At school, a teacher suggested they publish some of her
diary. They went through with it. This must have been tough to
have your diary—your personal diary—spread all over the
world. But she went through with it. She did it, not for the fame
and fortune of being a hero, but because she felt she had to! We
can only hope we would have done the same thing if we were in
her place. Now I have a question for you and me. When the time
comes to be a hero, will we be ready?

As part of our social studies exploration of global issues, students
investigated the effects of pollution on the health and welfare of
Eastern European nations. They became especially interested in babies
who breathe highly polluted air and have developed lung diseases. After
researching the causes of pollution and some of the ways industry and
government can control environmental hazards, they met in groups to
create a plan for cleaning up the environment in Eastern Europe. They
saw the relevance of their work to their own lives when they devised a
plan to clean up their own community.

While the students acted as environmental planners, they also
learned about scientists who had made a difference in the natural and
human communities. Science teachers found a great resource in the
book *Heroes,* by Betty Burke and Janet Cain, which highlights the contributions of important scientists. In sixth grade, we teach space as part
of the North Carolina competency requirement. Not only does the book
have a section for space heroes, but it also has sections about heroes in
medicine and inventions. Individually, students researched different
scientists and shared their findings in cooperative groups. Finally, the
class conducted a seminar on the value of each scientist's contribution
and his or her area of expertise.

No matter how many heroes students learned about, they tended to
single out one or two whom they especially admired. They did extra
reading and research on them and returned to them in their journals. To
share this expertise, we asked students to participate in a "carousel"
activity. We divided the class into two groups, and each group chose a

hero and became experts on that person. They researched the person's life history and contribution and illustrated his or her accomplishments on posters. On the day of sharing, they placed the posters around the room. Each member of one group acted as the expert for the day and stood with their poster to teach all the "visiting" students about their hero. The next day, the teammates exchanged places and the other group members stood with the posters and became the experts. This activity allowed each child to become both the "teacher" and the "student."

BUILDING THE "HERO WALL"

By weeks six and seven, students began preparing to make the tile wall. They started by exploring the question "Why am I a hero?" They reflected on the experiences of the ropes course, the stories told by community members, and the qualities learned from academic lessons and novels to find the heroic aspects within themselves. They chose the heroic quality that they thought was most important, such as knowledge, bravery, strength, or imagination, and wrote about it in their journals. Next, they drew a symbol of the heroic quality on a six-inch by six-inch sheet of paper.

After perfecting their design through rough drafts, they were ready to apply their image to a ceramic tile of the same size. The students brought their white tiles to life with brushes and brightly colored paints. All their hard work and creativity came to fruition in the designs they made. They were as varied as the students: a lightbulb on top of a book represented knowledge, a swimmer showed determination to make the team, tools represented hard work, and two girls with their arms around each other illustrated unity. But still, the students only saw the tiles as individual, discreet objects. They knew that together they would form a "Hero Wall," but they were not sure what that would look like. On the Saturday before the culminating activity, the teachers gathered to attach the tiles to an inside wall that leads to the sixth-grade wing. We would have liked to have had the students involved in the tiling process, but it was too difficult to orchestrate with two hundred students. When we finished the wall, we covered it with a large cloth. The next few days, the entire school community waited eagerly for the draped wall to be unveiled.

During the seventh week, the air was charged with anticipation. Students knew the culminating celebration was right around the corner, and they still had work to do. To meet the requirements in the "Hero's Journey" rubric, some students had to finish pieces of work, such as their life map, descriptive essays about heroes, or their science and social studies essays. Some students had to finish learning all the signs for the "Hero" song. When students completed the rubric, they launched into making their hero medals. Each child molded a piece of clay into a circle, and then personalized their medals by writing in the clay while it was wet. A final coat of gold spray paint and the red-white-blue ribbon made the clay look like an Olympic gold medal. The students were ready for the celebration.

On the evening of the culminating event, more than two hundred parents, students, teachers, and community members crowded into the gym, eagerly awaiting the arrival of our sixth-grade heroes. Excitement grew as the music from the movie "Rocky" filled the air. All guests rose to greet the 180 sixth graders entering the gym carrying his or her own hand-made medal. The students formed a large circle around the gym floor and invited a parent or significant adult to join each child. As they filled the floor, the students asked them to hold their hero medal. Then a hush descended on the crowded room as the song "Hero" by Mariah Carey began to play. Looking directly at them, students signed the powerful lyrics to his or her adult. Many eyes filled with tears as parents shared this special moment with their child, celebrating the joy of being a sixth grader and a hero. As the song ended, adults placed the medal around their child's neck and offered praise and appreciation.

After the song, the audience returned to their seats and listened to students describe their work through vignettes they had written. Emphasizing world peace while remaining sensitive to the diversity of cultures in our school and community, students sang "Let There Be Peace on Earth" to the group.

At the invitation of the children, the audience moved into the foyer for the unveiling of the "Hero Wall." Spotlights shone on the wall, and each student looked for the tile that depicted the heroic characteristic he or she had discovered during the past weeks. They searched through the colorful images of roses, eagles, peace signs, globes, lions, hearts, lightbulbs, and scenes of people working together, taking journeys, and accomplishing great tasks. Even though the students had seen all of the tiles individually, they were amazed by how inspiring they became when they formed a whole wall.

After sharing this moment, enthusiastic students grabbed their parents and ushered them to the halls hung with weeks of work. Eagerly, they searched for their own creative masterpieces and presented them with a sense of great accomplishment. The school had been transformed into one large gallery opening, complete with an enthusiastic audience, food, fresh flowers, and tablecloths.

The expedition has a lasting effect on students. Seventh and eighth graders continue to visit the "Hero Wall" down at the sixth-grade wing to point out their tiles to friends and visitors. Students tell us that the song "Hero" by Mariah Carey brings back memories of lessons and activities they successfully completed. "A Hero's Journey" is one sixth-grade experience that students will remember, as one student explained:

> I think the hero unit was the most important thing we did. My favorite part was making the symbol of what we think a hero meant to us. I think we should do the heroes unit again. Others need to learn who heroes are. They're not just movie stars, football players, basketball stars; it's about friends, family, and others. That's why I think the heroes unit should be passed down.

THOREAU AND TRIGONOMETRY: DESIGNING A CITY PARK

KATHERINE STEVENS

$\mathcal{A}$s Tony walked across the stage to receive his second scholarship, his aunts and uncles stood and cheered. Tony had no idea when he began our learning expedition on landscape design that he would find his life's focus and have a job waiting for him when he returned from college. Now here he was accepting the school's award for service and compassion as well as the two scholarships.

Tony was not the only student with surprises. A few weeks earlier, Vicki presented our plan for a neighborhood park to the Dubuque Park Commission. Vicki, who began with us in the fall as a freshman, had not attended school during the seventh and eighth grade and had struggled with gaps in learning and social skills. But by the end of the expedition, she had the confidence to speak to city officials and to appear in a television feature on our landscape design.

The transformations in these students happened during the time they worked on converting a nearby vacant lot into a city park. The two went hand-in-hand. I had seen this happen many times in my work at Central Alternative High School in Dubuque, Iowa. Central serves at-risk youth who either self-nominate to come or are sent by other schools because of low attendance, behavior problems, or special physical needs. As the students delve into learning expeditions such as environmental design, they come to see themselves as learners capable of high quality work and as young people who have something to contribute to the community. But as a teacher, you never know in the beginning just how things will come to pass.

I remember clearly how all of this began and how nervous I felt in the face of unknowns. I had invited a new math teacher, Terri Engelberth, to team with me, because although I believed that mathematics could be successfully integrated with English in an expedition, I did not how to do it. I only knew that the traditional way of offering math kept students from seeing how integral it was to daily life.

Terri and I met one day in the gallery at Central to try to plan an expedition. "Now what?" we wondered as we sat looking across the table at one another. She brought knowledge of geometry and trigonometry. I brought experience teaching about nature writers and romantic poets. We knew we wanted the students to create a product that had a real use and lasting value. In past years, students had created gardens at Central as one project in a learning expedition on naturalist writers. It was a service to the school to maintain them, but I found it hard to sustain students' enthusiasm for weeding. I decided to shift my focus to other design projects. For some time I had been eyeing a strip of vacant land near the school, wondering if we could turn it into a city park. When I shared the idea with Terri, she saw all the mathematical possibilities. I began to see all the literature students could read as part of the expedition. We had found our main project.

Service was the fabric that held the academics together. We knew that a service project falls flat unless it is tied to something real. It is not meaningful to most students to rake leaves for the neighbors around school, but it becomes significant if the students build ongoing relationships with them. The same is true of school service projects. Not only does the service need to be real, but the learning also has to be authentic and meaningful to the project. When service works with academics, it does so because both are intertwined and mutually dependent.

Our belief in the combination of service and learning was confirmed as we watched the expedition unfold. The expedition proved to be a great success, although there were the expected days of failure and rethinking. The whole Central community encouraged our students throughout the process by admiring and making suggestions on the designs hanging in my classroom. Students in and out of our class got caught up in the excitement of the project. Many Central students wrote notes to the park commission, like this one by Chris:

> I grew up near a park and it gave me a place to play with my brothers. It gave me a swing to dream on, to fly up and touch the sky. It kept me off the streets and on the field. These are the reasons we need a park in this area … it would give these children a place to go and a place to think.

In the end, the students created a conceptual design for Central Park that was resoundingly accepted by the city park commission.

FROM ALDO LEOPOLD TO COST ANALYSIS

The environmental design learning expedition began as a fifty-minute block that students could take for either math or English credit. In preparation for their major project of designing the park, students honed their math skills of perimeter, area, volume, scale, and proportion. Using principles of geometry and trigonometry, they found, graphed, and plotted the sun's angle of inclination and shade lines from each of four trees in the gardens during morning and afternoon hours. Students later used these charts to make their selection of plants, shrubs, and vines for the gazebo.

Through these steps, students used the shape of their landscape designs to develop cost analyses of the equipment they would need in the park, the plants and planting supplies, and the construction of four-foot-high berms. They also determined both the amount and the cost of materials they would need for the park, such as chain-link fence surrounding the perimeter, asphalt and stone for the path running throughout the park, sand and woodchip mulch for the playground area, and a three-inch layer of mulch to cover all flower beds. Finally, they had to estimate the labor costs for all the above. Students completed these skill requirements not because they were supposed to learn math, but because they needed accurate figures for the proposal they would present to the city park commission.

Students also read the literature of nature writers such as Aldo Leopold, Henry David Thoreau, and Albert Schweitzer. Throughout the expedition, students reflected in their journals on the reading, their interactions with the community, and the work planning the park. We read from a variety of works, including *A Sand County Almanac.* Our discussions focused on the need to establish a land ethic. This gave us a good context in which to talk about the best uses for the vacant area of land nearby. We read about birds, especially chickadees, and their need for shelter and food. We discussed whether businesses or billboards would be suitable for the hawks circling our bluffs and the deer herd grazing along our parking lot in the early mornings and late afternoons. We read from Albert Schweitzer's journal, *For All That Lives,* and discussed and wrote about the connectedness of all life. It was a combination of readings, skills, and an authentic project that tied us together as a community in the expedition, though a sense of growth as individuals, and growth as a community, took time to germinate.

Tony and Vicki came to us with different needs and skills. Tony planned to graduate from high school in May, though he had no idea what to do next. Vicki was just beginning her high school career, and had huge gaps in learning and social skills. They were as different as night and day. Tony was quiet, gentle, full of humor, and protective of the weak. Vicki was loud, pushy, and demanding. Tony was an artist, and had thought of becoming a cartoonist. He had written his senior portfolio career paper on animation and was creating sketches for Central's third quarter magazine, *The Central Issue.* Yet still, his career plans remained vague to him.

Vicki was as sloppy as Tony was creative; she lacked confidence in her ability. She had come to Central to learn, though she did not yet realize how much she needed to know. Vicki needed immediate praise for each piece of work she did and correcting of each problem before she went on.

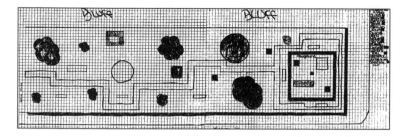

Vicki Roach, a student at Central Alternative High School in Dubuque, Iowa, designed this park for a vacant lot nearby the school based on community surveys that assessed the residents' needs.

She did well in math, but English came harder for her. She could read the story problems, though she often missed an important word. When the word was pointed out to her she was able to complete the work. She had read so little literature that she rarely saw beyond the literal meaning of passages from Aldo Leopold's *A Sand County Almanac*, or from the journal passages in Albert Schweitzer's *For All That Lives*. She was completely baffled by Henry David Thoreau's *Faith in a Seed*, although she was not alone in that. Despite her struggles, she began to get drawn in by the process of taking ideas from class and applying them to a real-life issue.

NEIGHBORS OPEN THEIR DOORS

Once we had practiced the skills thoroughly, we began working on the park project. We were fortunate to find a landscape designer, Wayne Klosterman, who helped us get started. Wayne had designed several of the city's parks, and he brought the city outline for park proposals to us. At this first meeting, we realized how much we needed his professional expertise, and he was kind enough to join our class meetings four times. Each time he left us with an assignment, and each time we were challenged and stretched beyond ourselves.

The first assignment called on the students to contact the Dubuque Department of Transportation and find out when the rest of the buildings on the property were scheduled for removal. They also needed to know when the property would be available for purchase and to whom the property would be offered first. They had to find out all entrances to the property, the traffic count, and the speed of the traffic passing the proposed park land. Any environmental problems with the property also had to be identified up front. As we discovered, the transportation department is not one person, and not just one person had all the answers we needed. Sometimes the transportation personnel we spoke with did not know which of their departments really had the answers. The students persisted and finally discovered that the buildings would be removed in the summer, that there was no schedule yet for offering the property for sale, and that the property would be offered to the previous owners first and then offered to the city of Dubuque. This last piece of information troubled us, but since there was limited access to the site, we hoped that businesses would choose not to relocate there. The site had no environmental problems, and the traffic pattern would not inhibit park construction.

For our second assignment, students created a questionnaire to find out if neighbors wanted to establish a park in the vacant lot. If people decided on a park, students needed to know what they wanted in it, if they had special needs for the park, and how many children in the area might use it. Students also wanted to know if people had concerns or worries about the presence of a park in the neighborhood. In our conversations with Wayne, students had learned that local input was essential for the success of a community project. Students made sure to include questions in the survey asking if neighbors wanted to be involved in the planning, and if they would attend neighborhood meetings in the evening.

We had already set a deadline of completion in five weeks, and had only three days to finish the survey. We made a map of the area, divided into groups (one staff member per group of students), and chose sections to survey. Since our students had not conducted surveys before and were nervous about meeting strangers, they worked in teams of two. After the first few homes, students became bolder and were able to knock on doors alone.

When we found people at home, they gladly filled out the surveys, and were thankful for the park plan and pleased to participate. Elderly people were especially happy about the idea of a neighborhood park and were eager to talk. These warm responses meant a great deal to the students. In the past, Central has had a reputation in Dubuque as a place for troubled youth or as a school that gives diplomas away. Central used to have an open campus policy and, unfortunately, some students caused problems in the neighborhood, which made neighbors concerned about their presence. But once expeditions started taking students out into the community, perceptions began to change. People who had contact with Central saw that the students were engaged in their learning and produced high quality work. Now, when the environmental design students knocked on doors with the purpose of trying to help the community, people appreciated their efforts.

Because of the warm welcomes and invitations to stay and talk, my group only surveyed three blocks on the first day. We only had two hours per day to conduct the survey because many of our students rode the school bus or had jobs. When Terri and I regrouped at the end of the day, I learned that the other teams had also covered limited ground. We decided to tighten the survey area, eliminating the area south of the highway (as many of these neighbors would have to cross the highway and drive to the park) and on the bluff to the west (which contained many businesses, hospitals, and extended care facilities). Even with our changes, we only completed five blocks in a semicircle to the west, north and east.

On the second and third days, Tony was on my team, and he quietly took the lead. The area we were canvassing included apartments above stores, and we saw a lot of children, younger than school age, with no place to play. They ran in and out of the neighborhood bar and up and down the rickety stairs to the apartments. When we first read Thoreau's *Faith in a Seed,* many students had a hard time understanding that the growth of a tree could be a subject for reflection. But as they walked around the neighborhood, saw children without a place to play, and spoke to neighbors who wanted a quiet place to visit or sit in the sun, they began to see the value of reflecting in nature. Students had learned through our reading and conversations with neighbors about the healing role nature can play in people's lives, and creating a park for these children became a natural outgrowth of that knowledge. Students wanted this work to be the best possible, for only in that way would the city consider their design and make a positive change in the neighborhood.

TRANSLATING NEIGHBORS' IDEAS INTO PARK DESIGNS

We compiled the results and discovered that 99 percent of all returned surveys asked for a park. Twelve neighbors wanted to be involved in the planning, and eighteen would be available for evening meetings. The neighbors wanted flowers, picnic tables, a merry-go-round, benches, green space, walking trails, slides, swings, trees, a fish pond and sand boxes. Many suggested a fence for safety and a drinking fountain. Some encouraged the students to think more about traffic and parking accessibility in the neighborhood. When we shared these results with Wayne, he said, "You know what the neighbors want. Now design it."

Designing a park involved measuring the area and deciding where the various elements of the park should be placed in the area. We drew those measurements on graph paper, and set a scale, but gave students no direction regarding placement of objects. Wayne told us that paths in the park had to be ten feet wide, and he gave us the area for "jungle gym" equipment, and for slides and swings. He said that the "diggers" would be in sand, but that most of the other equipment would have a woodchip base. He told us the depth of soil in berms and said to plan for lots of trees and flower beds. With this information, students were ready to let their imaginations roam.

We set the date for the first meeting for neighbors to give input on our designs, and that gave each of us a deadline. We worked separately and shared ideas. Students measured, did rough drafts on graph paper, and then each created their final design for the park using the figures Wayne had given us. When we finished, we were amazed by the variety of the designs. Some had straight lines, some used curved. Some had things grouped closely, while others had park areas spaced with trails between them.

In preparation for our neighborhood meeting, we decorated the staff workroom with plants and books and laid the designs on tables. We planned to begin the evening with a brief introduction, then students would stand by their work and explain their conceptual designs to neighbors circling the room. Wayne arrived early, and praised all the students on the quality of their plans, but he singled out Eric and

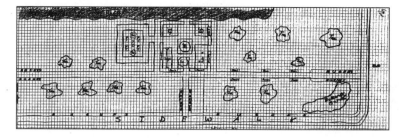

After surveying neighbors about what they would want in a neighborhood park, Eric Christ designed this park for a vacant lot nearby Central Alternative High School in Dubuque, Iowa.

Tony for their design work. Vicki missed this first neighborhood meeting. It was just as well; her design was unfinished.

Then the neighbors arrived, and they too were very complimentary. They also gave us many good suggestions. Some wanted to see water included in the park, either as a waterfall trickling down the hillside or a pond big enough for fish and ducks. Many thought a drinking fountain was a necessity. Others mentioned the possibility of building a gazebo and bird feeders. Some neighbors believed that garbage cans, a fence along the bluffs, and park lighting would make the park safer. Many people suggested building a meandering walking trail and placing flower beds near the benches and paths. By the end of the evening, we had collected a number of great ideas to consider and discuss as we revised our plans.

While Terri and I put the room back together, students returned books and plants to my classroom. Tony disappeared, and we assumed he had gone home. But as Terri and I went out the door, we found him and Wayne deep in conversation. Later we discovered that Wayne had taken Tony aside to talk about his talent in design and to find out more about him. This night was the beginning of a wonderful mentor relationship. Wayne encouraged Tony to develop his artistic abilities into landscape design. He also helped Tony choose a design school, and offered him a job when he finished his course work.

Like Tony, Vicki was also beginning to shine. Slowly, she gained confidence in her work. The more involved she got with conducting the survey and planning the park, the more she realized she was doing something real and important. In fact, the work proved so important that a landscape designer, a park commissioner, and a variety of Central's neighbors were interested. Vicki learned that I did not give immediate responses to her journal work because I collected them at the end of the period. I encouraged her and told her to always read what I said at the end of her work, because I wanted to share all the thoughts her writing brought to my mind. This was a different kind of work for her. Writing reflections required her opinion, her interpretation. She gained confidence as she realized she had valuable things to say, that she too, like the authors we read, was a writer.

PREPARING FOR THE CITY PARK COMMISSION

We could not finish the park proposal by the end of third quarter, so we continued working into fourth quarter. Our next focus was to revise our conceptual designs to match the neighbor's ideas. Students decided that they wanted to do individual revisions incorporating the neighbor's suggestions. Again, we were amazed at the variety of designs. Once we had completed the work, we hung the designs around the room and invited Wayne along with Gil Spense, director of Leisure Services for the city of Dubuque, to join our class. Gil had been a supporter of our work from the beginning. He wanted the corridor along the new construction of Highway 20 to be landscaped and commercial-free. He wanted a park right where we wanted one, and he was pleased with our new drawings. Wayne gave us more figures, suggestions for design, and a new piece of information. There was water available. A hotel and fast food restaurant had not been demolished with the other buildings, which meant that their water lines were intact. Water meant that the waterfall and drinking fountains neighbors had requested would be economical.

Keeping this new information in mind, we created one single plan for the park that incorporated the best of all the designs. We had no trouble reaching design consensus once Wayne and Gil explained why particular concepts worked best. For instance, we wanted the playground near the park entrance, but we had to consider safety. Wayne and Gil pointed out that one student's design addressed this problem by placing a small picnic area between the play area and the gate. We decided to incorporate that solution into the final plan. We also agreed to fence off the park from the highway and to have one gated entrance. Inspired by the nature writers we read, we included plenty of benches for reflection and a long, meandering path through the trees. Many of the benches would be surrounded by flowerbeds, so parents could chat in a peaceful, pretty environment while they watched their children play nearby. Finally, in response to overwhelming demand, we planned a pond and a waterfall, but made sure they were located far from the playground. Three students, Tony, Eric C. and Eric S., drew the final design. As the three artists worked on the final concept, other students completed unfinished assignments and journals, leaving their work frequently to offer suggestions or answer our draftsmen's questions.

Our final design was presented at a second neighborhood meeting, and again the neighbors were thrilled with our concept. At this meeting Tony explained the conceptual design. Neighbors wanted to know how to help, so we made copies of the petition we had asked them sign, and they promised to collect signatures for us. In the meantime, we gathered support from other Central students, and included their reflections in the final proposal to the park commission.

On the day of the presentation to the park commission, each student had a part to perform. Vicki led the presentation with a description of our survey. Tony explained the process leading to the final conceptual design, including the neighborhood meetings. Other students presented the petitions and explained our final conceptual design. Two neighbors spoke on our behalf, and on behalf of the final design. The final proposal contained reflections from students not in the expedition. For instance, Russ wrote:

> *The one thing in Dubuque, Iowa, that is needed is parks. Our town does not have enough places where young children can play happily and the parents don't have to worry. In my opinion the parks need more equipment and a better choice or selection of trees, flowers and/or other plants. The corner of Bluff and Dodge is an ideal place to have a park or rest area where chil-*

dren and parents or others may relax in beautiful surroundings.
One thing we do not need in this town is more billboards and/or
businesses cluttering up ideal space for beautiful surroundings.
The reason this particular corner is so ideal, is because first, it is
boring to look at, and second there is no nice park to play at in
this area of town. No, so that's why this would be a good spot
for a park.

The park commission accepted our proposal. The future is dependent on the transportation department and whether or not the city
chooses to purchase the land. Our presentation made the front page of
The Telegraph Herald, and two weeks later the Iowa portion of the five
o'clock news on KCRG. Tony had graduated by then, and we could
not reach him in time to join us in the taping for Channel 9. Vicki took
his place, and she eloquently explained the park proposal and our work
with the neighbors. In the interview, you could see that Vicki's experience using her math skills and learning to articulate her opinion based
on reading had given her much more confidence. She earned all her
credits third and fourth quarter, which was quite an accomplishment
for her. She speaks of how proud she is of her work and how proud
her mother is. When Terri and I saw Vicki on tape, we cried. We were
proud too.

There are many ways to help students care enough to do service.
You can offer credit or demand that they complete a project, but that is
not really service learning. It is better to draw students in through
their learning and sense of compassion. Readings of naturalists such as
John Muir and Henry David Thoreau and romantic poets such as
Wordsworth, Keats, and Shelly, all bring to mind the healing role of
nature. Once students view nature as a healer of body and soul, they
want to provide access to nature for everyone. A neighborhood
park fills that need, especially if it is in the middle of a busy city and
located next to a bluff replete with a variety of plants and wildlife.

Sometimes all it takes is a few students and the pressure to design
an expedition, and the belief in service as a way to learn, and all the
paradigms shift.

BECOMING SERVICE-MINDED

High school students in Peggy Chessmore's crew were sick of the trash that littered their school, the Umonhon National Public School on the Omaha reservation in eastern Nebraska. The crew—a group of eleven students who met four times a week with a faculty advisor—decided it was time to take action. Chessmore describes the process of the students making a difference.

The first thing students did was make a commitment that they themselves would not litter for one week. At first they did not think they could do it. It was easy to identify the problem, but it was difficult to say, "I can make a difference." We focused on that commitment for about a week. The students started to get really frustrated, because it was not making a difference. They would pick up the trash one day, and the next day it would be a mess again. So we said, "Well, what can we do about that?" They came up with the idea of putting up posters.

Students developed their own themes and ideas, and then made the posters, colored them, laminated them, and hung them around the school. Some read, "Keep Our School Clean," or "Have Omaha Pride." One showed a very clean locker area with no trash in the hall. Another had a sketch of the front of the school with trashcans and recycle boxes. They all showed what the school could look like if everyone did their part to clean up. They reminded us of what was possible, what could be.

Now, weeks later, the problem has not gone away, but it is a lot better. Students are more aware of their impact on how the school looks. Graffiti on the walls and writing on desks and tables has almost stopped. I hear students say to one another, "Don't write on that," or, "Don't do that," whereas before, everybody did it. Now a junior high school crew is working on trash pickup. I think we are making progress.

I attribute the changes to Expeditionary Learning—to the Expeditionary Learning design principles of Intimacy and Caring and Service. Those are concepts that we did not have here before. It was hard at first for my crew to become service-minded. They wanted to play games, talk, and goof around. Now they realize that they are expected to help, to be part of the solution.

Expeditionary Learning has helped the school—teachers and students—change what we focus on. We want a clean school. We do care about our environment and the natural world. We can give service and compassion to the environment as well as each other. We can make a difference.

Bay Ridge, Brooklyn: Painting a Community Portrait

Bayan Ebeid and Laura Kelly

*W*hen I.S. 30 opened its doors as a new middle school in the Bay Ridge neighborhood of Brooklyn, New York, many community members expressed alarm. Here was a new public school taking over a local building, and in the minds of some of our neighbors—especially a nearby senior center—this suggested noise, vandalism, and little accountability. While these sentiments made us feel uneasy about opening our doors, they presented an important learning opportunity we could not overlook. We decided to design our first learning expedition to address this real community need—the need to allay the fears of local residents who strongly suspected our presence would change their quiet, residential, middle-class neighborhood. Our task was to replace this concern with trust and friendship. We wanted to convey to the area that the students and local residents had much to offer one another. After some initial brainstorming, we decided that oral history would be a good way to build our first bridge.

We soon decided on a project of compiling oral histories and painting portraits of local senior citizens at the Bay Ridge Center for Older Adults. What better way to lay the framework of friendship, service, and authentic learning than to elicit the wisdom of community elders? Students would learn firsthand matters of historical significance in a local context. They would see history through the eyes of those who have lived it. Our expedition, "Bay Ridge: Revere and Restore," was beginning to take shape with an armature of sturdy guiding questions: What was daily life like in Bay Ridge in the early part of this century? How do we effect change, and how does change affect us? When is change progress? What is the cost?

In addition to knowledge in the content areas, and the skills and practices they would require, it was paramount that the students learn to: demonstrate compassion, caring, and service to others; understand other people's ideas and look at one's own ideas from different perspectives; and establish and maintain relationships with local community members.

Exploring these questions and qualities led to a rich interdisciplinary study. The English, social studies, and Spanish classes began an inquiry into mythology and folklore, two of the district content areas for sixth grade. We would soon discover, ironically, the mythic proportions of some of the tales our participating community members told us. The math teacher dug into archives to retrieve information about life in Bay Ridge when our neighbors were eleven years old, and students then compiled this information into flow charts. Technology students incorporated these findings as well as others into an impressive multimedia display. Finally, all of this hard work culminated in a gallery opening for the community that included oil paintings, interactive technology, statistical data, and a performance installation.

The following chapter focuses on the work of the two authors. The creative writing teacher, Bayan, and her students interviewed the elders and documented their oral histories. Laura, the art teacher, guided her students through the process of learning to sketch, stretch canvas, and paint oil portraits of local senior citizens. Each has described in her own section—and in her own voice—her experience with the expedition. Together, we write about the unique power of service to elicit student work and develop relationships that exceeded all our expectations.

JOINING THE NEIGHBORHOOD THROUGH ORAL HISTORY

In my creative writing classes, I launched the expedition by telling students about some of the concerns people at the Bay Ridge Center for Older Adults had about our new school. I asked them to brainstorm ways to alleviate some of these worries and ways to give back to this new neighborhood we were now a part of.

"Why don't we go over and introduce ourselves?" said Joseph.

"Maybe we could bring over a gift," said Emma.

"How about inviting them over to our new school?" said Lauren.

"Why don't they like us?" asked Michael. "We didn't do anything wrong." This was a hard question to answer. I tried to explain that having a middle school in Bay Ridge meant that people would have to adjust to something new and unknown in the community. Many residents were not used to a large number of young people in their area. Perhaps, I explained, they were worried about children playing in the streets and jostling into them on the sidewalk.

The students knew they did not want our neighbors to feel uncomfortable with their presence. "Let's go and introduce ourselves as new 'harmless' additions to the community," they decided. I told them that their ideas would dovetail very well with the project we had planned for their expedition. We could use our introductory visit to begin the process of collecting oral histories.

But in order to be ready for interviewing, we had a lot of skill building to do. I started our work by reading aloud the following quote from the author Christina Baldwin: "With compassion, we see benevolently with our human condition and the condition of our fellow beings. We drop prejudice. We withhold judgment." The students and I discussed the quote's relevance to society and specifically to our "Bay Ridge: Revere and Restore" learning expedition. Many students knew that the elders we would be interviewing might have disabilities we would need to consider. Some of the seniors would be in wheelchairs, some would be hard of hearing, and others might have bad vision. We discussed ways to address these situations.

"We should yell as we ask our questions because we assume that they might be deaf," said Jenna.

"We might scare them away," said Laura. "Maybe we should pull up a chair or kneel on the floor if they're in a wheelchair because they might be intimidated by us if we stand over them."

The students then discussed the information that they would be seeking from the senior citizens. The topics ranged from background, education, and family life to what the community of Bay Ridge was like during their adolescent years. Then the students worked in groups to transform their outlines into question form, making sure to stay away from questions that only gave one-word answers. Working collaboratively, we organized all the questions in chronological order. The students decided to keep the more personal questions toward the end, knowing that the interviewee would feel more comfortable answering them once a relationship had been established.

While all this was taking place in class, Mike Grimaldi, the physical education teacher, and I made arrangements with the Bay Ridge Center for Older Adults. Mike and I went to the center to speak with an audience of about one hundred senior citizens to explain our learning expedition. We told them that our students would like to interview them to learn about what Bay Ridge was like when they were the children's age. We said we believed they would be a wonderful firsthand resource to our students. Most of our audience responded positively. We passed out a sign-up sheet, set a date and time, and went back to tell our students. They could hardly wait.

Since we had a couple of days left to prepare before the actual interviews, I asked the students to go home with a copy of the twenty interview questions and perform and tape mock interviews with their parents. As students completed these assignments, they brought them in and we listened to them as a class and held critique sessions.

"I think the way Mark introduced himself in the beginning by

Laila Akther, a student at I.S. 30 in Brooklyn, New York, made this sketch from a photograph of a Nigerian girl as part of a series of exercises on portraiture in preparation for the students' oil portraits of local senior citizens. This sketch is Laila's first drawing in the series.

telling his name and the school that he attends made his interviewee feel more relaxed," said Dana.

"I actually liked the way Polina addressed the person that she interviewed by their first name whenever she asked a question or made a comment," Chris said. The students benefited from this activity because they learned what to do and what not to do for their future interview with the elders.

After a whole week of listening and critiquing the tapes, interviewing one another as well as teachers, and performing "do's" and "don'ts" interview skits, we were prepared for our visit. Every two students had been assigned to one elderly person before we left, and each pair was armed with a disposable camera and a tape recorder. I could tell the students were nervous as we walked over to the Center, but they began to relax when Susan Lavin, the director, met us at the door. She told us the senior citizens were excited about their project and were anxiously awaiting their arrival. Susan matched up the partners with their elders, and for a good forty-five minutes, all I saw was students taking notes, snapping pictures, plugging in and turning on tape recorders, and laughing with their new friends. Some elders draped their arms around the youngsters while students sat listening to stories of favorite childhood pastimes.

I smiled as I walked around and overheard bits and pieces of conversations. Even though our project was just beginning, already I felt as though my job was done. It seemed as though the students no longer needed my guidance. They took on the roles of reporters and were getting the information they needed for their histories. They were on a first-name basis with the seniors, and I even overheard them talking about the next time they would be stopping by. When the students got to share a snack of milk and cookies, the atmosphere became even more relaxed and homey.

At one point, Susan Lavin came over to me and said, "This is absolutely wonderful. The kids are just so lovely and they really mean business. They're doing their assignment for class, forming a bond with their new friends, and they're just so polite! Let's continue this because everyone is truly enjoying it."

The time came for us to leave, and the senior citizens were disappointed. They enjoyed having company and sharing their memorable experiences with curious listeners. As I looked around the room, I saw students taking group snapshots of their partners, the senior citizens, Susan, and our principal Linda Viggiano. The students and their new friends shared hugs, exchanged addresses, and gave warm good-byes. As we walked out, the seniors called, "Come back soon. We had lots of fun. Thank you for coming."

MINING THE NEIGHBORHOOD'S PAST

Back in our building, teachers, aides, and security guards gathered around us to hear about our visit. Students quickly told them how positive it had been. Then, back in class, we reflected more deeply. Many students were moved by the elders' willingness to share their memories and the pride they took in talking about their past. For some students, the highlight came when their senior citizens said they reminded them of favorite grandchildren. Other aspects of the interview were not so easy. Some children encountered seniors who were unwilling to participate, were hard of hearing, or could not remember certain times in their lives.

We listened to some of the interviews on tape and students laughed along with their classmates' reactions and remarks to the answers. At the same time, they complimented each other on the way they clearly articulated questions. They especially liked hearing when their classmates did not necessarily follow the script of questions, but simply followed the course of the conversation.

Now that the interviews were completed, we had a major task ahead of us. What do we do with all of this information? We decided we would write biographies of the elders, and students began by taking notes of the taped interviews. They focused on the most significant aspects in the person's life and on the parts of the interview that dealt with what Bay Ridge was like during their adolescent years. They created outlines of all the information they wanted to use in the biographical sketch. We had read biographies as a class, and we discussed the elements of good biography writing so students would know what to include in theirs. Each member of the interview pair wrote an individual biography; then together they chose the best pieces for a joint product. Students shared these with other groups to get feedback and critique, and then wrote final drafts incorporating the suggested revisions.

Laila Akther, a student at I.S. 30 in Brooklyn, New York, did this exercise in "opposite hand drawing."

At the same time students were working on these biographies, they also wrote reflection pieces on what worked and what did not work for them during the interview process. We built in time during classes for conversations among students about how the service expedition was progressing. Their questions and ideas helped push the expedition in new directions. Since our students were being trained

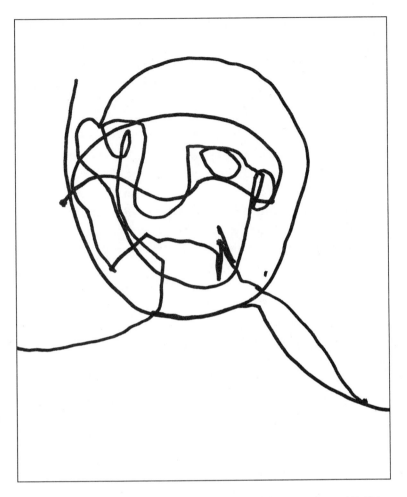

As part of a series of exercises in portraiture, Laila Akther, a student at I.S. 30 in Brooklyn, New York, sketched this face without looking at the paper.

in technology, they decided to create a Microsoft Powerpoint presentation highlighting the most interesting information from their biographical sketches. The presentation seemed like an excellent way to highlight the students' oral history and writing skills and to share the information they had gathered about Bay Ridge with the community.

This is where the computer teacher, Katherine Tsamasiros, became an asset to the project. She aided the students in assembling all the media, which included the digitized photographs, electronic art, and text. She showed them how to access the Microsoft Powerpoint applications. The students selected a template to work with and inserted the various media into specified areas of the template. The students then had the opportunity to choose how the overall presentation would look, including transitions, time between each slide, and order of slides. They each reviewed the biographies they had written to choose highlights of the senior's life to include in the presentation. They also chose how to incorporate digitized photographs of the elders that students had scanned into the computer. After many drafts and revisions, their presentations were finally ready for the gallery opening.

THE ART OF REVISION

As the students worked on the oral histories in their creative writing class, it was my responsibility to facilitate the painting of portraits in oil. Before they could even begin to think of applying paint to canvas, however, we had to lay months of painstaking groundwork. Most students came equipped with minimal skills, possessing that cryptic, primary language of figure drawing with which we all are familiar. It gives me great satisfaction to watch them now as they compare their very first draft to their final product. Their expressions are a hybrid of wonder, faith, empowerment, and pride.

I wanted to begin by demystifying the skill of drawing. I asked them to draw draft after draft after draft of the same subject, a life-size photographic portrait of a Nigerian girl. I felt that if the subject were constant, yet the skills we used differed each time, we would be better able to chart our growth. We were inspired by the words of the mountain climber Richard Nelson, "You may learn as much by climbing the same mountain one hundred times as by climbing one hundred different mountains." Through multiple drafts, we developed our skills of drawing, color theory, manipulating oil paint, and learning to draw what we see, rather than what we think we see. Many times we had to rescue drafts from the wastepaper basket after someone tossed them in frustration. It is much easier to tear down and deconstruct than it is to create. Each day I was asking these children to breathe life into a piece of paper. It was an excruciating request. It was hard to see my gentle student, Hussain, cry quietly after I refused to accept his words "I can't." I swallowed hard, pushed his drawing paper pimpled with tears back in front of him for his twentieth attempt and said "You will." I always acknowledged their discomfort and assured them that, with their faith and perseverance, they would master the skills that would allow them to create images they were pleased with.

We all kept journals, one for words, and one for images. At times they became the receptacles of disappointment, fear, pride, and progress. Amarah, one of my students, wrote in her journal: "If you think you're not good at art, don't believe it. Everyone is an artist deep down. You just have to uncover it. Put your mind to it and you can do just about anything you want. Just reach deep down and pull hard." We read the journals of Vincent van Gogh and Paul Gauguin, seeking inspiration in their work, learning humility through their struggles. We recognized through their writing that their powers of expression were not limited to the canvas. These artists became wonderful exemplars of the art of literary articulation, reflection, and creating images with words. They were helping me to confirm and convey the belief that art is not merely a modality, but an intellect.

We looked at portraits in oil created by van Gogh and Gauguin using simple guidelines for viewing art: What do you see? How does it make you feel? How do you think the artist felt about his subject? Support your answers with details from the painting. With this recipe, we began to have interesting and intelligent conversations about paintings.

There were moments when I quietly wondered if perhaps I had set the stakes too high. After all, oil painting with seventy-five eleven-year-olds with limited space, time, and money, was a lofty, if not insurmountable, goal. Few middle school students ever have the opportunity to paint in oil. It is a costly and challenging medium. But I believe that students produce higher quality art when they use the tools of artists. I carried on in spite of myself, with a little solace in thinking that this is just the way Expeditionary Learning likes it—slightly out of reach. We did, however, improve our skills enough to undertake our task of painting portraits in oil.

BREATHING LIFE INTO CANVAS

Our classroom became a beehive of activity as students stretched and primed their canvases in preparation for the portraits of the seniors. The passion, precision, and cooperation with which they worked was intoxicating. I watched in amazement as an extra pair of hands would appear when a student had difficulty both tugging and stapling a canvas, or, when a batch of gesso (canvas primer) was exhausted, someone would instantaneously whip one up. All this occurred without my ever having to issue a directive. It was exactly what I had dreamed this experience would be for these children, but I never imagined the power it would have over me.

When all the canvases were ready, each student selected a photograph of a senior citizen they had a particular affinity for. Not every child had had the opportunity to interview the seniors. It was just a logistical impossibility. In the true spirit of oral tradition, however, all those who had firsthand contact with the elders were required to tell those who did not the tales of their subjects. It was a wrinkle that turned into an asset, as it allowed the students to practice the art of oral tradition. This, coupled with extensive work on the impact of line, light, and brush stroke when rendering age and capturing individual characteristics, helped us prepare for the portraits in oil. The photos became a permanent part of our daily lives for months. I remain bewildered how, with oil- and turpentine-stained hands, constant shuffling, and interclass sharing, these photographs survived unscathed. It was almost as if the students had imparted the reverence they had for the elders into these two-dimensional photographs.

With the photos of their elders in hand, the painters began to practice steps of portraiture. They each completed approximately four drafts in pencil on paper, four drafts in color on paper, a charcoal drawing on canvas, and an underpainting on the same canvas. Once

Laila Akther, a student at I.S. 30 in Brooklyn, New York, drew this portrait as an exercise in "light and texture."

they completed that process, they were ready to begin painting in oil. Slowly and painstakingly the portraits emerged. I was so impressed that I was often moved to tears, not only by the paintings, but by the painters themselves. The quiet dignity with which the students devoted not only to their craft, but to their subjects as well, exceeded my greatest expectations. In past portraits, the students often noticed how they seemed to paint an element of themselves when painting subjects. Indeed, it was true of this project, yet something had changed. It was not an element of their image that they had endowed this painting with, it was an element of their spirit. A gift, I suspected, that would be returned tenfold.

As magically as the portraits began, they ended, each child somehow sensing its completion. I never challenged their decisions of when their work was complete. I did not have to. I was always in agreement with their instincts. We had worked many months creating an atmosphere of trust, respect, compassion, and high standards. I now had to let go and allow them to flourish.

It is a curious thing to think back to the beginning of the expedition, when the students and I discussed what would be done with their paintings when they were finished. We decided we would auction them and perhaps donate a few of the paintings to the senior center. When I asked how many students would donate their canvases to the cause, 99 percent of the students raised their hands with little hesitation. I would later come to find that less than 5 percent of the students were willing to give their canvases to auction once they were completed. The 5 percent who said they were willing to auction their work confided in me that they had arranged with their parents to offer the highest bid.

This, however, did not mean the abandonment of the service component of our expedition. It merely compelled us to examine more closely the concept of "service." Upon careful consideration, we concluded that our service component, in its original form, would have represented a closing of a chapter, an obligation met, a good deed done. I am grateful and humbled by what our service component turned into and continues to be long after the expedition has come to a close. Service for us was not merely a donated oil painting, but the gift of compassion, recognition, friendship, and respect. A gift whose patina grows richer each day through the ongoing relationships that began with this expedition and have continued into the next year. True friendship is reciprocal. This we learned through our expedition. These were not merely people to be talked to for our own purposes, then sent on their way with a lovely parting gift. They were, and are, an intricate thread in the delicate fabric of our communal lives. We are richer for serving one another.

With this significant change in our course charted, we had only to await our authentic audience. The audience was responsible in part for the level of quality in the students' work. Not only would teachers, parents, Expeditionary Learning representatives, and the community at large be in attendance, but the very subjects of the expedition would be present. This coupled with high expectations and the somewhat privileged medium of oil painting became the recipe for stellar results.

We barely managed to contain our excitement and pride until our gallery opening, busying ourselves with creating, printing, and mailing invitations. We had already done fieldwork at the School for Visual Arts in Manhattan, where we had learned about curating a gallery show. Now we prepared our own. Our portable gallery of installation walls, which we commissioned from students at Coop Tech High School, arrived just as we had envisioned. Students finished and displayed their interdisciplinary projects and watched the replies to our invitations roll in.

With sparkling cider and cheese refreshments, Benny Goodman music, an inviting rocking chair for story telling, and multimedia works of art on display, we opened the gallery doors to our audience. No one could have prepared us for what was to come. The elders poured in, enthusiastically examining the projects and offering great praise for their skill and craftsmanship. Several of the seniors beamed and giggled as they discovered themselves immortalized in oil. I overheard two women in conversation marvel at the amount of times "the Captain's" portrait had been painted. They surmised, with a chuckle, that this newly acquired fame would catapult the Captain's ego into mythic status. As I glanced across the room, I noticed Mary, a senior neighbor, sit down in the rocking chair to hear one of the students tell the stories

Laila Akther, a student at I.S. 30 in Brooklyn, New York, used "light mapping" in this drawing, which forces students to look critically, rather than passively, at the subject.

she had learned during the expedition. Mary rocked back and forth rhythmically, languishing in the reverence and accuracy of the tale.

Then, subtly at first, the focus of the gallery seemed to shift as each community elder began to seek out his or her student counterpart. It almost appeared as if the entire scene was staged. As the pairs of child and elder moved about the gallery, many arm in arm, one did not have to hear a single conversation in order to understand what was said. It was choreography at its most sublime, it was performance art at its most provocative, it was a story told to be told again. It was a living gallery.

LOOKING BACK AND LOOKING AHEAD

As we write this a year later, we can report that the relationships forged during the expeditions did not end with the gallery opening. That was only the beginning. Now students make frequent visits to the senior center, they make stationery for the seniors, and help them write letters to loved ones. They visit the seniors when they enter the hospital, and they invite them to come to the school to celebrate the culmination of expeditions. Students feel perfectly comfortable visiting the senior center, and the seniors know they are welcome in our school. Watching these connections grow over time has taught us teachers an important lesson about service. A one-time visit to a center for seniors might introduce students to the life of the elderly, but returning throughout the school year has opened their eyes to the power of making a difference in someone's life. It has been in continued relationship with the senior citizens that students have learned commitment, respect, and reciprocity.

It is interesting to realize in retrospect that the service component was the catalyst for the expedition, not a contrived, last-minute addition. With a real community need as a starting point, the students produced quality work that far exceeded our expectations. These children had the opportunity to see history through the eyes of the people who lived it. They had real peoples' lives as a barometer and that escalated the quality of work, both their writing and their painting. As personal and spiritual as art is, it is meant for an audience, and these students had the most authentic audience they could by showing it to their subjects. They knew these were not people who were going to exit their lives. They were going to continue to sit next to them at the senior center, invite them into their classrooms, and share their learning with them. These were relationships that would endure, and that is why the students worked so hard.

But there is also one more essential ingredient to the success of the expedition. As we prepared for our gallery opening, Laura wrote the following in her journal: "My wish is that my students, with gentle guidance, will emerge and thrive in a place they never knew before. I have begun to understand what it feels like to leap without looking. It is called faith. I will offer these children my arms as I gently coax them to leap."

SCIENCE

THE AQUARIUM ARCHITECTS

KAREN MacDONALD AND
CHRISTINE GRIFFIN

The call came in the middle of the school day. It was Don Perkins, the president of the Gulf of Maine Aquarium Committee, who wanted to know if a group of King Middle School students would present their designs for a proposed aquarium to his environmental and education subcommittees. Perkins had seen the students present their designs before as part of their "Dream On" learning expedition, and he had been so impressed that he wanted the architects and community members working on the aquarium to see the plans themselves. Of course, the students quickly agreed to meet that very day. They scurried around the school to gather their floor plans and proposals. There was no time to get nervous. An hour ago the students may have been discussing a novel in language arts class, but now they were presenting to a new group of decision makers, adults who were eager to spend time with sixth graders and hear what they had to say. The meeting was a hit. These sixteen students had, in reality, become a focus group for the Gulf of Maine Aquarium Committee. If, in fact, this project were going to succeed in Portland, students such as these knowledgeable, excited twelve-year-olds would need to be willing to spend their money to visit the aquarium. They would need to be repeat visitors for the aquarium to be a long-term success.

The students were able to contribute to this community effort thanks to the many long hours of researching, drafting, revising, and writing they had done for their "Dream On" learning expedition. The expedition, in which students become architects for their community, calls on students to become active decision makers in the world around them. Sixth-grade students arrive at King Middle School in Portland, Maine, from surrounding inner-city schools and the islands in Casco Bay ready for a new beginning. They are assigned to one of two teaching teams, called houses, and they stay together as a group for their three years at King. As members of these houses, students learn to make a difference in their world.

When the group of sixth graders who worked with Don Perkins first arrived at school in the fall, they entered a renovated King Middle School. The wing that they would share, the computer room with a connecting work lab, the atriums letting in an abundance of light, the new stage, even the outside landscaping had all been ideas offered by our students three years earlier as they participated in our initial "Dream On" expedition. The final product for that expedition had been to design the new sixth-grade wing of King Middle School and present this vision to the architects who were working on the renovation design.

There had been many positive aspects of that expedition, not the least of which was the service students provided to the architects and staff members working on design options. While many elements of the expedition needed revision after this first effort, it was clear to us that the service was a strong motivator, and that it provided the students with a great sense of pride and satisfaction as they walked the halls of the newly renovated building. We had seen students giving tours to their friends, pointing to a design feature and stating, "This was my idea." The students had stretched themselves in their work to impress the professional architects, and in the process they surprised their peers, their teachers, their parents, and themselves. As we reflected on our initial efforts with "Dream On," we became convinced that the service was a powerful motivating force. We needed to recapture this

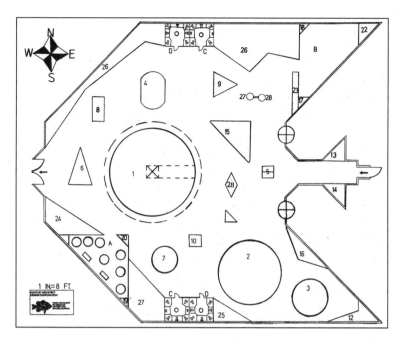

Aaron Huntley, a sixth grader at King Middle School in Portland, Maine, created this blueprint for the Gulf of Maine Aquarium.

element as we revised our plans for the upcoming school year, but the renovation of the school was now complete. What would this year's "Dream On" expedition give to the community? How would we "renovate" our expedition to make it meaningful and successful for the new sixth-grade students?

An opportunity for our revised "Dream On" expedition arose through an article in the *Portland Press Herald,* our local newspaper. A group of business leaders and community members were seriously pursuing a plan for a local aquarium. Their efforts were gaining momentum, and their next step was to work with architects on a potential design. The idea of connecting with the Gulf of Maine Aquarium Committee and asking students to design an aquarium became the seed of our latest "Dream On" expedition.

Brainstorming, webbing, planning, gathering materials, contacting local resources, and scheduling meaningful fieldwork soon followed.

As our plans jelled we realized we had an even stronger expedition than before. In order to complete the final project successfully, students needed extensive knowledge about aquatic life and habitats. Bringing science into the expedition made this effort more interdisciplinary and more academically rigorous than the first one. We planned to have our students complete three final products: a floor plan of their vision of the Gulf of Maine Aquarium, a written proposal to describe details of the floor plan, and an oral presentation of their work.

PURPOSEFUL FIELDWORK

Even before the actual kickoff in early November, students grew excited about their upcoming expedition. They entered classrooms decorated with blueprints, tool charts, aquatic life posters, and aquarium pictures. We, their teachers, had also enlarged and posted the newspaper article that had spurred our interest in the aquarium. We worked hard to foster a sense of the students' responsibility to help out the aquarium committee. They wrote business letters to aquariums around the world asking for pictures, features, and, if possible, blueprints. They wrote friendly letters to a middle school in Baltimore, asking students for information about their local aquarium. The majority of our sixth graders had never been to an aquarium. These activities helped in our efforts to gather resources and also helped students begin to see what it takes for an aquarium to be successful.

Our kickoff activity was a trip to the closest aquarium, the New England Aquarium in Boston. The sixth graders entered the building with a questionnaire in hand. After receiving information from other aquariums, each student had written three important questions to investigate during their fieldwork. These questions, along with those developed by teachers, went into the final draft of the questionnaire. Questions about lighting, exhibit space, flow of traffic, and features that encourage learning needed to be answered before they completed their tour. The students met with the curator of exhibit design and learned how aquarium staff put together the exhibits. A small group of students toured "behind the scenes" where they viewed the inner workings of the aquarium and all of the machinery and background space required to take care of the animals. This was fieldwork at its best, focused and purposeful, and it was absolutely necessary for these students to see this model before they began their own design. We watched as students viewed the aquarium with a critical eye, visiting each exhibit to gather information, and then taking a step back to analyze how effectively it was done.

On the way back to Portland it was evident through listening to the conversations that the students were eager to design their own aquariums. Most of the students lived near the proposed sites and were very familiar with the area. They had only positive comments on the tourists it would bring in, the improvement it would bring to the area, the business the area stores and restaurants would receive, and how it would help to put the "port" back into Portland. We realized how proud they were to live in Portland, and how much they thought this would improve their community. As our bus slowly made its way through Boston's busy, bustling streets, only a few people commented on the city's beauty and activity. These students were focused on getting to work on ideas for improving their own city.

Immediately after we returned, all of our students assembled working portfolios, which are color-coded folders that provide information about the overall trail they would be taking to complete the expedition. The portfolios became more and more valuable to the students as the expedition rolled along. Moving from class to class became easier; instead of carrying four to five different notebooks, each student carried his or her portfolio. It held all of the students' product descriptors, work in progress and final drafts, notes and information sheets, and a list of what they still needed to do. At a quick glance, they could tell where they were in the expedition and where they were going.

A REAL-WORLD AUDIENCE SETS THE STANDARD

Phil Dyer, the math teacher for our team, was in contact with Don Perkins prior to the start of the expedition. Perkins agreed to look at the ideas developed by the students. Not only would their parents and teachers receive this work, but members of the community would actually listen to their ideas. This would clearly motivate students to do high quality work. In middle school, students tend to focus on their peers within the walls of the building and center their actions on what will impress them. These walls were gone during this expedition, since their peers were not the only ones passing judgment on their ideas. The atmosphere was more serious because of their role in providing ideas to the Gulf of Maine Aquarium Committee. Students started asking questions about Perkins. When will he be coming? How will he share our ideas with the rest of the committee? Do you think he will like this idea? We quickly realized that they were hooked.

Besides providing the important real-life connection, Perkins shared information on the four potential sites for the aquarium. We sent a group of ten students, accompanied by two teachers and a video camera, to investigate the four proposed sites. (Staff availability dictated sending a small group out to complete this fieldwork.) At each site they videotaped the landscape and added comments on the strengths and weaknesses of the site based on the Gulf of Maine Aquarium Committee's criteria for assessing these potential locations. The video and their personal reflections were shared with the rest of the student body so that each student had a potential site in mind at the beginning of the design process.

During the next week, students opened architectural firms at King Middle School. Students designed logos and company names and established themselves as presidents of their own architectural firms. They printed business cards in the computer room. In math class the students learned the skills of drawing to scale from director of school renovations, Charlie Pressey. They learned about universal symbols, drafting tools, and drafting skills from an architect, Jeff Verreault. They did extensive work on geometry skills including area, perimeter, and volume with Phil Dyer. A second speaker from the Gulf of Maine Aquarium Committee spoke to the students regarding the effort in Portland to bring an aquarium to the waterfront. This provided another chance to remind students of the real-life aspect of their work. He shared his excitement at being able to return to King in January to listen to their creative design plans.

As skill work was taking place, we introduced and reviewed product descriptors for the final products. A product descriptor, similar to a criteria list, sets the standard for the final product. The product descriptor form lists the parts of the product, the specific attributes that the teachers are looking for, and the number of points each part of the product will earn toward a possible grade of 100. This tool, originally developed by John Samara and Jim Curry, breaks a product, such as a brochure or a book review, into the specific elements that make up the product and explicitly outlines the criteria for each of these parts so that the students know exactly what is expected of them. As a teacher-team we developed product descriptors for all three major products: the floor plan of their aquarium design, the written proposal, and the oral presentation of their work.

As the expedition continued to progress, some students felt like they were going to work in the morning instead of school. They were punctual, organized, and ready. Attendance was at an all-time high, discipline problems at an all-time low. The students wanted to be there. They did not want to be fired. Students wanted to hear more of what the teachers had to say, because they saw the immediate purpose of the lessons. If they missed a day, they might miss important information that would help them with their design. Speakers came frequently and gave demonstrations of how to use the architectural tools.

One strength of this expedition was the richness of the science content. Kim Verreault filled her classroom with resources related to aquatic habitats in general, as well as books on very specific topics such as blue holes, coral reefs, and mangrove swamps. We asked each student to research five aquatic habitats and detail the habitat as well as the animal and plant life that thrived in the region. They would need this content as they developed their designs and described it for their written proposals. Research time also included the Internet, where students found information on their topics and visited fantastic aquarium sites around the world. This process helped students begin to focus their ideas and relate them to the sea animals that would inhabit their aquarium.

When they had all the tools, skills, and materials, the students met an inspiration, Joe Hemes, an architect with Blatt Architects in

Portland. He had entered an aquarium design in a national architectural design competition. In his design, he planned to take an existing abandoned structure in the city and turn it into a productive building. He chose Fort Gorges, a Revolutionary War island fort seen from every shore of the city, and designed an imaginary aquarium at the site. His design was created solely for the purpose of the national contest, and he graciously agreed to share his creativity with our students. Through a slide show, Joe Hemes presented his designs, his blueprints, his artistic renderings of his dream and provided the inspiration, enthusiasm, and creativity the students needed to dream on. Now that they had seen a professional example of exemplary work, they were ready to begin their own design process.

Ever since their visit to the New England Aquarium, the students had been thinking and developing unique ideas for their aquarium design. You could hear the discussions in the hall, in the classroom, and in the lunchroom. Plans started to take shape, and you could hear a sense of pride and ownership in their vision. As teachers, we enjoyed stepping out into the hallway to find the conversations between students focused on the work of the expedition. It was important for them to carry these ideas from class to class, not put them away because they had changed rooms or teachers.

CRITIQUE AND REVISION: TOOLS OF THE ARCHITECTURAL TRADE

There was a heightened level of excitement in the air the day that students started outlining their floor plan ideas on drafting paper. One particular student was having difficulty sitting still in language arts class and concentrating on the assignment at hand. When asked if he was having a problem, he replied, "It's just that I can't wait to get to math class. We get to start our floor plans today!" The students displayed a passion for the expedition and the day-to-day skill work that led up to the point that was now coming to fruition.

Due to the nature of the design process, the students had to spread themselves throughout the Windsor wing of King Middle School.

About one half of the class could remain in the math room. We borrowed several large tables and set them up in the hall and in our project room. Visitors who walked through our hall during the expedition were amazed at how focused, yet excited, these sixth-grade students were. They would invariably stop to ask a student what he or she was doing or how it was coming, and before they knew it they were involved in a twenty-minute session with this new "architect" who was very eager to begin sharing his or her ideas with an audience.

Throughout the design process the students would informally discuss and critique design ideas as they worked on their floor plans. Many had to adapt and revise their original visions once they started to work within the limits of the project, which included a set area of 30,000 to 35,000 square feet and a scale of 1 inch to 8 feet. They also had to make sure their design matched their research on aquatic habitats. Yes, there were points of frustration for students. It was challenging work, which required a marriage of creativity, scientific knowledge, and exact mathematical calculations. But minor bumps along the way were expected and allowed students to experience a situation where perseverance paid off.

Once the designs were in full swing, we created large blocks of time for students to work. Our double classroom was opened up and students spent several hours at a time working there. We also found the cafeteria, with its long tables, to be a great space for our work and students often spent the morning down in that area. Certainly a lot of energy was flowing and it was contagious. Students and teachers alike could feel the excitement grow.

As the sixth graders put their pencils, rulers, protractors, and T-squares to work on the first draft of their floor plan, we used the language arts class to examine the elements of a written proposal that would accompany their design. We reviewed a product descriptor with the students that they used to examine and critique proposals completed in previous years. This allowed them to see what our expectations were and what it would take to reach that level. As educators, whenever we repeat an expedition, we use models from previous years as exemplars. We want the students to clearly understand the standards we have for

The Pool of Life is based on Maine tide pools. Animals such as the periwinkle, green sea urchin, cushion starfish, crumb sponge, red starfish, hermit crab, frilled anemone and rock eel will be featured in this exhibit. This exhibit contains some seaweed to help the animals adapt to their new environment quickly. The water will be salt water and the temperature will range from fifty to sixty degrees Fahrenheit. The tank will be a circle shape and have a smaller coral reef tank in the middle of the exhibit. The approximate area measurement of this exhibit is 1,280 square feet. The volume measurement is 19,088 cubic feet. Two steps will be placed around the four-foot-high tank for younger children who want to get an even closer look at the fun.

...The crumb sponge is built with no stomach or brain although it has many branching channels inside its body. In order to eat, it filters food out of the water through thousands of small sponge holes. Another animal found in a tide pool is the northern yellow periwinkle. This species is very common in various tide pools around the world. Its cone-shaped body has only one foot, so it gets around fairly slowly. The frilled anemone has stinging tentacles that only a sea slug can eat. This animal is related to the jellyfish.

Though the public is quite familiar with the atmosphere of a tide pool, many people still do not know the small, yet important information of life inside this rather small environment. As you walk around The Pool of Life you will gather this information in fun and unique ways.

Krista Robinson, a sixth grader at King Middle School in Portland, Maine, and the president of Big Bang Architects, wrote a proposal for an aquarium slated to be built in Portland. Above is an excerpt from her plan that outlines the Pool of Life exhibit.

them. If it is our first time through an expedition, we make a few models ourselves, some weak and some strong, to use in critique sessions. In this case, a proposal written by a former student for the renovation of King Middle School was a model for a critique session. (Of course, it was used anonymously, and with permission.) After reading the proposal together, the students worked in small groups to critique the work, using the product descriptor as a guide. Each group then shared their ratings and rationale. We charted their observations and discussed the overall strengths and weaknesses of the piece. We ended by returning to the product descriptor and discussing what they would do next if this were their piece of writing. This was a critical point in the expedition. Everyone needed to understand the standards for quality work.

Direct writing instruction was integral to this phase of "Dream On." These students had not completed much informational writing at the elementary level, so they needed practice turning research and notes into a piece of writing that informed, and engaged, their audience. We modeled the note-taking process and the students did practice activities. Follow-up work included instruction on turning the notes into interesting and informative paragraphs. Again, we used the modeling approach. We held mini-lessons on the difference between recopying and revising. Students reviewed examples of engaging writing as well as dull, repetitive proposals. Most of the language arts classes at this time began with a short writing lesson in an effort to strengthen the quality of the students' work.

It was critical that the typing and revising of this proposal became a part of their computer work. The computer instructor at King works closely with each team of teachers and tailors his instruction to the needs of the students. He is able to cover his computer curriculum through much of the project work completed during expeditions. Students had the necessary class time for their word-processing needs.

For the students, much of their day (math class, science class, language arts class, computer class) was now focused on the expedition. Our priority was to guide all one hundred students through the completion of the final products: the floor plan, the proposal, and the oral presentation. We used our team meetings to review the status of the expedition, discuss any necessary changes in the schedule, and share information on the progress of individual students. Throughout the day students heard the same message from all of their teachers. The work for this expedition was their priority and our priority, and we needed to work together to bring it to a successful conclusion.

As the students neared the completion of the first draft of their floor plan, we scheduled a large critique session. Local architects graciously gave a morning of their time to meet with individual students and review their plans. We gave each architect information on the parameters of the project, and they completed a critique sheet for each student so that he or she would leave the session with written feedback. It was a great morning for all involved. The architects loved the excitement and enthusiasm of the students. Once again, the students found a new audience with whom to share their vision. These architects proved to be a wonderful connection for our students, and the students were able to educate these professionals about some of the exciting learning occurring in a local public school.

We had already scheduled a presentation day with a guest panel including Don Perkins, and as the deadline drew near, the pace of the work increased. Students began to produce final drafts of their floor plans and their proposals. Now every class was devoted to "Dream On." Students typed and edited during their computer class time and all the extra periods we could reserve. They constantly peeked into the computer classroom to see if there were any free computers. If there were a few available, you could be sure that they would tip-toe into the room and quietly get to work. The hallway was full of students working at tables, trying to make error-free final drafts of their floor plans. White drafting erasers became a hot item among students.

At this point in the process, it was evident how much the service was driving the work. Often, this stage is when we see students fall behind, lose interest, or express frustration with a project. The connection with the community kept these students focused, raised their expectations, and pushed them to have their best work ready for presentation. When we viewed the proposals and floor plans as they neared completion, we were amazed. They showed the quality and precision of the blueprints shared by the visiting architects.

Teamwork among the teachers is critical during any expedition, and this one was no exception. When one hundred students needed lengthy, typed proposals edited and revised, we had to share the work. Six teachers (math, science, social studies, language arts, special education, computer) divided the students so that each had approximately seventeen to work with throughout the editing process. We met with students before school, after school, in class, at lunch, and in the hall. In other words, we met anytime we could. Every day there were six folders placed in the computer room, each labeled with a teacher's name. If a student wanted a teacher to look at her work, she had to place it in her folder by 2:30 p.m. Students started appearing at our classroom doors at 7:00 a.m. Some of our island students started taking the 6:15 a.m. boat over to the mainland and were waiting at our classroom door when we arrived. We were asked to stay late so that students could type on the computers or work on their floor plans. The pace intensified as the due date loomed. Slowly, but surely, the revisions took place and the completed proposals and floor plans appeared, shared with great pride by their creators. But the work was not yet complete. Students began to move their focus from planning to presenting.

Once again, skill building became a necessary part of this expedition. Delivering a formal oral presentation required some new skills, and we needed to provide the necessary instruction. We began by reviewing a product descriptor with students. The language arts teacher modeled some oral presentations, and the students critiqued them using this tool. We scheduled practice sessions in which each student gave a "mini" speech focusing on one of the necessary skills, such as eye contact. Finally, each student was paired with another for a run-through of his or her oral presentation. The partner gave praise and made suggestions and the speaker had time to revise before the presentation day arrived.

Oral presentations took place in two phases. The first required each student to present his or her design to the homeroom group of approximately twenty-five students. Students had access to an easel, podium, and pointer for their presentations. Each student had three to five minutes to share the highlights of their aquarium design and persuade the audience that their ideas were worthy of examination by the aquarium committee. Teachers used the product descriptor as their assessment tool in grading the presentations. As the presenter spoke, the audience members completed feedback sheets. Although the teacher's grade was the one that went into the rank book, the students were equally interested in what their peers had to say.

This was quite an experience for the students. Many were nervous, since they had never before stood in front of their peers to present their ideas. Also, it was important for them to do a good job. They had worked incredibly hard on this project, and they wanted to present it in the best light. As educators, we were proud of all of the students that day for completing a challenging problem and seeing it successfully through to the end.

CONTRIBUTING TO COMMUNITY DECISION MAKING

We scheduled our guest panel to hear presentations the next Thursday, and since their time was limited we had to narrow the presenter list down from one hundred to sixteen. Each classroom selected the four students they felt could best represent the class. The maturity of the group was evident as the students chose excellent representatives who would be sharing outstanding design ideas with this adult audience.

The final sixteen students presented to the guest panel in our school cafeteria. They presented as if they were the presidents of their own architectural firms, and this was their chance to impress the potential client. Adding to the reality of the experience was the presence of Don Perkins, who was a panel member along with Mike McCarthy, principal of King, Angela Joliffe, teaching strategist, and Pam Brann, teacher for the gifted and talented program. As the students entered the cafeteria they were not looking for their parents or their principal. "Where's Mr. Perkins?" "Where's the aquarium guy?" they asked over and over.

The students spoke for well over an hour. They showed poise and

Speech on the Gulf of Maine Aquarium

Hello, my name is Allison Beal, president of McKechnie's Modern Architects. I am here today to speak to you about some of our plans for the Gulf of Maine Aquarium.

First, I am going to share with you what is probably the most exciting part of the aquarium, the wondrous exhibit, Turtles of the Reef. It is located here (point) in the central part of the aquarium. Children and adults alike are enthralled by the beauty of the Hawksbill and Green turtles inside. The tank has some very special features, which are the four alcoves indented into the tank. These spaces allow the public to get a sensation that they are actually inside of the tank (point). There is a cartoon video, some computers at different heights, and a poster, all about turtles.

The second thing I am going to speak about is the exhibit, Your Own Little Fish Tank. This exhibit speaks to the public about the care and sanitation of fish tanks you have, or are going to get. It is located here (point) on the left wall of the aquarium. The exhibit is in an enclosed room, and tanks surround visitors on all sides. In these tanks, there are many varieties of fish that the normal person could care for in their own home, like goldfish, guppies, angelfish and catfish.

Allison Beal, a sixth grader at King Middle School in Portland, Maine, gave a speech to community members and representatives of the Gulf of Maine Aquarium Committee. This is an excerpt from her speech.

confidence beyond their years. Their fellow students supported them throughout the morning by helping clip floor plans on easels, picking up dropped note cards, and arranging visuals. Many parents joined us to videotape and photograph the event. The enthusiasm and commitment that the students had for this project had clearly spilled over to home because parents arrived without a formal invitation. And since this activity took place during the school day many had to leave work to attend. But even more amazing to us was the pride and respect the other eighty-four students displayed. They were attentive and interested for the entire session and they complimented their fellow classmates when we returned upstairs. One student in particular, who was not a presenter at this phase, made it a point to commend as many of the presenters as possible. He said he thought they did a great job, and he knew how hard it was because of his own experience presenting to his classmates.

Don Perkins was a gracious guest, standing at the end to make a positive comment about each of the sixteen designs. The students were thrilled to have the opportunity to present to this community decision maker and loved receiving his accolades. However, this praise was not given lightly. Perkins was indeed impressed by the presentations and immediately arranged to have these students meet with representatives of the full Gulf of Maine Aquarium Committee. The students knew how important this invitation was. Their exciting ideas and their first-rate presentations had provided them with the opportunity to present again. This was not something arranged by the teachers. These sixteen students had earned their way into a Gulf of Maine Aquarium Committee meeting to present their ideas. It was more than we all could have hoped for at the onset of the expedition.

At the first meeting between committee members and the sixteen students, the sixth graders were nervous as they presented. Speaking quietly at first, they slowly gained their poise as they walked the committee through the highlights of their designs. But during the question and answer period the group really came to life. They became excited and animated as they answered questions, explained their own creative exhibits in more detail, and provided feedback about the current plan and design ideas. The meeting was so successful that Don Perkins called the following week. He was sending his environmental and education subcommittees over to King. Could the students meet with these people and repeat their presentations that very day? Once again, despite the last-minute nature of the meeting, their presentations to these community decision makers were a hit.

The next invitation was a little more formal, with more advance notice. The architects who had been hired by the committee were eager to talk to the students. They reserved a conference room in downtown Portland, and the sixteen students rode to the meeting with parents and Phil Dyer. Two hours later the students returned to the second floor of King Middle School excited and proud. They relished every chance they got to share their vision. The parents who provided the transportation could not get upstairs fast enough to tell us that the students had been superb. Those of us who were left at King Middle were actually a bit jealous, wishing that we could have witnessed the meeting.

But their work for the committee still was not complete. The final large-scale gathering took place at King Middle School. At this time, the sixteen young "experts" got a sneak peek at the potential aquarium design from the actual architect. Now the tables were turned as the students asked questions and provided feedback. They were polite, but probing as they discussed the importance of technology and the use of changing exhibits. These young people were truly providing a service to the committee and the community at large. This was not some extra activity tacked on to the regular school program. Service was embedded in this expedition naturally, and that is what made it so powerful. These sixteen students earned the right to represent their classmates at this level, and they felt the weight and responsibility of being spokespersons for the group of one hundred students. It was a powerful experience, one they spoke about eloquently a year after their expedition ended.

In many ways, the "Dream On" expedition has yet to end for our students. Don Perkins called Phil Dyer and invited two students to sit on the Gulf of Maine Aquarium Committee as part of the decision-making process. He felt the input received from students had been very valuable. Now representatives were needed to bring ideas from the students to the committee, and vice versa.

Phil Dyer thought it was a wonderful idea and had several students in mind. First, however, he needed to check with the parents. The meetings often took place in the middle of the school day, and he wanted

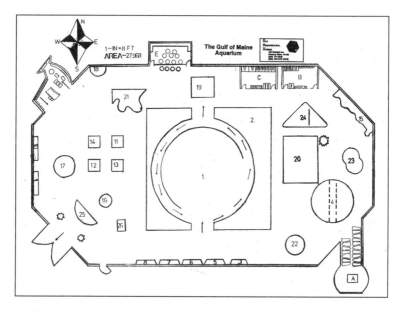

Robert Sax, a sixth grader at King Middle School in Portland, Maine, designed this blueprint for the Gulf of Maine Aquarium.

parental support before he approached the potential candidates. Both sets of parents were extremely supportive and excited and willing to help in any way they could. Phil Dyer approached the two students and they eagerly agreed. Students were now literally at the table with the Gulf of Maine Aquarium Committee and spent the remainder of the school year attending monthly meetings.

According to Allison, one of the student representatives, the first meeting was a bit difficult. Since they were joining a committee that was already functioning, the students felt somewhat lost during the early discussions. However, once the committee solicited their input, a level of comfort and confidence developed that continued throughout the year.

The two students, Allison and Robert, continued to bring design ideas back and forth between the one hundred students and the committee. They stressed the importance of technology, hands-on stations, and a connection with Maine aquatic life. When they returned from a meeting, students would pump them for information: "What does the design look like now?" "Have they settled on a location yet?" "Tell me about the exhibit plans." It was important to all involved that Allison and Rob truly be representatives, bringing the information back to the others, and they fulfilled these responsibilities completely.

At one particular committee meeting, the group discussed the selected location of the aquarium. This information needed to remain confidential for a period of time, so that final details could be completed and an appropriate press release prepared. Rob and Allison were asked not to speak about this information, along with the rest of the committee. Allison said it was difficult to keep quiet, especially when students or adults would ask her directly about the location. But she kept the information confidential, not even sharing it with her parents.

The work of the committee continues. A site and design for the aquarium are now agreed upon and the committee is focused on securing the significant funding required. Rob and Allison continue to attend committee meetings, and both look forward to the day when the actual construction begins.

All of our students look forward to visiting the Gulf of Maine Aquarium. They will certainly feel a sense of satisfaction and accomplishment and will recognize their input in many direct and indirect ways. They should also recognize that the energy and excitement that they brought to the local committee was as important as any specific exhibit design.

"Expeditions have brought a lot to the community," stated Krista, a King Middle School student, speaking to a group of teachers who recently visited our school. It was a statement that took us a bit by surprise. As educators, when we reflect on our work with Expeditionary Learning we tend to focus on the academic gains that the students have made through this approach. But Krista is right. The community has gained a great deal through the service that Windsor students have provided through the five in-depth expeditions they participated in over a two-year period. These young people have been able to reach beyond the school walls in many important ways to make the connection between academic content and real-world problems. Youth service is powerful, and through "Dream On," these students felt the power that comes from being a participating member of the community at large.

LISTENING TO ROBINS

JEANNE ANDERSON AND
KAREN WOHLWEND

*E*ach year, we listen carefully to the interests and concerns expressed by our kindergartners. We know that at some point we will embark on the expedition "Creatures Great and Small," which will explore the animals in the world around us. The paths in the journey, however, are always different from year to year. The impetus for our expedition comes from the interests of the children. One year, "Creatures" started on a blustery, frigid February day in Iowa. The winter had been mild when a sudden burst of snowy weather with subzero windchills caught us by surprise and trapped a flock of twenty robins returning north prematurely. The birds hopped across the snow drifts, desolate little plumped-up balls of fluff with feathers rippling in the -20° F winds. The kindergartners shifted their attention from the possibilities of snowballs and snow forts to the plight of the robins. Their questions became guiding questions for our expedition:

Would the birds be able to survive? How do they stay warm? How do they live without houses? How do they find food? Why do the robins fly away from us? And, is there a way that people, especially small children, can help?

These questions led us into our study of other animals in our Dubuque neighborhood, nearby woodlands, and throughout the world. Along the way, students wrote a guidebook for local birds, built bird shelters for the robins, and returned ladybugs to their natural habitat. These service projects formed the heart of the expedition. They gave the children a purpose for pursuing their learning, a purpose that was meaningful for *them*. From small beginnings—shivering birds in the snow—children learned to be caretakers of their world and have respect for all living things. They learned to make a difference appropriate to their level of development and to be members of a community that includes both humans and animals.

MAKING SERVICE MEANINGFUL TO YOUNG CHILDREN

As early childhood educators in an Expeditionary Learning school, we often struggle to mesh complex ideas and meaningful service in a way that is accessible for young children. Often early childhood curriculum is oversimplified and teaches children things they already know. Or conversely, the lessons become too abstract and the children cannot relate or construct their own meanings. Our challenge is to help the children design an expedition that is meaningful to them. When investigations emerge from the interests of the children, they tend to be developmentally appropriate and, at the same time, more rigorous than activities that adults create for them.

During our "Creatures" expedition, the children became interested in the material through their service for the robins. Now they were eager to learn more. Children often spent the entire time at the science center observing and recording ladybug activity. They pored over nature magazines and naturalist guides to find new species, noticing similarities and differences in structure. Our job as teachers was merely to act as guides, providing support, networking, and clearing obstacles out of the way of the children's learning.

It took us a few years to adopt this approach. Our first years of planning expeditions were characterized by detailed curriculum maps, tabbed manuals, and hours of weekly teacher preparation. *We* chose all the activities, books, and research projects. We assigned children to teacher-directed jobs and groups. The time requirements for coordinating materials, schedules, and teacher planning began to overwhelm us. We had assumed all the ownership and responsibility for learning. Once we gave ourselves permission to allow children to take leadership roles in the classroom, the expeditions became fluid and ever-changing.

We first experienced this epiphany five years ago in the midst of an expedition on seasonal changes. We had planned snow stories, winter activities, journal prompts, and teacher-directed projects. We felt these projects were premier examples of Expeditionary Learning. It was, in fact, frenzied activity that left the teachers exhausted and the children harried. These teacher-directed products were impressive, but allowed little room for imagination and passion on the part of the children.

The children themselves brought about a change in our thinking. One day, we asked the children what *they* wondered about. The range of responses was remarkable. When children shared their "I wonder" responses, the curiosity became contagious. Each question sparked another.

"I wonder what happens to the moon during the day."

"I wonder how long it takes to get to the moon."

When the children left that day, we looked at each other and said, "This is what we should have been doing all along!" We scrapped our road map for the expedition and followed the questions that the children had posed. "I wonder" became an expedition about changes: daily changes, changes in physical properties, time changes, and even seasonal changes. The children became fully engaged because the study came from their own interests. We had placed the responsibility for learning with the children—where it belonged. Taking a few unexpected pit stops, pausing occasionally to refuel, students showed us where they wanted to go.

We took these lessons to heart when we planned this year's "Creatures" expedition. We mapped out a loose framework, recognizing that the children would lead us along paths of their choice. We planned to study animals in our neighborhood, woodlands, and on other continents. Our investigations would go in-depth, focusing on a manageable number of animals rather than learning a little about a great number. After exploring the wilderness close to home, the children would go on a safari around the world through books, videos, and exhibits. We brainstormed a list of projects from which the students could choose. Our challenge would be to remain watchful for authentic ways for the students to protect the environment. We wanted them to learn that they can make a contribution of true value to the natural world, but we knew the best service comes out of real need and true interest. We decided to wait and see what service ideas the children generated themselves.

LEARNING LEADS US INTO SERVICE

We began our study of local birds by reading about robins and other songbirds, such as cardinals, goldfinches, blue jays, and bluebirds. The children listened to bird calls and closely examined photographs and drawings of birds. The students had an added connection to birds, because our school, Audubon Elementary, was named for the naturalist John James Audubon. It was as if his thick text filled with intricate bird illustrations had been written especially for them.

A park ranger from a nearby nature preserve helped the children to look closely at the shape of each bird's beak to determine the type of food it needs. Birds with short, conical beaks crack seeds; robins use their longer, pointed beaks for digging up worms; and predatory birds such as owls have sharp, hooked beaks for tearing meat. The children would later use this information in creating their own bird identification guides.

We learned from the park ranger that birds often face a scarcity of food and cover during Iowa winters. Once the children discovered that people can make a difference by feeding the birds and providing shelter with bluebird boxes, they were eager to help.

First, they struggled with what to feed the birds. One child remembered feeding bread crumbs and Cheerios to ducks at a pond during the summer. When prompted to recall the beak shapes of the songbirds we had studied, several children suggested seeds as a good choice. The conversation turned to the types of seeds that we might use. As we recorded on chart paper, the children generated a long list of seeds that resembled an index for a gardening catalog. We narrowed the list to sunflower seeds, corn, and thistle seeds.

Next, parent volunteers helped us collect pine cones from a nearby park, which provided the bases for simple and environmentally friendly bird feeders. Upon returning to school, each child tied yarn around the pinecone, slathered it with peanut butter, and rolled it in the seeds. We carefully packaged the finished bird feeders and sent them home with the identification guides.

In the following weeks, the children and their parents identified the birds that visited the feeders. Children returned to school with excited reports of the birds they had seen. Their excitement told us that we had succeeded in nourishing the children's sense of wonder about everyday surroundings.

We wanted to make a connection between home and school with our expedition. The families of young children are a key resource in service. At times, young children must rely on adult guidance and support to carry out projects. Children in our program live in an urban setting with few green spaces and little opportunity to observe the natural world on their own. Asking parents to help gave them a chance to share in their children's excitement when they saw a bird build its nest or a squirrel bury acorns.

The children learned to be careful observers during frequent walks around Audubon's neighborhood. Whenever we were outside together, someone would notice a bird and call it to everyone's attention. We used Tana Hoban's book, *Look Look Look,* to focus the children on the detail in their surroundings. In the book, children examined a close-up view and then tried to guess the object. After reading the story, we explored the school grounds, armed with cardboard paper towel tubes. By limiting the view to a two-inch circle, we discovered the patterns of veins in a leaf, the speed of ants crawling in sidewalk cracks, and the diversity found in pea gravel. Throughout the expedition, children learned to view their neighborhood with new eyes, look with wonder at a familiar setting, and discover the small animals that are underfoot but were never before noticed.

David Bentz, a kindergartner at Audubon Elementary School in Dubuque, Iowa, drew this sparrow for the "Creatures Great and Small" learning expedition in January.

SERVICE LEADS US INTO QUALITY WORK

As children began to notice birds at home, we encouraged them to draw and record their observations. When they brought these drawings to school and shared them during community times, other students called out, "I want to do that, too." Although we had planned a list of possible projects, we decided to place those on the back burner and build on this flurry of excitement.

"Well, since you are interested in the drawings, we could do this as a class project," we suggested. "We could make a book." When the students readily agreed, we began establishing guidelines of best work for the book.

"Is this something that we want to put on scrap paper and staple together or should it be something that we put into the computer?"

As David Bentz's motor skills and observations began to improve, his drawings became more detailed, as demonstrated in this revision of his sparrow done in February.

we asked. The children decided to make a polished field guide like the ones they had been using for their research. We then asked the students to suggest the best way to start the book and the steps involved in making it ready for publication. This helped gather student input, but it also helped them understand the stages they would have to go through to complete the project.

Students began making contributions to the field guide based on the research we did during group time. For example, when we studied the cardinal, we examined the feathers, crest, beak shape, feet, and size as well as its food, nest, and habitat. Next we created a sketch in group time, with children advising the teacher as to the size and shape of the cardinal's body, crest, markings, and colors. The children then created individual drawings and captions. We consulted authentic sources such as one of

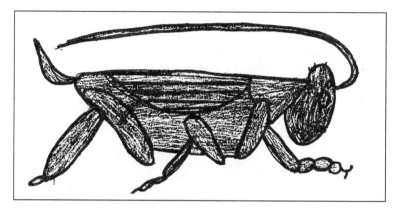

David Bentz's detailed illustration of a field cricket, created in May, shows vast improvement over a year of practicing revisions and observation skills.

Audubon's bird field guides, a hardcover book of more than two hundred pages. In examining Audubon's naturalist style of illustration, we pointed out the difference between "scientific drawings" and "cartoon drawings." Children could see a need for accuracy in their depictions, since it would help readers differentiate birds in the wild. At the close of center time, we would gather and report new information that the children had found. This gave the children an opportunity to share their work with an appreciative audience of peers, which was a significant factor in increasing the quality of the work throughout the expedition.

By the time the students started working on their field guides in early spring, they were used to the process of revision. We had spent a lot of time during the year talking about how to make best quality work. We began in the fall by asking individual students, "What do you think you could have added to this picture?"

"Well, I could have added hooves. Or I should have made it a different color," a student might reply, and that would start a conversation about the work.

We would never say, "You need to go back and erase all of that and add hooves." That kind of feedback is not appropriate for kindergartners. We simply taught them to look and search for best quality work. Soon they started doing it by themselves. They wanted to do two or three drafts of the same piece. By spring they were giving us very nice products, because they had learned to look for detail and revise. In the beginning of the year, that level of detail was in their heads, but they learned to put it down on paper. They became very aware of their work, and are now picky about what goes into their portfolios.

Peer critique was another skill we tried to build over time. In the beginning of the year, the children might have said, "Oh, that's a really cool bird," or, "I like your cardinal." But we encouraged them to look for detail, to notice the feet, the feathers, or the beak. When we modeled giving feedback, we stressed elements like background, composition, and shoreline, so the students realized these were things they should look for. By the end of the year, they knew how to use this vocabulary. They would say, "I can tell that there are individual feathers. I can see that in your picture. And that really makes your picture interesting."

The peer critique became very important in driving the quality of work the children did, but it also deepened our sense of community. When we first started sharing work, the students usually wanted to show their work to the adults in the room. But over time, they became more and more interested in hearing from their classmates. The language they learned in peer critique sessions began to emerge spontaneously throughout the day. When we gathered in our circle with our journals flipped open, children got very excited about each other's work. They would lean over and say, "I like how you put six legs on this bug," or "You really worked to make sure that that looks real." We had given the children a way to talk about their work, but we were amazed with the way they adopted it and used it to support their classmates.

SERVICE EXPANDS OUR CLASSROOM COMMUNITY

One unexpected result of service in our classroom was the connection that children made between caring and respect for classmates and concern for the animal world. Just as the children were learning to have compassion for other students, they were also learning to care for animals. Each form of compassion seemed to strengthen the other.

Every year, we begin kindergarten with the goal of becoming a true community. In September, we work to establish a climate where children are encouraged to see the other children as people with feelings as valid as their own. Young children, as egocentric beings, have difficulty imagining that other people are more than animated objects. When two children have a conflict, we help them notice each other's emotions and needs. We help children take another's perspective by directing the attention to the feelings of the other person. "Look, he's really sad. He's crying," we might say. When we appeal to the child's innate sense of compassion, it often results in an outpouring of sympathy for one's victim. The more understanding they gain from each other, the more compassion they have.

Similarly, when the children started to learn more about the birds around them, the classroom conversations centered on caring and compassion for these creatures. This was a triumph. We began having parallel discussions about humans and animals.

> *So why does it help if the zebras stay together in a herd?*
> "The zebras turn around backwards so they can kick the lions away."
> "So the babies … so the babies are in the middle, and the lions can't get 'em."
> "Like the elephants."
>
> *The elephants do that too, don't they? They stand together in a circle to protect the calves.*
> "With their tusks."
> "'Cause they're sharp and the lions can't get in."
>
> *You thought of some good ways that animals help each other by working together. Can you think of other ways?*
> "Monkeys take turns holding the babies."
> "The teenager monkeys do."
> "People do that."
>
> *Do we do that? Do we help each other?*
> "Yeah, when I watch my baby brother."
> "But I can't 'cause our baby's head's too wobbly."
>
> *Your baby is pretty new, isn't he?*

Throughout the expedition, children were continuously gaining a new respect and concern for living creatures. They handled tiny ladybugs and insects with newfound gentleness and respect. Bugs were no longer summarily squashed but rescued and removed outside to their natural habitat. In addition to whole-class service projects, children began doing their own spontaneous service for the natural world. One child gathered acorns and stuffed them into his bookbag on the way to school. After school, he would dig small holes in his backyard and plant them to create an oak forest, his contribution for the birds and wildlife.

This kind of tenderness eventually spread out and strengthened our own classroom culture. We began noticing more signs of genuine concern, caring, and respect for others. By fostering a climate of helpfulness toward the natural world, a sense of generosity permeated our class. Not only did the commitment to service derive from the classroom community, but the sense of community in our group grew stronger as the result of service.

A TYPICAL DAY

Each day began with community time and agenda building. The children participated in planning the activities for the day, taking ownership of the agenda for the class. During our "Creatures Great and Small" expedition, both kindergarten classes met in a common area to share expedition discoveries and ideas. As we focused on each habitat, we studied individual animals in depth. The children researched and drew the featured animal in Safari Guides created by each child. A wealth of resources, such as Internet sites, community networking, videotapes like the "Eyewitness Explorer" series, and excellent nonfiction literature, helped us with our research. We encouraged the children to look closely and share discoveries as they worked with these materials during center time.

During group time, we modeled "investigating and observing" and "scientifically recording" the physical character of animals. We started with a photograph or an actual animal, inviting the children to look closely and discern the important features. At times, we would compare and contrast animals using webs, Venn diagrams, and other graphic

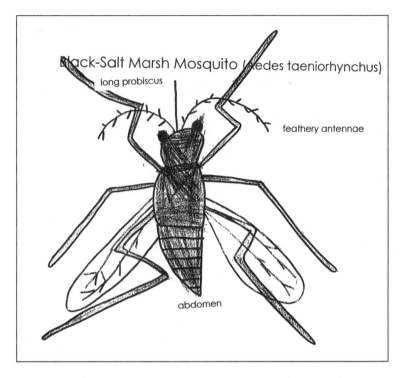

Black-Salt Marsh Mosquito (Aedes taeniorhynchus)

long probiscus

feathery antennae

abdomen

Arthur DelCastillo, a kindergartner at Audubon Elementary School in Dubuque, Iowa, drew and labeled this illustration of a black salt-marsh mosquito for the class field guide to animals and insects.

organizers. We also used exemplars of work generated by the children as they worked independently at centers. We were often surprised at the depth of scientific detail that the children included in their representations. The children asked for magnifying glasses at the art center so that they could draw the wing cases on the ladybugs. It was important to them that their drawings had an accurate number of spots for each ladybug.

At daily learning centers, the children were free to choose animals to study in more depth, or to focus on other aspects of the expedition such as exploring globes and maps. The children amazed us with their intensity and concentration while leafing through the various magazines and literature that had once been force-fed by teacher direction. When allowed to pursue investigations of their own choosing, children develop ownership and a high degree of pride in their work. It has a power that spills over into their time away from school. Many children brought in booklets, made of loose-leaf lined paper, backs of grocery receipts, or old envelopes, stapled or taped together. These books were filled with drawings that the children felt a need to repeat at home. We set aside time for sharing the ideas and items that children brought in from home.

We often integrated math into the expedition through the discoveries that the children themselves made.

BEN: Look! There's a baby ant!
JOM: And there's a tiny one!
LAKIN: There's an ant; it's following an aphid.
MEGAN: I see six bug bites on that leaf.

Can you show me?
MEGAN: (Pointing) One, two, three, four, five, six.

So something has been eating this plant.
MEGAN: I think it needs a ladybug.
AMANDA: Hey, this one has eight.
DARCIE: Something took a big bite, a BIG bite!

Do you think that is a bite or a tear in the leaf?
BEN: A tear.
DARCIE: A bite.

Each day, we continued to offer a range of literature that supported the expedition with multiple opportunities for choice. Our classroom library included book tubs categorized by each species, with magazines such as *Your Big Backyard* and *Ranger Rick,* nonfiction and fiction trade books, and naturalist guides. The children added to the collection by choosing books from the library that related to our topic. They first discovered John James Audubon's bird guide in our school library and excitedly carried it back to the classroom in our book wagon.

FROM FEATHERS TO FROGS

The children's understanding of birds laid the groundwork for a wider focus to the expedition. They brought their compassion for birds to the study of other wildlife. We fostered this capacity through realistic fiction such as the Mousekin stories, in which children develop an attachment to the characters who struggle in a natural setting.

In order to see a variety of animals in our region, we traveled to a nearby nature preserve. Although located at the edge of our town, it was an unknown world for many of the children. Videotapes and photographs recorded the excitement of these first ventures into a wooded preserve.

The children found a napping raccoon nestled high in an oak tree as well as a tiny frog in a small pond. When we spent some time watching the frog in its pond, the children noticed money that had been tossed into the water. We used the opportunity to underscore the impact of our actions upon nature.

BEN: It's a frog! It's a frog!
PAIGE: It's under the rock you're stepping on!

Is it under this rock?
PAIGE: It's a tiger frog.
MELISSA: I don't know where to see it.
AMBER: It's right there.
ROY: There he is!
PAIGE: It's a tiger frog.

I want to you to see the frog eggs that are in the water. Look, he's coming up! Everyone that couldn't see ... he's in the middle of the pond. See this long string. Those are all frog eggs. The eggs are in the long threads on this plant in the water.
MEGAN: Why is there money in there?
SAM: Nickel, penny, nickel, penny.

Money is like trash to the animals that live here. People should not throw money into the pond. It's like throwing trash into their home.
MEGAN: Yuk.

During our fieldwork at the nature preserve, we learned of the threat of garlic mustard to woodland areas in our area. A transplant from Europe, garlic mustard was originally planted in herb gardens in the United States. Its seed pods produce offspring in such abundance that it now threatens to crowd out many of the native plant species, leading to a decline in soil fertility and the area's ability to support diverse wildlife. The park ranger showed the children a carpet of garlic mustard that covered the forest floor as far as we could see. Later, during fieldwork at a local arboretum, the children uprooted some of the weeds along the path.

AT THE Y IN THE PATH

We need to vote. Point to the way that you want to go and I'll count. Six want to go this way and ten want to go that way.
JOM: But that way leads us back to the waterfall.
TYLER: Yup.

Jom says this is the way that we've been and this way is someplace new. Now you can choose again which way you would like to go. Eleven people want to go this way now. This time we're going to go this way. Be careful not to touch any of the plants here.
JOM: 'Cause they're poison.

They might be itchy.
JOM: Now what way?
TYLER: That way or this way?
CHRISTOPHER: This leads us back.

I think they both do.
PAIGE: Now we're on a big bridge!
LAKIN: That path has a bridge too.
MELISSA: There are some mushrooms—wild!
JOM: What happened to the water?

This is a place that has water when there is a lot of rain but when the ground dries out the water does not stay here.

Remember when Mr. Walton at Swiss Valley talked to us about the problem with too much garlic mustard? Look! There are garlic mustard plants everywhere!
PAIGE: Holy cow!
(Later, along the same path)
TYLER: Hey, there's more of that stuff!
CHRISTOPHER: The mustard stuff. It's bad for the other plants.

Maybe we could pick some of the plants right now.
CHILDREN: Yeah!

Our final service project tied "Creatures Great and Small" to our first expedition, "Everything Grows and Grows," which includes the study of trees over the course of the year. During "Everything Grows and Grows," the children learned skills of planting, caring for plants, weeding, and rudimentary plant identification. In May, the children closely examined the mini-habitat around trees in our schoolyard. As they studied insects in and around trees, they learned how plants and animals affect each other.

Our investigation of ladybugs began with close examination of these insects with magnifiers. We learned about the stages of growth of a ladybug, identified the body parts, and used magnified illustrations and photographs to clarify the concepts. The children compared ladybugs to other insects and learned how they differ in structure and habits. They developed their own classification schemes, pondering such questions as: "Are spiders bugs too?" "What about slugs and snails?" One child even saw similarities between insects and starfish.

To study ladybugs more closely, we ordered a batch of them for our class. When they arrived, the school secretary gingerly brought the cardboard box, punched full of air holes, into the classroom. Amid confusion and curiosity, we opened the box to find a mesh bag of ladybugs huddled in a mass.

KRISTOPHER: Look how many there are!
TONI: I bet there's a million!
DAVID: Not that many.

ZACH: One's getting out!

We better find a good place to keep them in our room. I wonder what they need?

EMILY: I bet they're hungry. We should feed them.

ALEX: I have some of my sandwich left in my lunchbox.

ARIELLE (GIGGLING): They don't eat people food!

I think that we have some books in the reading corner that will tell us what ladybugs eat.

One of our immediate priorities was to learn to care for the ladybugs. We learned that they needed air and water, but not too much water as they can drown in a tiny droplet. We took great care to provide enough moisture through misting. The children learned that although we can keep the ladybugs alive in the classroom containers, they would not flourish in this artificial environment. They were eager to release the ladybugs into their natural habitat. How different this attitude was from the traditional bug-catchers in early childhood science programs.

The role of ladybugs as natural predators of aphids provided a chance for young children to help protect plants in nature. Through class discussion, the children debated about possible sites. Some children wanted to take ladybugs home to their own yards; others wanted to release them on the playground. Since we had so many bugs, each child took two ladybugs to release at home with their family. We agreed to release the remainder of the bugs at the local arboretum, a site that could benefit from 150 ladybugs.

AT THE ARBORETUM

LAKIN: An ant!

There's that ant. I wonder where he's going.

AMANDA: There must be aphids.

I don't know. It doesn't look sticky. Remember if it has aphids, it's going to have sticky stuff on it from the juice being sucked out of the plants.

JONATHAN: It's sticky.

Do you think that's sticky or is it water or dew?
JONATHAN: It's sticky.
JONATHAN: Look! There's an ant! I found an ant!

Are you sure it's an ant?
JONATHAN: Yeah, it's crawling like a ant.

Okay. We need to take a really close look at the leaves and see if there are any aphids on them.
TYLER: Look at this!
DARCIE: I found another ant!
AMBER: Look! There's one!

Okay. The friends that found the ants...
BEN: Look! I found another one!

If there are ants on the plants, then what does that mean?
CHILDREN: Aphids!

I'm going to give someone a ladybug and let's put it on this plant.
SAM: One's crawling out! One's getting out!

Christopher, can you take this container over and put one onto the plant?
CHRISTOPHER: Oh no! One [ladybug] just flew!

That's Okay. It will find some aphids by itself.
JOM: Oh my goodness! It's crawling all over.
TYLER: I can find some aphids.
CHRISTOPHER: It's on the plant.
JOM: It's just checking every single plant!
CHRISTOPHER: It's back on my hand!
JOM: It likes you, Christopher.
PAIGE: Yeah, it likes Christopher.

WINDOWS INTO YOUNG CHILDREN'S THINKING

The reflection component of Expeditionary Learning presents a challenge in early childhood classrooms, particularly kindergarten where writing skills are limited. We struggled to develop a program that encourages reflective thinking, coupled with teacher guidance and support. Through trial and error, we have discovered and refined several avenues that are successful for our children.

Displaying student work: Once limited to bulletin board displays of children's art work, we now include reflective drawings, photographs, portfolio contents, and documentation boards. Documentation boards are an adaptation from Reggio Emilia schools (early childhood centers in Reggio Emilia, Italy) which document the child's progress in thinking through their language, drawings, and writings. Documentation boards provide a summary at a glance of fieldwork and cooperative projects through photographs, drawings, and transcripts of the children's language. These displays are at child's eye level so children can revisit their experiences again and again. They serve as a springboard for conversations about student progress with parents, administrators, and visiting adults. We used pocket charts next to the documentation boards to display photographs and drawings that the children brought in. For example, during the study of birds, one child brought in a series of photographs of birds at his feeder. Another brought a sack of birdseed to share with everyone and we displayed a small amount in a bag in the pocket chart. This served as a powerful way to recognize the service contributions of individual children.

Transcripts: As often as possible, we try to tape record and transcribe children's discussions of their work. At first we used the transcripts as a means for communicating with parents, to give them a peek into the child's day. As we began to do more and more recording, we saw the value of in-depth documentation. Expedition vocabulary and concepts were evident in the conversations between children and in self-talk. We then added transcripts as a checkpoint along the way, for reflecting on what we had learned and to summarize important

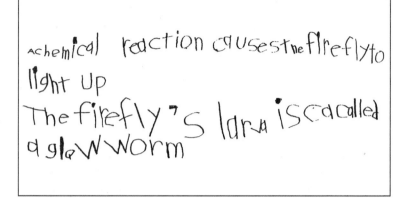

A chemical reaction causes the firefly to light up The firefly's larva is called a glow worm

Arthur DelCastillo, a kindergartner at Audubon Elementary School in Dubuque, Iowa, described the Pennsylvania firefly's glow in his contribution to the "Creatures Great and Small" field guide.

information in a group setting. The transcripts not only show the extent of vocabulary and depth of knowledge, but show how all members of the community make a contribution.

We have always been "kid-watchers," alert for signals that show development and understanding. Too often, we only have the time to jot down snippets of what we see, or we rely on memory. Transcripts provide an accurate and permanent record of a moment of learning.

Replaying and Retelling: Videotapes and literature provide background information for class investigations. We also videotape the children as they engage in fieldwork and classroom conversations. We play videotapes of fieldwork on the following day to help gel the children's discoveries and ideas. They allow the student to relive the experience and see the event from another perspective. Conversations during and after the videotape reflect the level of students' understanding and provide opportunities to build upon current knowledge. We also create a transcript of the video, which requires that we listen closely to the individual voices during the group experience, lending further insight into student thinking. We send copies of the transcript home for families to follow up, and we place them in each student's portfolio as a tangible artifact of the fieldwork. Group stories, written after the children have reflected on their fieldwork experience, allow children to share and organize the collective thinking of the group.

Journals: After sufficient reliving of experiences, children record their ideas in their journals through drawings and developmental writing. We use the journals to assess the ways that children express their thinking, the levels of their drawing and writing, and understanding and misconceptions that trigger new instruction. We use a checklist of stages in developmental writing to assess the progress that children are making. For example, children at the beginning of kindergarten often use scribbling or random letters to represent their ideas. As the year moves on, the children are incorporating expedition vocabulary that they locate and copy from the classroom environment. They also begin to have the confidence to spell on their own, using letter sounds, spacing, and punctuation at an emergent level.

Retracing our steps: Process is very important for young children; often more important to them than the end product. For example, when a young child paints, the end product may appear to be a sea of brown and gray paint. In this painting, a rain storm obscured the original and underlying flower garden. Children paint fluidly and the paintings may undergo constant change as they work. By recording the steps in children's work, we enable them to see the process that they created. We also gain a new understanding and respect for their thinking processes.

Expeditions are more than the sum of their parts. Expeditionary Learning can be life changing for all learners involved; children, teachers, and families. This power comes from the interaction of all the design principles. To view service learning only as one part of the expedition to be checked off, is to misguide the community of learners. Our goal is to create a community of learners committed to lifelong service to their world.

"What's in the Water You Drink?"

Cheryl Sims

"What's in the water you drink?" I asked my eighth-grade earth science classes.

"H₂O," one student responded.

"It's nothing but water," said another.

"Would you drink water from your bathroom sink?" I asked.

Some gasped in horror as they exclaimed, "No, way!"

Others shrugged their shoulders and said, "Sure, why not?"

I was curious why some thought it was acceptable to drink bathroom water and others thought it was repulsive. "After all," I continued. "It's just hydrogen and oxygen, nothing more, isn't it?"

As they debated a response to my last question, I challenged them to figure out a way they could determine if there was a physical difference between kitchen and bathroom water, or if it was just a psychological hang-up of some people. The students gathered in small groups, then shared their solutions regarding the kitchen-versus-bathroom water dilemma as a whole class. They decided that in order to settle the debate, they would have to test samples of water from each student's kitchen and bathroom.

There was only one problem I saw with this approach. Based on their responses to my earlier questions, I realized they had no idea what they would be looking for. What is in water besides hydrogen and oxygen? Why do we not just drink water from a rain barrel outside our windows instead of relying on the city to pump water through pipes from reservoirs to our homes? Who takes care of our water? How do we know our water is truly safe to drink?

This is how I introduced the "How Safe is the Water We Drink?" learning expedition to students at School for the Physical City. My two earth science classes consisted of fifty-two students from all over New York City with various levels of academic skills and social behaviors. Some of the students had been in my classes before, but some were new.

Those who were my former students knew my preference for incorporating service into their expeditions. True to form, I reviewed the water expedition with them and informed them that they would be expected to do a service project on New York City's drinking water toward the end of the expedition. I find that service learning coincides well with applied learning goals from the city's New Standards, which ask students to design, organize, and implement projects that demonstrate their ability to assimilate and accommodate knowledge. I also find that watching students perform service is rewarding because usually they end up doing things I did not imagine they could do. I have a sense when we start that something good will come, but the students always exceed my expectations. Service allows the students to go beyond my teaching abilities.

I told the students that my goals for them during this expedition included having them conduct a scientific experiment, set up and monitor controls and variables in an experiment, and write a narrative procedure. In addition, I wanted students to look at the process of designing an experiment and analyzing data from it, to represent information in more than one format, to reflect on their own learning, and to find ways of using their knowledge to help others. I had an idea of how these projects and assignments might turn out, but as usual the students exceeded my biggest hopes.

EXTENDING THE WALLS OF THE CLASSROOM

The expedition on water quality lasted approximately twelve weeks. At the beginning of our journey, students read water-related research, watched videos, and held discussions on the origins of water and the process it goes through to get to our homes. We made arrangements to go to the Department of Environmental Protection, which is responsible for supplying New York City's water.

To prepare students for their trip, I asked them to brainstorm questions about their drinking water. In addition, I let them know that the trip was designed to give them ideas of how to go about doing their own testing; therefore, I expected them to pay close attention to the processes conducted in the lab for controls and variables.

When we arrived, our tour guide took us through a chemical analysis and two microbiology labs. The students saw samples tested for pH levels and microbes. I quizzed them after each lab tour about their observations of the controls and variables used. Toward the end of their visit, students watched a slide show that illustrated field workers testing water from water-sampling stations and from reservoirs both in and outside of the city.

Having the students prepare questions before the field excursion helped peak their interest when they arrived at the lab. The attentiveness of the lab personnel also contributed to motivating them, as did the equipment that surrounded them. When they went to the microbiology lab, they were surprised to learn that microorganisms could live in the water supply. When they looked under microscopes at some microbes potentially found in water, it sparked a lot of inquiries. One student exclaimed, "Oh, my goodness, you mean this stuff is in water? Do we drink this stuff?"

Students asked questions about why certain procedures were followed, such as heating instruments before using them and incubating cultures for set periods of time. They came away with the notion that it was vitally important to implement controls when conducting experiments in order to reduce contamination. They also wanted to know why water comes out of the faucet cloudy, and how they could get their water checked if they suspected something was wrong with it. Some of their questions were answered at the lab, while others had to wait until the students completed their own research.

After the visit to the Department of Environmental Protection, students generated even more questions they wanted answered: How safe is the water in schools? Does the quality of drinking water change from borough to borough? Do filters really make a difference? If so, what are those differences? How can one tell if bottled water is better than tap water? What is the quality of water served in food places? They also included the question I posed to them initially: is there a difference between kitchen and bathroom water? If so, what?

FOLLOWING LEADS: THE RESEARCH STAGE

To answer these questions, students did research through the Internet, textbooks, a Mayo Clinic CD-ROM (released by the Mayo Foundation for Medical Education and Research), and newspaper and magazine articles. In addition, they made phone calls to government agencies such as the Department of Environmental Protection, the Environmental Protection Agency, the New York City Board of Health, and even the Food and Drug Administration.

As they contacted these agencies, they were put on hold and transferred to other numbers, only to end up at the Department of Environmental Protection information line again. The experience taught them about the nature of bureaucracy. When students contacted the Environmental Protection Agency to ask questions about New York City's water, the agency referred them to their local branch, which is the Department of Environmental Protection. The New York City Board of Health also told them to contact the Department of Environmental Protection. The Food and Drug Administration told the students to contact their local water supplier if they wanted information about their city's water. This was both shocking and disturbing. We got the impression that no one really checks up on the Department of Environmental Protection. What type of checks and balances system, we wondered, is the government using to protect our water?

How Safe Is the Water You Drink?

Question: Which is better, bottle or tap water?

Answer: Depending on the source of tap water, you will have a greater chance of finding a pH of more than 7 as likely to get neutral water. Bottle water was more consistent at pH of 7. All of the samples of both bottle and tap were in range of the state standard for pH levels. Tap water had more traces of chlorine than bottle water. In other areas they were close to the same percentage. Therefore, drinking bottle or tap water mostly relies on a person's taste.

Question: Do filters really make a difference?

Answer: Our results show that sometimes filters really do make a difference. When it comes to pH levels, filtered water had more samples that were neutral than the other samples of water. More filtered samples turned out to be soft water than unfiltered samples. This means that higher concentrations of sodium are found in filtered water. Also the filtered water had fewer samples with chlorine than unfiltered water. If you don't want minerals in your water such as chlorine, iron, and copper then buying a filter is better for you. Some filters remove microorganisms too, but not all do....

Question: Is school water safe to drink?

Answer: Seventy percent of the school water tested turned out to be soft water. Soft water could be a good thing to drink unless you have a health problem such as hypertension, then the sodium in the water would pose a health risk. School water turned out to be similar to filtered water in that it had no detection of iron, and very little copper....

Eighth-grade students at the School for the Physical City in New York City compiled a whole-class study in which they reported the findings of tests they conducted on residential and commercial water. In this excerpt, the students addressed questions commonly asked about water quality.

Students also acquired information about drinking water by writing to bottled water and filter companies. They compared brochures from companies such as Deer Park, Poland Springs, Evian, Perrier, and Dannon. By the time students finished going through the pamphlets and brochures, they had some understanding of the role of propaganda. The students found the companies' marketing schemes amazing. One company, they discovered, fortified its water with caffeine. They were surprised to discover that you do not have to drink coffee or cola to get a jolt, you can just drink water.

However, it was the information that was lacking on the labels that really concerned us. For instance, Dannon sells water that contains sodium. They do indicate on the label that sodium is an ingredient found in their water, but they did not include a warning that people who suffer from hypertension should not drink that product. When students did their own water testing, they were surprised to find that Perrier contained copper. Through extensive research, students found that copper in the water was not a health risk for most people in the world, but for people with Wilson's Disease, drinking that water could pose a major safety concern.

ESTABLISHING TESTING PROCEDURES

After checking countless sources, students were ready to design their water-quality test. I ordered several hundred collecting jars so students could standardize their collection of water samples. I also ordered a few Tap Water Tour Testing kits from a science supply catalog, but I was not particularly happy with them. I pointed out to my students that the handouts accompanying the kits were geared more for elementary school than middle school. The kits called for students to collect water in any container from home without any concern for contamination of samples. If the students used only the kits, they would have dropped tablets into their water samples, shaken the bags, recorded the colors, and checked a chart to find out the elements present in the water. That would have essentially been the end of the investigation. They would not have known if what they found posed a health risk.

The students seemed to understand the limitations of the test kits, especially after they had visited the Department of Environmental Protection facility and seen real water-quality testing. Nonetheless, we knew there were some useful things in the kits. We discussed how to meet our objectives using the components of the kits. We decided to use some reference materials in the kits that gave basic explanations of chemical compounds, the color chart, and the tablets and testing bags. We discarded the lab sheets. Students would keep track of their experiments using charts of their own design.

After deciding on materials and reviewing information about elements, students were almost ready to start testing. However, they needed one more preparatory step, the standardizing of sample collection.

As students learned the concepts of controls and variables as well as reduction of contamination of samples, they knew that they needed to have samples collected in the same manner in order to make their tests valid. They had learned that water acquires contaminants and forms bubbles when stagnant in pipes. To test water quality they needed to run the water long enough to flush the idle water. One group of students came up with the idea of filling each sample jar to a specified level after allowing the water to run for ten seconds. They then decided how to mark the jars and store them.

Many of these ideas came from the classes' visit to the Department of Environmental Protection, but some of them came from reading college papers students found on-line. These college papers, which reported actual research studies of well-water tests, proved to be a good model for the students. They were easily accessible, and by simply clicking an icon, students could read text and view charts and graphs. I asked students to review the papers' formats and look for information that would inform their own testing.

During group discussions, we compared the information we got from the college papers with the work we saw at the Department of Environmental Protection, and we talked about what best practices these tests had in common. Students then wrote a list of proposed test standards and shared it with the other class. After long discussions, both classes agreed on their test protocol.

CONDUCTING EXPERIMENTS

Once students finished their initial research on chemicals for their tests, determined their method of testing, developed their guiding questions, and collected their samples, they were ready to perform their own water-quality test. They collected samples from all five boroughs in New York City, from homes, places of worship, community centers, restaurants, and schools. To obtain the samples, students wrote a letter to each potential client requesting their participation in the study.

My room was filled with hundreds of water-sample jars kept in boxes stacked on top of each other. Students wore disposable gloves and goggles to protect themselves and their samples. They used distilled water to rinse equipment after washing. They lined tables with paper towels, something they had observed at the Department of Environmental Protection facility.

In each class, I asked a group of students to read how to handle the testing bags and tablets and to give demonstrations for their classmates. One thing they emphasized was not touching the inside of the bags or breathing into them. In their initial examinations of the bags, they noticed a color change in pH when they blew into a tested sample. They realized that carbon dioxide would interfere with the test results, and they cautioned the experimenters to handle the testing equipment with care.

Between the two classes, students ran more than 155 tests on drinking water. They learned from reading state standards that the Department of Environmental Protection runs 141 tests per day on New York City's drinking water. Due to time constraints, some samples did not get tested; however, classes ran enough tests to get a general sense of how scientists conduct scientific investigations and how to draw conclusions based on results.

The water tests were designed for students to determine the presence of copper, iron, chlorine, calcium, magnesium, and sodium, as well as ascertain the pH levels of the water. I would have liked students to investigate the presence of lead in the water, but the kit did not come with any indicators for that element. I checked the cost of equipment suitable for doing a lead inquiry and discovered it was far too expensive. Again I brainstormed solutions with the students. After some debate and several phone calls to agencies, we decided to send a

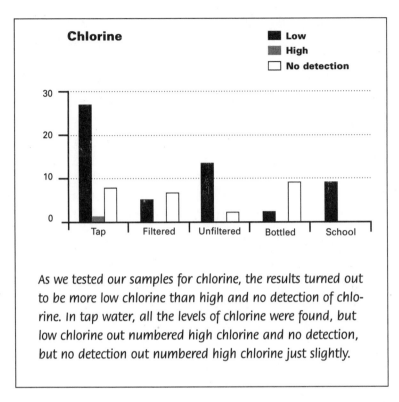

Chlorine

Low
High
No detection

Tap | Filtered | Unfiltered | Bottled | School

As we tested our samples for chlorine, the results turned out to be more low chlorine than high and no detection of chlorine. In tap water, all the levels of chlorine were found, but low chlorine out numbered high chlorine and no detection, but no detection out numbered high chlorine just slightly.

The following graph, taken from a whole-class report, illustrates the levels of chlorine found in water tests conducted by eighth graders at School for the Physical City in New York City.

couple of samples to a laboratory in North Carolina that did the lead testing for free. The results of those samples came back negative.

As they worked in their groups, leadership roles emerged. I remember one student who was transferred to our school after the school year started and had trouble fitting in with her peers. She was relatively quiet and withdrawn, and she would often not hand in assignments. I began to notice a change in her when we started studying the periodic table of elements, which we did prior to the water study. Her interest picked up and so did her class participation, and she began handing in assignments. This newly found interest continued to grow as we began the water study.

By the time we started testing, she became our standard bearer. She would patrol the classroom to see how students performed their experiments. She was quick to complain if she found a student not following the prescribed procedures. She would suck her teeth, then lecture the offender about the proper method for handling the material. She would even make certain that if the student needed to start over that he or she washed the containers and rinsed them with distilled water before continuing. Many students endured her lectures and paid close attention to what they were doing. She was persistent and thorough in her duties. Though she seemed to lose patience from time to time with her peers, she would always find a way to calm down and model proper handling techniques if a student needed her help.

This kind of attention to detail was essential for keeping our tests valid. Students began to realize that mistakes in procedure had consequences for their results. For instance, one group testing kitchen and bathroom water failed to take samples of each from the same households. They had to get new samples from the same household, mark them properly, and perform their tests again. The second time around, they were extra careful.

COORDINATING TWO CLASSES

With two large classes working on multiple small-group projects, I acted as facilitator for all the different activities. I kept a sign-out sheet in the room where students let me know if they went to make copies, use the phone, or go to the library. They understood that they had to be responsible for themselves and their learning. I checked on them sometimes, but I often did not have time to do that. Instead, they checked on and helped each other. They were responsible about signing out because they knew I trusted them. They would come back and report about what they discovered.

Someone might say, "I found a bottled water called Johnny Java and it has caffeine in it. I really want to get in touch with the company and find out more about it." I would ask, "What do you plan on doing?" She might reply, "I got some information on the Internet, but now I want to call them to have them send me a packet." They did not ask, "Cheryl, can I do this?" They said, "I need to do this in order to get my work done." And I would say, "Okay."

I emphasize with students that I want them to live up to expectations for quality of work, for conduct, and also for responsibility. They know that as a class, we are working toward certain goals. They are responsible for seeing them through, and for fostering good learning habits. It is not acceptable for them to lie back and say, "The teacher has to do things for me," or, "If I don't make it, then it's somebody else's fault." They know that they have choices to make, and that they need to make good choices. Besides, an infectious thing was happening in the classroom. Students wanted to find answers to all the water questions we were uncovering in our research. Peer pressure was in the air. When one group got very excited about their discovery, others did not want to be outdone.

My role during this group work was to be a liaison for both classes. For instance, when a standard was set in one class, we had to make sure that the other class knew and agreed to it before the testing could proceed. Each water sample collected was distributed to students who needed it for their specific tests. This meant that if a group in one class needed a water sample from Staten Island, but no one in that class lived in Staten Island, then they would get the sample from someone in the other class who did.

I was not the only source of communication between classes. Students set up a bulletin board that posted information on reference Web sites and copies of text regarding a particular issue about water quality. When someone found information that related to one of the questions, the person would post the text or source on the bulletin board for whomever needed it. Since the board was a community board, anyone who used the information would take it down and copy it or take notes, then repost it for others to use. I felt this way of communicating illustrated the design principle of Intimacy and Caring, for students had to be conscience of others' needs when using the bulletin board.

Students also communicated through computer files and folders. The computer files contained pieces students wrote regarding their class work, and the folders contained graphs and charts based on results obtained in small groups. That information allowed students in one class to ask questions and share resources with students in the other class who were working on the same issues.

BUILDING A CULTURE OF COLLABORATION

The collaboration that emerged during the expedition had taken a long time to build. Getting students to respect each other, work together, be compassionate, and be persistent with their efforts is a yearlong task. These things do not happen by themselves. We work on social interactions just as much as we work on academics. For me, this is where the design principles come into play. I always keep the principles in the back of my head as I teach, and I constantly look for signs of their presence. If I do not like what I see, then I change an activity or lesson to address the issue of my concern.

For example, just before we began our water study expedition, I noticed that one class was less able to work cooperatively in groups than the other. One concept I emphasize with students is that competition is the opposite of cooperation, and that anytime they have difficulty cooperating it is because competition is getting in the way. Therefore, they would have to identify where competition was evident in their conflicts and identify sacrifices they would make to accomplish group goals. For middle school students this is a hard lesson to learn, but not impossible.

The class that struggled with working in groups was a very competitive class. I decided to ask them to work on a project that would have time constraints and would challenge each and every one of them so they were all on equal footing. The project I chose required them to create a mural related to their science studies. I explained that my goal for the mural was to improve the culture of the class. I got a drop cloth made of canvas material, some paints, blank transparency sheets, and copy paper. I gave them three weeks to complete the project with the following guidelines:

~ Everyone in the class had to participate.

~ No decisions about the project could be implemented unless the entire class reached consensus.

~ Everyone's opinion had to be respected.

~ If a disagreement occurred between any individuals or groups, they had to appeal to the class for a solution.

~ Students were responsible for facilitating the process.

At first they thought I was off my rocker when I told them I wanted them to do a mural. They felt my expectations of the whole class working together to do an artistic production with a science theme in just three weeks was not possible. They did not think they could get that much cooperation among the class, or that they could produce a mural that people would like. They protested and I insisted. Finally, they relented and began the mural.

Students used a calendar to make a timeline for the work. They hung the timeline so they could keep track of their progress. Their first challenge was to decide what would go on the mural. After some deliberation, they voted for a water cycle theme in an urban setting. Next they generated a list of jobs, and students volunteered to become facilitators, painters, suppliers, scribes, artists, supporters, cleaners, or projectionists.

As students worked, the roles shifted. For instance, those who were facilitators found themselves painting or cleaning, and those who were artists found themselves in leadership roles. A gradual blending took place and halfway through the creation of the mural no one held a defined role, but everyone pitched in and gave opinions as to what to do next. All the while they had to adhere to my strict rule to listen to ideas or settle a dispute collectively, otherwise the work could not continue. They recorded their progress in their journals on a daily basis. They wrote about their work, and how they felt about it, as well as how they saw their social interactions change among their peers.

The mural was completed on time, although they did have to rush the last two days with the finishing touches to meet the three-week deadline. The end result was amazing. The mural depicted a reservoir outside of a city supplying water through pipes that went to a pump station, and then to a city block. Over the reservoir, a low pressure system moved in the direction of the city. The students titled it "How We

Get Our Water." Everyone who saw it was impressed. The students felt pride as they looked over their work. Their journal entries and their debriefing comments described how they found themselves working with students they normally did not associate with, and that they did not mind doing it.

We hung the mural in my classroom over the windows to function as a curtain to keep the glare of the sun off the computer screens nearby. This was only one purpose the mural served. It also was a reminder to that class of what they could accomplish if they were willing to work together to meet challenges.

INTERPRETING DATA SCIENTIFICALLY

Students relied heavily on their new collaborating skills when they had to analyze the results of their tests. Not only did they have to be aware of what went on in their groups, but also what the other groups and other class were doing, in order to draw comprehensive conclusions. To do this, students had to learn a new vocabulary. They used words such as controls, variables, contaminants, and microbes. One of the toughest changes in their jargon took place when they were explaining the results of their experiments. They had to learn the difference between using judgmental words such as "good" or "bad" and nonjudgmental words such as "positive" or "negative" results. The latter terms indicate something is either present or not present as a stated fact. The former terms are inferences as to the quality of what they were viewing.

Students had to wrestle with the issue of factual statements versus inferences when they analyzed water samples for hardness. When they reported the outcome of their data, some of them made statements that soft water was good, and hard water was bad. I asked them how they knew hard water was bad. They were under the impression it was bad because the majority of samples tested were soft. I challenged their way of thinking. I wanted proof that their assumption was correct.

They knew that hard water contained more calcium and magnesium than soft water, and that soft water contained more sodium. Yet those facts did not explain if hard water was good or bad for con-

In a report entitled "Is School Water Safe to Be Drinking?" eighth grader Jody Kitcher assessed that the water at School for the Physical City was safe, but a little hard. The excerpt above examines the growing concern people have about water quality.

sumption. Everyone started searching on-line and looking through the Mayo Clinic CD-ROM for answers. They could not find anything substantial one way or another.

Students continued to probe further. They contacted local college chemistry and environmental studies departments. To their surprise, the experts did not have an articulate answer for them of whether hard water could be harmful for consumption. It was as if no one ever considered the question. The complexity of getting at a concrete answer frustrated the students, but it also motivated them to dig deeper.

Although they could not make a judgment about hard water directly, they deduced that if hard water were bad for people's health, someone would have been aware of it by now. They also knew that people who suffer from high blood pressure should not drink soft water; therefore, their alternatives would be either hard water or distilled water. They came to the conclusion that hard water was fine to drink.

Researching the effects of calcium, magnesium, and sodium lead them to discover interesting facts about other elements found in water. One in particular was chlorine. Most students had always been taught that chlorine was a good thing. It was a way of cleansing water, like in a pool. When they found it in their drinking water, they were not concerned. However, some of the information they encountered in their research warned that high levels of chlorine could foster the growth of a parasite that could be fatal to people with immuno-deficiencies. They even found some articles about people who died from drinking tap water because of the parasite. So why use chlorination as a method of treating our water supply? Because, they learned, science and technology have not come up with a better system for treating drinking water.

For many of the results they examined, the students discovered that individual health issues determined if a water sample were harmful or not, but for the majority of citizens, the water was safe based on the elements they tested. However, since not all contaminants were tested, students still knew they had to recommend to participants to have further testing done if they wanted to know more about their water.

COMMUNICATING THE FINDINGS OF THE WATER TEST

After they tested the samples, students wrote reports of their findings. Students had to do quite a bit of writing for this expedition, including their individual reports, an overall report, letters, and brochures. In previous years, I had not focused on writing in science. Yet I noticed that more students crossing my path had difficulty writing coherent sentences. Improving students' technical writing skills became one of my teaching goals for the year. I paid particularly close attention to those students who struggled to write a paragraph. I used a standard practice of Expeditionary Learning to improve their writing skills. Together, we developed a rubric of what good writing looks like. Then students looked at samples of student work and took notes about the quality of the work based on the rubric. It helped that the models they were looking at did not come from a textbook. They were the work of real students, pieces that we viewed as good examples of writing.

After looking at the sample work, students recorded their reflections on how their own writing compared. They were very honest. They looked at it and said, "Okay, I know mine isn't where this model is." Then we started to ask questions like, "Well, what do you need to do in order to get it there?" I reminded them that all those skills they learned in humanities class still counted in science class. As soon as it became clear what they had to do to make the work better, they did it. They revised as much as they needed to, and by the time they had written one or two successful papers, they started to feel it was something they were able to do. Since everybody was revising their work, no one felt, "I'm the only one who has to redo stuff." Revising became the norm.

Having clearly stated, high expectations made a great difference in their work. By the end of the water study, all students had experienced some degree of progress in their writing. The biggest improvement came from the students who started the year barely writing complete sentences and were reluctant to do any writing at all. Those students were willing to put greater effort into their writing than they had in the past. Soon they were writing coherent sentences and developing paragraphs as well as revising their work.

Writing a number of varied reports helped them hone these skills. When it came time for them to write their individual reports, we collaboratively developed a criteria list that explained that their reports had to reflect the work of the group, provide information on their water source, and describe the type of tests they performed to answer their inquiry. They also had to show their data in more than one format. This meant including charts and graphs to help explain their results. Clarifying all these steps and expectations helped students understand what they needed to do in order to write a high-quality report.

Students also learned that test results reports were like math problems: answers had to be double-checked. With their reports they had to check their data and graphs against their conclusions. This method of checking did not always uncover an error. However, when students con-

June 15, 1998

Dear Participants:

Please allow us to thank you for using your water for our testing. We appreciate your patience and participation throughout this project. Our final results are the following:

We are happy to report that none of the water we tested showed any traces of dangerous elements which could be harmful to you and/or your customers. Our tests were conducted by students of School for the Physical City as precisely as we could make them. We were able to test water samples for chlorine, copper, and iron levels, as well as for hardness and the pH of the water. The majority of the samples tested neutral for pH, and the few that didn't were in state guidelines for pH levels. Most samples had little or no chemical detection of the elements listed above.

Our results were submitted to the Department of Environmental Protection (DEP) for review. We did not have the capacity to check water samples for lead or bacteria. If you would like to have your water tested for those areas of concern, you can call DEP at 1-800-DEP-HELP. They will test your water for free. You can also go on line at www.ci.nyc.ny.us.com for more information on DEP services. We are enclosing a brochure created by students you might find helpful.

Thank you once again for your participation.

Sincerely,
(The Eighth-Grade Class of School for the Physical City)

Eighth-grade students at School for the Physical City in New York City sent this letter to people who had submitted their water to be tested by the students.

solidated reports by groups, they uncovered some discrepancies. Students had to recheck raw data in order to get at true values for their analyses.

In addition to group reports, I asked them to write a group scientific report that would contain both classes' data. I wanted their work to be of the same caliber as the college papers they had read. Students divided into several groups, those who:

- ～ went through the individual reports to select information for the overall report
- ～ went through everyone's graphs and charts to make certain that data among groups agreed
- ～ wrote the introduction for the paper
- ～ looked into the history of the city's water supply
- ～ looked into the cost of supplying water
- ～ wrote the main body of the paper and the conclusion

Students had no problem graphing small quantities of samples, but when they had to compile data from two classes to integrate into the overall report, they became confused. The more variables they had to contend with, the more disorganized their data, and the more errors occurred. I put the brakes on their work, and we had a review session on how to chart and graph information with several variables. I had them do the work by hand, then transfer it into a computer file.

While the official report was being constructed, other students created brochures and posters of their water study for the final presentation. The brochures and posters summarized the individual reports and contained graphics of the results. Unlike the individual reports, however, specific information about the source of their water sample was left out to respect the privacy of those who offered their water to be tested.

To notify participants about the quality of their water samples, students distributed letters and a brochure, which they voted on from all the brochures constructed. They selected it because it contained general information about the water testing, yet it contained specific information about health facts. Also they liked its design.

They put the letters and brochures in envelopes to either mail or hand carry to a client. One student, whose household participated in the study, took his letter and brochure to his father's job. When his father saw the brochure and read the letter, he showed it to his co-workers who read the material and inquired how they could get brochures to take to their families and friends.

PULLING IT ALL TOGETHER

I had managed to bargain with other teachers in the school about scheduling so I could have both classes concurrently work on the design of their final presentation. Students brainstormed ideas, then voted on them. They decided to set up the school's gym into a gallery with chairs in the middle in auditorium-style. As they talked about their ideas, one student sketched the gym and began to layout a floor plan based on the conversation. Adjacent to the chairs, they placed tables to display their posters and brochures. In front was a space for student spokespersons, a water demonstration table, a table with microscopes and slides of protozoans found in water, and behind the speakers was the mural of a water system.

I was surprised by which students said they would be willing to present in front of the whole audience. Many of them had started out the year barely participating in group discussions. They would never raise their hands, and if I called on them they would shrug their shoulders, look at the floor, and say "I don't know." But later, during the water expedition, a lot of these students wanted to participate in small group discussions and give their opinion about issues. They started speaking out in whole group activities. The change seemed to come when they realized they knew what they were doing, that they understood the process of testing and analyzing water. They felt like they actually had something worth sharing.

Soon the day of the presentation arrived, and all the students were ready. After they ushered the audience to their seats, one student, the master of ceremonies, called everyone's attention to the front of the room. At the beginning of the school year, this student had struggled with his writing and was not very interested in science class or school in general. School was a place for him to hang out with his friends rather than a place to learn. Sometime during the water study, he emerged as a leader of his group, and he began to take his work very seriously. He actually volunteered to stand up in front of a public audience and be the emcee at the final presentation. He did a wonderful job. He explained the project and announced speakers and demonstrators.

The audience included a representative from the Department of Environmental Protection and one from the Environmental Protection Agency, clients of the water study, parents, students from other classes, school faculty, staff developers from local colleges, and Expeditionary Learning staff members. They all listened intently as students spoke about their work and demonstrated how they conducted their tests using a sample of school water. At the end of their talk, students presented their official report to the Department of Environmental Protection representative, who commented on how substantial and thorough the students' testing procedures were. She said she was surprised and pleased at what they had accomplished, and she wished the commissioner of her agency could have been there to hear the students speak so articulately about a technical subject.

When the first part of the ceremony was over, the emcee instructed the guests to browse at the tables where they could review work and ask questions. Many people were impressed with the comprehensive responses they received and with the eagerness of students to share what they had learned. They were amazed that they could walk up to the students and ask them questions—not just about what was in front of them, but also about anything they wanted to know about water—and the students responded with confidence. Audience members walked away with the impression that these students really took this work seriously, and that they did a lot of in-depth research. They could tell the students really knew what they were talking about.

When I first wrote this curriculum, many people thought I was expecting too much from my students. After all, they were only in eighth grade. But by the time they finished the final presentation, we knew they had done more than test water samples and report results. They had broken new ground. They had uncovered information that cannot be found in textbooks or on the Internet. They found answers to tough questions that a lot of people had never thought of exploring. They also discovered that when they have trouble finding answers, if they persevere, they will accomplish a great deal of learning.

WHAT IS SERVICE?

At the Service Institute held in Wappinger Falls, New York, Cheryl Sims helped a group of teachers understand what constitutes meaningful service through an initiative she does with her students.

Sims, a teacher at School for the Physical City in New York City, gave participants examples such as "Someone gives blood to the Red Cross during a blood drive," "Some teens paint houses in a dilapidated neighborhood and get paid for it," and "A Peace Corps volunteer builds shelters in a war zone for refugees and hates it."

She then asked them to decide if they thought each example was service. Once they gathered into groups of "yes," "no," or "maybe," the teachers had to explain their decisions.

The initiative, adapted from curriculum developed by Susan McCray for the South Bronx High School Outward Bound program, provoked debate and raised many other questions: Does service have to be voluntary? Is it enough if your intentions are good or do you have to make a measurable difference? Is it still service if you receive something in return?

As the teachers grappled with these questions, a list of service attributes emerged. They charted these on a continuum to illustrate that while service can be superficial sometimes, it can also address real community needs and deeply impact students' academic achievement and character development.

This continuum might be helpful for planning service in expeditions. For instance, where does a plan to visit homeless shelters fall on the continuum? If it were just one visit, it would fall to the left of the continuum's first component, but if it were connected to an extended oral history project that looked at hunger and housing in a community, it would be on the right.

Different aspects of the same project may fall at different places along the continuum.

Similarly, the same project may progress over time. Students may start a project because a teacher suggested it, but as they get immersed, the motivation can become intrinsic.

Service Continuum

Service as an event————Integrated with academic content

Low impact————High Impact

Nice gesture————Addresses an authentic need

Short-term relationships————Sustained relationships

Extrinsic motivation————Intrinsic motivation

Agrees to serve————Desires and identifies how to serve

Expects something in return————Surpasses personal gratification

Attitude of service only during service————Attitude of service is generalized

Limited ability to take action————Empowerment

Limited understanding of community served————Respect for and knowledge of community served

Putting Down Roots: Erosion Control on the South Platte River

Wendy Ward

*M*uddy, hammer in one hand and emptied bucket in the other, Caroline made her way up the loose, steep slope of the South Platte River's bank, reached back and gave Dylan a hand over the lip of the eroded riverbank. From the top of the bank, they could see over one hundred willows they had helped plant, trees whose roots would someday hold the fragile earth at that riverbend in place.

A learning expedition on time and erosion had brought these seventh-grade students to the South Platte River and given them the chance to see their work spread out around them. What started as a classroom study of erosion became a part of the Denver-area landscape, and these students and their classmates became workers in service of the riverbed. As students at the Rocky Mountain School of Expeditionary Learning (RMSEL), they were accustomed to providing service to their community. RMSEL has a service portfolio requirement that students must fulfill before they pass through each major transition from kindergarten to high school graduation. Yet no matter how often students become involved in service, each project touches them in unique ways. The work on the South Platte River not only brought to life geological concepts, it also helped the students see their own power to mend their surrounding world.

TRIBUTARIES

"Time," a seventh- and eighth-grade spring expedition, was guided by the questions; "What is time?" "What are the costs of time?" and "How can time be measured?" In humanities, students read *Fahrenheit 451, The Giver,* and *Heartlight* and developed their own theories of time. Students then wrote creative fiction illustrating how their unique perspectives on time would play out in the lives of their various characters. Meanwhile, in math and science, students explored the source of time through a study of planetary motion. This study culminated with students designing calendars for other planets in our solar system based on their understanding of how increments of time are defined. Next, we looked to Earth itself and explored how the Earth developed and continues to change over time. This geologic study was the launching point of our erosion-related service work at South Platte Park.

The broad topic, time, could have lent itself easily to a variety of other service projects. For instance, Rainbow Bridge, a local group that connects young people and elders, was quite keen to work with us. Our students could visit elders in nursing homes, interview them about their lives, and compile oral histories either on video or in written form. Tantalizing and time-related as this project was, we decided to focus our attention on erosion for a number of reasons.

First of all, erosion was a major theme in our study of geology, whereas the focus of elders' life stories seemed a bit more diffuse. Second, the logistics of matching all the seventh graders with video cameras and elders seemed a bit more challenging than simply handing each of them a shovel. Most importantly, the learning goals of our erosion control work were more tangible, more easily identified and assessed.

Deciding to focus on erosion control was far easier than actually finding an erosion project that the students could work on. Although we did not plan to start our service work until April, I began seeking resources in January, which proved to be just soon enough. Any teacher with a fondness for phone tag can imagine the thick pile of message memos and the numerous sprints to the telephone booth that ensued as I contacted over thirty organizations, seeking the perfect erosion-related project. City officials directed me to private contractors, few of whom were interested in twenty-two enthusiastic middle school students descending on them. Underfunded park conservation officers had neither resources nor ideas to offer us. Phone call after phone call, referral after referral, I eventually landed in the nest of South Suburban Parks.

Not only was South Suburban Parks interested in having my students work with them, but they also had a community-relations officer whose very job it was to create service opportunities for the likes of us. We arranged for our group to spend four consecutive Wednesdays working at South Platte Park alongside the resource rangers on erosion control-related projects. I received a carefully worded memo from their community relations office, detailing the dates, projects, and personnel with whom we would be working. After my long search, I was relieved to finally connect with such an interested and interesting organization.

STANDARDS

Two broadly stated standards defined by the Colorado Board of Education became the main governing ideas of this expedition:

- ~ Students know and understand the processes and interactions of Earth's systems and structures and dynamics of Earth and other objects in space.

- ~ Students know and understand the interrelationship between science, technology, and human activity and how they effect the world.

While we were not able to delve into all aspects of the above standards, students developed a depth of understanding of these principles through our focused study. By looking specifically at the issue of erosion, students gained first-hand knowledge of one force which shapes the Earth; additionally, they learned of a specific role humans and technology play in Earth's constant changes by being involved themselves in erosion-control efforts.

For my own use, I narrowed the above standards into measurable learning goals and designed the expedition as a whole, and this service work in particular, with the intention that students would:

~ understand erosion as one of many forces which shape
our landscape

~ understand the role humans play in promoting and
controlling erosion

~ learn some erosion-control strategies

In addition to these academic goals, I had other benefits in mind. I intended students to develop their skills at working together on physical tasks, improve their connection with the natural world, and even glimpse a field of employment they may never have considered.

TAKING THE PLUNGE

"Born of Fire," the National Geographic video, kicked off our geologic study one rainy day in March. After some rock talks and a few more classroom days discussing the forces that shape the Earth, the time came when I shared the good news that we would *not* be spending the entire spring indoors. I explained that we were about to begin a sustained service project at the South Platte Park. The announcement, which I thought would spark whoops and hollers of glee, was met by blank twelve-year-old faces and a variety of moans.

"Do we have to go?"

"I'm allergic to plants."

"*Every* Wednesday?"

I went on to explain how great it would be to be outside, how the rangers would be working with us, and how we would get to see firsthand so many of the things we had been discussing in class. I passed out the letter of explanation for their parents, along with the essential permission slips. The students took the papers and headed for the door, while I slumped into my chair wondering where my sales pitch had gone wrong. Was this worth the effort? Was the whole project going to turn into a fiasco? Why didn't they want to go?

Much to my surprise and delight, students began to turn in their permission slips the very next day. My limited experience had already shown me that the quicker the permission slips come in, the more enthusiastic the students are about the outing. I was hitting a return rate somewhere just shy of our class's ski day. So, I thought to myself, they are interested after all.

In class, our geologic conversations continued. We collected rocks and developed systems of our own to categorize them before memorizing the obligatory igneous, sedimentary, and metamorphic classifications. We studied various geologic forces such as volcanoes, earthquakes, landslides, and more. I introduced them to the concept of erosion, and we discussed its role in our changing landscape, though not in much detail. I promised that at the park, students would see evidence of it for themselves.

The Tuesday before our first service outing, I met with all the students and planned for the day. They had as many questions as I did about what exactly we would be doing, but my knowledge of willow staking was no greater than theirs, and so we were all left in suspense overnight.

DAY ONE

After arriving at school the next day and doing our last-minute preparations, the students and I met in a circle. I reminded them of what they should have in their backpacks, and asked what they thought they could do to make this day a success. Well-schooled in producing student generated norms, the students came up with all the right ideas about how they ought to behave: listen and pay attention to adults, stay with the group, work hard, and remember that we represent our school. I asked for a show of hands of all students who could agree to behave in the aforementioned manner. Knowing that the alternative would be a day under fluorescent lights, every one of them put five digits into the air.

The class was blessed by the presence of two Sallys on this day and most of our service days. Sally Carey, who had worked with RMSEL in the past as a service learning consultant, proved to be an invaluable asset. She knew many of the students from her previous work with the school and was well-versed in the goals and norms of quality service. She was joined for the first three weeks by Sally Ortiz, mother of one of our students. Her presence was also a great benefit; our student/adult ratio was down to eight to one before we even left the parking lot.

Arriving at South Platte Park, we were greeted by Kelly and Dennis, the resource rangers whose resources we became. After a short welcome and introduction, we divided into two groups: seven students and the two Sallys went with Kelly to plunge into willow staking, while the rest of the class and I went with Dennis to attend to the job of grass planting.

Dennis quickly demonstrated his knowledge of the natural land-scape and his ability to connect with students. Those first moments with him were enough to convince me that indeed this project was a jackpot. He took us to our work site on the banks of a few ponds. From there he gave us a small tour of the area, describing how the landscape had changed over time, how South Platte Park was created as a result of a great flood in 1974, and how the purpose of the park was to preserve wildlife habitat. Right before us was an example of that very thing. Here a few ponds had been shaped by the hand of humans, designed to control the water quality as it leached from the development project behind us into the lake beyond. Dennis explained the need for this water-collection system, as well as the threat to its stability: erosion. The solution to this potential problem was contained in the green garbage can awaiting our gloved hands: grass seeds.

A bale of hay, two rolls of jute matting, a barrel of seeds, some ham-mers and stakes, and a collection of rakes had been left on the road near the pond awaiting our muscles to move them. Once oriented to our work site, we collected our materials and brought them over to the slope where we would begin work. Dennis faced the sun and explained the step-by-step process of grass planting. Each student was assigned a job: the rakers first prepared the soil; the seed sprinklers next scattered the flakes of hope across the hillside; meanwhile, the cutters measured out and snipped an appropriate length of jute matting; hay spreaders sprinkled handfuls of the golden fibers over the seeds, for protection from hungry birds and blowing wind; finally, the students stretched the measured jute across the seeded area as hammer-wielding stakers tamped it down. Meanwhile, the rakers had begun again on the adjacent slope. In this way, we spent our morning, each with a job and a purpose.

Scattering seeds went faster than raking, and spreading hay went faster than stretching jute, so certain teams had lulls in their work. After some time, the rakers started envying the seed spreaders, and, for the sake of justice, we rotated jobs, and then rotated again, giving everyone a chance at what was perceived as the executive position: handling grass seeds.

Most remarkable about that morning was the behavior of the students. Tony, visually impaired, who sits in the front row of class every day clicking his pen, drumming his desk, and tapping his feet, became the master jute cutter, wielding the snippers with precision. Caroline, who seldom speaks up in class, took over the task of jute stretching with authority. She gently directed her assistant Dylan, autistic but keen to participate, as they worked together to cover the freshly planted seeds. It was these three students, not the highest academic achievers, who shone our first day in the field and to whom I awarded character kudos the next day at our schoolwide community meeting.

Within a couple of hours, we used up our supply of jute and had succeeded in securing the greatest part of the slope. Dennis declared our work done for the day, and we headed back toward the Visitors Center to meet the other group and see what they had done.

The muddy-kneed willow stakers, as it turned out, had cultivated quite a high opinion of themselves as hard workers saddled with the toughest job. As we toured their work site, we learned the fine art of South Platte Park's most commonly employed erosion-control strategy: planting willows on unstable banks. With pride, the students explained their work: pound rebar 18 inches to make a hole, insert a willow stake (a trimmed branch from another willow tree), and begin again. There was an air of superiority wafting from the willow stakers as we explained our grass-planting accomplishments. I left them to their pride and assured everyone that our jobs would change each week.

We were planting willow bushes along the banks. The roots of a willow will hold the soil in place when it rains, snows, or high winds occur.... I feel good about my work because Evan, Andy and I planted at least one hundred willow bushes, and it wasn't as boring as you think. —Daniel Walter

The notion of food sent the group running to fetch their lunches from our vans; they joined me on the benches of the Visitors Center porch, overlooking the park and the mountains beyond. During our lunch break, the head ranger told us some park history and thanked us for our work. He described how the forces of nature themselves, not humans, have dominion over the landscape. He also brought us up to date on the development of this wildlife habitat and efforts to monitor and modify the flow of the river. While just a sliver of the geologic history of Colorado, his description gave life to the pictures of continental plates and samples of sedimentary rock that had graced our classroom conversations. I thanked him for the work of his resource rangers, then asked the class to debrief our morning and prepare for the afternoon's journal-writing session.

"What?" "So what?" and "Now what?" were the questions I used to guide the discussion. We reviewed the definition of erosion in this particular context—the river moving earth. After the three questions were answered to my satisfaction, I asked the students to share their experiences that morning. The projects got mixed reviews. Willow staking was hard work, and grass planting boring, according to some. But I was satisfied to hear that many of them had somehow felt that they were actually *doing* something real—not pushing buttons or writing words, but changing the surface of this minute patch of Earth.

Our last activity at the park was solitude and reflection. Students grabbed their pencils, and I handed out a service reflection page that listed several questions at the top. Pencil, paper, and notebooks in hand, students scattered across the open field and the path between the Visitors Center and the river. As they spread themselves out, I took the chance, for the first time all day, to inhale the fresh air and notice the Rockies looming before us, to feel happy that here I was, at last, outdoors with these children, touching the Earth we had been studying.

I feel really great because I know that I did something to help out nature and I guess you could say mankind ... I just really liked getting out of school to help make a better place for wildlife. Another thing that I liked was that we had fun doing what we were doing. I also thought that the scenery was very beautiful and peaceful. —Caroline Maestas

Sunburned in spite of #30 protection, muddy, tired, and mostly happy, we returned to school in time to catch regular rides home. Thanking the two Sallys for their effort, we agreed that it had been a fine day, that Dennis and Kelly were gems, and that this service project was working out all right. Weary but inspired, I scurried to our after-school faculty meeting with a feeling of pride in my heart; after all my phone calls and worries and fears, we had found a meaningful service learning opportunity.

CLASSROOM CONNECTIONS

While we were spending Wednesdays in the field, our classroom work further enhanced students' understanding of geology and erosion. After an overview of the forces that shape the Earth, we delved into a study of rivers and their relationship with the landscape. One major product of this expedition, a portfolio piece, was an Erosion Lab in which students conducted their own investigations about erosion. After a year of carefully scaffolded science labs, students were prepared by this time to design and conduct their own from start to finish.

In this inquiry-based lab, students wrote their own hypotheses about erosion rates and then designed their own experiments to test them. Particle size (sand versus diatomaceous earth), volume of water flow (one versus more siphons) and slope of riverbed (how many books under the top end of the blue plastic river table) were some of the variables students chose. Lab partners agreed upon one or more variables to test and then devised their experiments and data collection plans. One group posited that sand would erode faster than diatomaceous earth. Another claimed that the more water volume, the faster the erosion. Still another hypothesized that steeper streams erode faster.

> **Overview of Erosion Control Strategies**
> We have gone to South Platte Park almost every
> Wednesday to do service for erosion control. This was a
> hard and strenuous process of willow staking, grass
> planting, tree wrapping, French drain, weeding, and
> trash pickup.
>
> Willow staking was a way to keep the soil from slipping
> into the lake. The first step in the process to willow staking
> is cutting your willow stakes at about a foot long. They
> must be at a slant to be able to put into the ground. The
> second step in this strenuous process is hammering a piece
> of rebar into the ground with a mallet (this is harder than
> it looks). Then you slide the willow stake into the recently
> made rebar hole.

Nathan Tittle and Evan Kutz, seventh-grade students at Rocky Mountain School
of Expeditionary Learning in Denver, Colorado, wrote a report about erosion
control strategies they used at South Platte Park. Above is an excerpt.

"How will you actually measure erosion?" I asked many groups who
presented me with dainty drawings of buckets and plastic trays. With
little prodding, most generated ideas about the volume of sand that was
moved a measurable distance, demonstrating their understanding of
the definition of erosion. Their plans approved, students were free to
set up their water buckets and river tables for their experiments.

There is something delightful about the pairing of water and children. No one left class these days completely dry, and the hands-on
nature of our labwork was engaging even for those less inclined toward
science. Working in small groups, young investigators puzzled through
the operation of siphons, the use of measuring tools, and the management of water containers.

All labs completed and typed, our floor mopped dry, we gathered to discuss and compare results. Each team of scientists reported the outcomes of their inquires, which I listed on the board, summarizing the work of each in a short phrase. Stepping back and reading over their results, together we developed our own theory of erosion: Erosion occurs quickest on steeper river beds, covered by smaller particles, when there is a high volume of water.

"Can anyone relate this to willow staking?" I asked.

"South Platte Park," students called out.

"Yeah, it was drastically reshaped by a huge flood," remembered one student. "A high volume of water led to significant erosion."

"But what about willows?" I asked.

"Willow roots hold the soil in place."

"Does this relate to particle size?"

"Well," considered one student, "it would be easier to hold larger particles in place."

"Given all this, what can or do humans do to control erosion?" I asked.

"We can stabilize banks and hold the earth in place," someone called.

"Can we control the slope of the riverbed?"

"No, not really. Even if we dam a river, it still has to find its way down to the ocean, so somewhere there will have to be a slope. We could line the slope with concrete."

"What about the volume of water? Can we control that?"

"We do," declared a student. "With dams."

"Should we?" I wondered.

Activities and conversations such as this served as one assessment of students' understanding of the three learning goals I had set forth: understanding erosion as one of many forces which shape our landscape, understanding the role humans play in promoting and controlling erosion, and learning some erosion-control strategies. Further, we were offered a launch pad for ethical conversations about humans' relationship with the land. Erosion control led to a discussion about water resource management, which is another wonderful and related topic whose surface we only scratched.

PARK PROGRESS

Week two, week three, and week four at the park all followed the same basic rhythm: meet first thing in the morning at school, break into task groups at the park for a couple of hours of work, lunch together on the porch, debrief, end the day with solitude and reflection. Our projects varied week to week and included tree wrapping (with chicken wire to prevent beaver attack), French drain building, trash collecting, weeding, and, our staple, willow staking. As time went on, students became familiar with the routine and the work, which had both drawbacks and benefits.

Getting to know our rangers Dennis and Kelly, our work groups became more cohesive, and I began to step aside and turn leadership over to them. With each visit, the student's familiarity with the park and its terrain increased, and it became more their place, not a foreign land. They grew comfortable with our schedule and were quicker to follow a lead to circle up or get to work. Over time, though, students snubbed their noses at willow-staking assignments and relished new opportunities. Within the context of our routine, they enjoyed change.

As we traveled to our service site in two vans, the students quickly divided themselves along clique lines for this part of the day. The first day out I sent everyone to work in van groups, just for the sake of simplicity. I soon realized that this error reinforced the unfortunate perception of the "cool" and "uncool." Week to week, I devised new ways to divide the class, seeking the perfect student combinations to maximize work attitude and learning opportunities.

Interestingly, there were several teams of students who loved being together but whose influence on one another was unpredictable: One week, Evan and Leighton were racing around the riverbank with a wheelbarrow collecting rocks at top speed; another week, they attempted to lose themselves in the woods rather than wrap trees. These attitude changes could be explained by a number of factors: interest in the task, ease of the task, weather, mood, and sugar content of breakfast cereal. With so many variables in the mix, I never did find a surefire way to ensure 100 percent positive participation, but I did recognize responsibility for the two factors I could control some-what, interest and ease of task. These two alone can be the success or failure of any service project.

WEATHER

I awoke Wednesday of week three to the promise of our worst weather yet. Sniffing snow, I considered canceling the outing for the day, but the prospect of spending an entire unplanned day indoors beckoned me to reconsider. With a quick reminder to bring coats, we were off to South Platte Park. This day we worked along the riverbank where park rangers and various teams of engineers had already employed a range of erosion-control strategies. Dennis gave us a tour of the length of the South Platte, and students saw the failure of the Army Corps of Engineers' metal and concrete barrier designed to reinforce the bank. They also witnessed the ineffectual rock pile approach. Dennis unveiled the day's work: willow staking, nature's remedy to erosion.

A group went down the bank to pound willow stakes while the rest of us were left above to clip new stakes to specifications. As the flakes began to fall, Tony came to me with a weather report. "Wendy, it's snowing." I smiled and nodded.

"Well, can we go back?" he whined.

"When we're done, " I told him. I scanned the group: uncomfort-able but working. The students kept at it. I was glad the weather had come out to greet us this day, reminding the group not only to dress warmly, but also that in spite of humans' efforts to control nature, to channel rivers and manage floodwaters, our Earth has rhythms and cycles all its own.

> *I feel good because I got to help people out and make their*
> *work just a little easier and I got to help out the environment.*
> *Today was really hard and cold, but some people have to*
> *go out there almost every day to do the same work we*
> *were doing.* —Homan Abbasi

CELEBRATION

Our last day at the park, we quit work early. Dennis and Kelly, naturalists at heart, had a special surprise in store for us; they had spotted a
pair of great horned owls nesting in a critical habitat area of the park,
an area off limits to the general public. As their way of thanking us for
our labor, they had arranged to take us to see these rare birds. Bringing
along a few spotting scopes, Kelly led the group north along the river to
a place where a thin trail dodged into the woods. At this point, she
warned the group to be silent, that our noise could frighten the birds
we were coming to spy on. Lips zipped, we headed single file into the
trees to a stream crossing.

Wet feet were imminent. The log across the stream clearly could
have been sufficient to keep one's feet dry had we arrived later in the
season, but on this day the crossing looked precarious. As this adventure had been cast as a special treat, and many of my students' ideas of
fun did not include leaping from a slimy log into an eddy of six-inch
deep water, I gave students the option of joining the owl-viewing party
or remaining behind, dry footed. A few ventured ahead without hesitation, assisting one another across the log. All had wet sneakers upon
reaching the other side. Kiyomi really wanted to join us, but was
unwilling to venture onto the log. At this point, the young Tim, a
loner's loner, was transformed into a gallant gentleman and hoisted her
up for a piggyback ride. He himself waded across the thigh-deep water
to deposit her, dry, on the other side. She giggled with glee. I myself
prevailed upon a few students to hold my hand as I made the log-to-
eddy leap. Then, about two-thirds of the group sloshed in our sneakers
to the owls' nests.

Once in the clearing where the owls had allegedly been nesting, we
scanned the trees for a glimpse of them. Everyone remained silent until
the birds were spotted—then the whispering ensued. Kelly and Dennis
set up their scopes to give us a good view. After fifteen minutes of
pointing and looking and adjusting, everyone had the opportunity to
see the birds. Later, Dennis explained the value of our work, which
helped to preserve these birds' habitat. While we did not have the time

Weedy Work

At South Platte Park, there is a serious weed population. The park is trying to establish native plants, especially tall grasses. But the weeds are taking over. We decided to pull the weeds to get rid of the biological pollution, and help the native plants grow.

You're probably asking yourself, what does this have to do with erosion? Most plants have deep rooting systems that hold the soil in, especially along the river bank. When we weeded, we worked along a river bank. Ray Sperger, one of the staff, went though the bank and tagged all the native plants with ribbon, so we would not pull native plants. We learned that weeds generally have shallow rooting systems that only hold in top soil. It was steep along the river bank so we wanted deep root plants to stop erosion. It is wiser to let the native deep-rooting plants grow instead of the shallow-rooting weeds. Some of the native plants that are in the park are: willows, cotton woods, foxtails, blue varvain, and soft-stem bulrush.

This excerpt, from a report on the interplay between plants and erosion entitled "Weedy Work," was written by seventh-grade students Cassie Phillips and Danielle Haynes at Rocky Mountain School of Expeditionary Learning in Denver, Colorado.

to discuss this, I hoped that the students understood that in their individual ways, they really were making a difference.

When we rejoined the waiting and dry group, I was surprised to see that many of them had ventured closer to the water, and two were actually on the log poised to cross. I took heart seeing that my city youth had glimpsed a taste of the risk and wonder involved in simply being outside.

PRODUCT

As if one thousand willows planted, a hundred trees wrapped, fifteen bags of trash collected, two French drains built, an acre of land weeded, and a hillside planted with grass were not enough of a product, I decided we should have some way of sharing our work at the park with the world at large. When I first presented this idea, students proposed a plethora of media for informing the public about their work: video, comic books, poster displays, and more. Intrigued as I was by this crescendo of creativity, I was well aware of the time constraints and wanted our Wednesdays to be spent working rather than merely documenting.

The students decided to make a book of our experiences. We brainstormed a list of topics and projects related to South Platte Park, and then, in pairs, students signed up to document one specific project or part of our experience. We shared drafts, held peer critique sessions, and revised. The final service album, as we came to call it, was completed while I was out on a week-long trip with another class. Although the album contains some nice information and many labeled photos, I was a bit disappointed with it overall. Somehow I had not succeeded in inspiring all students to do their finest work on their service writing. Nonetheless, this book of experiences serves as an easy way to communicate to others about our work. At year-end conferences, many students enjoyed showing their parents the photos and writings in this binder.

> *I think it's a great opportunity for everyone to do lots of work while learning. Plus, they feel good because they know they will really have an impact on the environment ... Of course, we chose to come here because we knew it would be a great learning experience, and it is.* —Mike Nolan

REFLECTIONS

Erosion is tricky to control, we learned. Even human societies erode, as ours well could have in the last weeks of the school year. Impelled to work together—one holding the rebar while another pounds it in, a team pushing the heavy, laden wheelbarrow up a steep slope, ten workers passing rocks down a human chain—students demonstrated improved abilities to cooperate and collaborate, and some of their potential spring fever was mitigated. We grew together, and our work served as the roots that kept us in place.

Each week, Kelly and Dennis were genuinely thankful for our labor. When it came to building a French drain to channel water and secure a slope above the lake, our group collected, transported, and placed two truckloads of river cobbles in a matter of hours, a task which would have taken the resource rangers at least a week working alone. While not all students were enthralled with the concept of manual labor, they were well aware that they were completing tasks no machine could do and that would not get done without us. We mattered.

Our service was real, Kelly and Dennis reminded us each week during our closing conversations, and this reality seemed to surprise the students. In their written comments they made it clear that they felt the power of their participation. They looked with pride through photos of themselves hard at work. Even now, months later, I hear them talk to younger students about their service work with an air of superiority, as though they really have something to brag about.

> *I think it is cool that I am able to play a part in preserving the wildlife habitat. I think my team worked very hard and accomplished a lot.* —Francis Grano

While this project and the learning associated with it were not precisely what I originally intended for this expedition, I was quite satisfied with the results. One important lesson I learned is that service cannot always be formulated to fit our precise learning goals, but that quality service experiences have merits well beyond what could be gained by simply remaining in the classroom. Although Earth's changes over time, specifically by means of erosion, was the theme which launched this service project, students ended up learning a lot about wildlife habitats and the relationship between development and the natural landscape—valuable lessons in any expedition.

Should I have the opportunity to repeat this expedition, I would keep most things the same. Technical writing is one skill that could have been further developed. Students' weekly reflections often included descriptions of the day's work, some of which were more coherent than others. Given the time, this would have been a great chance to encourage students to hone their skills at describing the exact procedures they followed, a skill needed to write high-quality lab reports.

In all, I would have to say I am proud of what we were able to accomplish this spring—meeting science standards as well as working in the out-of-doors. I give thanks for the kind assistance of South Platte Park's Kelly and Dennis, for the good humor of my students, and, most importantly, for Rocky Mountain School of Expeditionary Learning. It is a privilege to work in a school that believes students ought to grow up knowing that they can change the surface of the Earth.

WHEN SERVICE COUNTS

The Rocky Mountain School of Expeditionary Learning (RMSEL) in Denver, Colorado, demonstrates its commitment to service by including a service portfolio requirement for each passage from kindergarten through twelfth grade. Students meet this requirement through service inside and outside the school, and through service imbedded in learning expeditions as well as individual projects guided by a mentor. Faculty and community members assess service portfolios based on the quality and depth of the students' reflections and the number of hours or projects they performed. The passage requirements are:

- Kindergarten through second grade: Documentation and reflection on student's service experiences.
- Third through fifth grade: Documentation and reflection on two service projects, one inside and one outside the school.
- Sixth through eighth grade: Documentation of eighty hours of service and a reflection on one or more service projects.
- High school graduation: Documentation of a major service project and a reflection on the role of that and other service in the student's life. Students must conduct at least two hundred hours of service and include a resume of their service projects and hours logged.

Students have done a variety of service projects, including tutoring bilingual students in Denver elementary schools, volunteering in orphanages, working at homeless shelters, maintaining trail huts in the Rocky Mountain backcountry, building houses for Habitat for Humanity, and participating in personal care, systems management, and family coordination in elder-care centers. Below are excerpts of student reflections on their service.

Katherine Dalton
Service Reflection

I heard about Camp to Belong when I was looking for summer volunteer opportunities through the Denver Department of Social Services. I was referred to a woman named Lynn Price. I attended one meeting and knew instantly that participating in this program would change my life forever. Lynn explained that she herself had been a foster child who was separated from her older sister, Andi. After reuniting, they grew extremely close and decided to create a summer camp that would give foster children and their brothers and sisters a chance to meet and get to know each other.

Before I knew it I was on a bus full of screaming kids headed to Estes Park, Colorado. This week was definitely going to be a challenge, one I was praying I could handle. ... The first night was hard for everyone.

One girl in my cabin didn't feel well. I think it was hard for her to adjust to her surroundings, and we sat up all night. I held her in my arms, stroking her back until she finally passed out at 4:00 a.m. She didn't leave my side for the rest of the week. ...

Camp to Belong was the most challenging week of my life. Physically it was tough chasing after kids all day. This I could handle. What I wasn't ready for was the emotional test I was being put through ... I will always be grateful to them for teaching me that above all we are each only human, and we make mistakes and we all live under different circumstances. We all feel pain, anger, and joy. The connections we make as humans can either make our time here a pleasure or agony. That last week of my summer I could have stayed home, slept in, and hung out with my friends, but I chose to change my life and make a difference in the life of a child.

Tania del Rio
Service Reflection

I had never realized how important community service was until I came to RMSEL. In my very first year here, I went on a two-week trip to the four corners region to do community service for the Navajo people there.

At first, I thought it would be a drag to do work like planting trees, cleaning trash and fixing things, but I quickly learned that service work really makes you feel good and can actually be enjoyable, especially when you're working with friends. I met several nice people during that trip and I was happy to help out with things that probably wouldn't have been done otherwise. Planting the trees also turned out to be a very rewarding experience, for you're not only giving something back to the community, but to the Earth itself.

Back at school, I started to get more involved and interested in community service. I ran for student council and got elected the first year, although it fell through, and I was involved in peer mediation until that fell through as well the following year. Even though I didn't earn hours for either of these, I continued to do community service with my friend, Lisa. Together, we set up a recycling project for a couple months where we'd collect all the recyclables in the school and take them to King Soopers during lunch. Then, we headed two canned-food drives for the Salvation Army.

I think community service should be as stressed in other schools as it is in ours. Many people out there still consider it to be boring and tedious torture, and if they discovered it wasn't, our communities would be much better places.

STEWARDS OF THE ELEMENTS

CHRIS QUIGLEY, BRYAN STREET, AND CHRIS WEAVER

The Eagle Clan girl held on tightly to the madrona tree. "What kind of a test?"

Eagle looked at her. "You and your clan must go for three days without using water from the pipes. No sinks. No drinking foun-tains. No flushing toilets. If you succeed, you will be ready to start learning ..."

The boy looked at the great old turtle. "What kind of a test?" he asked.

"You and your clan must go for three days without using heat or electricity. No lights. No heat. No TVs, or computers. If you succeed, you will be ready to start learning ..."

The girl was sprayed with water, as Orca moved toward the shore.

"What kind of a test?" she shouted.

"You and your clan must go for three days without any food from the lunchroom or the store," replied the orca. "If you succeed, then you will be ready to learn. ..."

Three classes of students filled the floor of a classroom that Monday afternoon in early October, listening to the end of this strange story. Tom, the father of one of the students, read the story and told them that it had been handed to him at a gas station by a mysterious stranger wearing a brown cloak. "The story seems to involve your classes," Tom explained, "so I thought I should bring it over and read it to you."

Indeed, the story seemed to involve these students. The multi-age classes, two second and third grades and a third and fourth grade, went by the names of the Eagle Clan, the Turtle Clan, and the Orca Clan here at Pathfinder School, a public school in West Seattle with a Native American focus. But what did it mean, to go without water, electricity, and food for three days as part of a mysterious "test?" Surely, this was just a story.

When it was over, Bryan, one of the teachers, said, "Thanks, Tom, for bringing the story in. I really do not know what it has to with us …" A call over the intercom interrupted him. It was Carrie, the head secretary.

"I just got the strangest call from downtown," she said. "The district food service says that no lunches will be delivered for the next three days for any students in the Eagle, Turtle, or Orca Clans. They also said that none of you are allowed to bring any food from home! Do you know what this is about?" The room erupted into excited chatter.

The three teachers discussed with their students whether they should actually follow the directions of this "test," with its mysterious and unknown source. Some students protested, but most were excited to take a leap of faith. The teachers sent home a note explaining, as best they could, the situation to parents. That night, eighty-one children lay in their beds and wondered.

On Tuesday morning, the students arrived, lunchless, to find a series of new surprises. They flipped the switches, but there was no light. They tried the sinks, but no water came out. They turned on the computers, but they were dead. The hallway drinking fountains did not work. They hurried down to the bathrooms, but each bathroom had a sign on the door: No Eagles, Turtles, or Orcas Allowed.

By 9:15 a.m., each of the three clans was gathered on its meeting carpet in the dim light, with its teacher unrolling a blank sheet of butcher paper on the wall and saying something such as, "Well you guys, we are in quite a predicament. We had better make a plan."

What transpired over the next seventy-two hours is difficult to describe in brief. The continuation of the story had charged the Eagle Clan with responsibility for the element Water, the Turtle Clan for Fire (which seemed to include electricity), and the Orca Clan for the element Earth, which seemed at this point to mean food. Student messengers ran between the rooms to see if the three clans agreed on this organization of duties, which they did.

After some brainstorming, the Eagle students identified "bathrooms" as the most intense need. In the middle of an animated discussion about using the bushes on the lower field, one child said, "Hey. Maybe we can get a port-a-potty." That student called the Honey Bucket Company from the classroom phone, and, remarkably, a port-a-potty could be delivered within the hour. The news spread to the other clans. Everyone was vocally (and, later, otherwise) relieved.

The Turtle Clan concluded that lacking electricity would not cause too many difficulties. The students gathered extra sweatshirts and coats for what was looking like a cool and drizzly day. But soon a much more serious duty appeared. A messenger from the Eagles came in to say that a group of them, accompanied by two parents who luckily were at school that day, were heading to the creek in Schmitz Park to fill containers with water for drinking. "But the water won't be clean," the Eagle student said. "It has to be boiled to be safe. Can you guys figure out how to boil water?" Coincidentally, the school had a fire department permit to build "recreational fires" on the lower field. The Turtles started organizing to find and transport firewood from students' homes and a local construction site.

Meanwhile, any Orca students who had gardens at home were discussing how they might gather enough food for lunch that day. One of the mothers, who happened to be at school, offered to take a group of students to her house to make bread and churn butter. Another group knew where to go to dig up potatoes. The Eagles got water for them, but the Turtles told them the fire would not be ready that day to cook the potatoes. It was agreed that the potatoes would be the main course for lunch on Wednesday

And so it went. Small groups of students were out all over the neighborhood with parent helpers. They almost always found what they needed, but often the families who had the food or materials they desired asked the children to do some work for them in exchange. On Wednesday and Thursday, the Turtle Clan tended the fire for most of the day and struggled to figure out how to support the big cooking pots and hold down the tarp that acted as a windbreak. Families produced salmon that they had caught and venison that they had shot as food "not from the store" to be cooked on Thursday.

Then, on Thursday afternoon, when at last the meal was finished and the exhausted children sat on the floor of the dim lunchroom, the secretary walked in with a box that had been, once again, mysteriously delivered. It contained a note of congratulation, and a small award for each child: a necklace bearing an Orca, Turtle, or Eagle bead. The students had passed the "test." But the expedition had just begun.

PHILOSOPHY AND STRUCTURE

In the above account of the "test," the reader will have detected evidence of behind-the-scenes, pre-experience engineering. The three teachers who planned this expedition are believers in constructivist learning and emergent curriculum; we see the teacher's planning role as one of providing students with opportunities for rich discoveries and meaningful actions of their own choosing. How much a teacher engineers and how much space one leaves waiting to be filled with student-initiated surprises is a matter of the developmental level of the students, and the teacher's experience, personal philosophy, and teaching environment.

Constructivism brings an interesting spin to service learning. In the words of Expeditionary Learning's tenth design principle, one of our primary functions is "to prepare students with the attitudes and skills to be of service to others." One of the most important capacities behind meaningful service is the ability to identify and act on one's own values.

Yet how can students discover their own values in service projects that are chosen only by the teacher? If we do not give our students the freedom and opportunity to discover their own values and to choose actions based on those values, then our students may not experience service as an opportunity calling for creative action, but instead as a duty calling for compliance.

Pathfinder School follows a three-year cycle of schoolwide "generative themes." The theme for this school year was stewardship. Our dictionaries defined the word as "responsibility for wise use or protection." The student understanding of the word amounted to "to take really good care of something," which they could understand in terms of being a good steward of a pet or of the coat racks in the hallway. What would be new to most eight- and nine-year-olds, we knew, was the idea of taking good care of water, or electricity, or food. But we vowed in our earliest planning sessions *not to raise the question of what this might mean,* at least not before we all had many weeks of experiences behind us.

We based this vow on our understanding of constructivist practice. We could tell the students how to take care of water. We could ask them how to take care of water. But the importance of taking care of water would ultimately be built on each child's understanding of water, what it means, and how it works. Our job as teachers was to provide as many experiences as possible in which our students could build their own understanding of the element they studied, their relationship to that element, and, near the end, their interpretation of what being a steward of the elements might mean in practice. In familiar other words, self-discovery was primary.

The remainder of this chapter tells the story of the rest of the expedition. Each teacher wrote the account of the experiences of his own clan; our various voices will be evident, as will differences in our teaching styles. The clans worked largely independently, but gathered together each Thursday afternoon so that two clans could watch a presentation, skit, or report performed by the third clan, on a rotating schedule. The students also shared information in inter-clan individual oral reports, which were evaluated by the listening students in small groups, based on a rubric and criteria created by the students.

We owe a deep debt of gratitude to the mysterious and unknown author of the Story, for, lo and behold, new chapters arrived, remarkably, just at the moments when our clans were groping for the next big step.

CHAPTER TWO ARRIVES

Eagle spoke first, "So why did you come to see us again?"

"We wanted to tell you about the test!" said the Eagle girl. "About how the clans are doing! You have to hear about carrying the water jugs up the trail ..."

"... and digging up potatoes and how the kids brought herbs for the soup ..."

"... and how the plastic rope melted over the fire and the pot almost fell, but we put up a grate and cinderblocks ..."

"Don't worry," said Orca. "We know about all these things. Human beings think they are all alone, but really there are many ears and eyes listening and watching."

"Well then," said the Orca girl. "What we really need to know is, are we stewards of the elements now?"

The animals were quiet for a moment. "That depends," said Eagle. "What have you learned from this test?"

The Eagle Clan girl spoke first. "I learned that we need clean water to live."

"Yes," said Eagle, "as I also do. Tell me this: Where does your usual water come from?"

"Well," said the girl, "it comes from the sink."

"And before that?"

"Well, from the pipes. You know, from the plumbing."

"And before that?"

"I don't know. From rain, I guess."

"To be stewards of the elements, you must find out where your water comes from, and where it goes. "

Turtle boy spoke up. "I learned how much we need fire, for heat and light and cooking."

"Where does your fire come from?" asked Old Turtle.

"Well," said the boy, "It's not really fire. It's electricity. It comes from a switch."

"And before that?"

"In wires, I guess. Electric wires."

Old Turtle seemed to smile. "To be stewards of the elements, you and your clan must find out where your electricity comes from, and where it goes."

The girl from the Eagle Clan was thinking. "Well," she said, "I learned that it's a good thing we have all that food from the lunchroom, because it's hard to find our own!"

"How does your food get to the lunchroom?"
asked Orca.

"Well … I don't know! Maybe the cook gets it from the store …"

"To be stewards of the elements," said the Orca, "you and your clan must find out where your food comes from, and where it goes."

THE EAGLE CLAN: WATER'S JOURNEY

The "test" was over, but it would be a long time before it was forgotten. My goal for the next phase was that the students understand and be able to explain where their drinking water comes from and where it goes, including the natural water cycle and the city system that brings water to us. I asked each student to draw a map showing the journey water took from the creek at Schmitz Park to the school, and where it went afterwards.

Next I walked to the sink, turned on the faucet, poured a glass of water, and took a drink. I said: "During the 'test' you got water from the creek at Schmitz Park, so you knew where that water came from. But does anybody know where this water (pointing to the glass) comes from?"

I listed their ideas on the blackboard and then had them vote on which one they thought was the actual source for our drinking water. The most popular choice was "the ocean," with thirteen votes, followed by "geysers" with ten. Other ideas included "the Mississippi River," "any river," and "the ground."

Next I asked them, "How can we find out the answer?" The students suggested calling a water expert. They prepared a script, one student volunteered to call my contact at the city water department, and soon we had the answer: The Cedar River watershed.

"Would you like me to call and see if we can visit the Cedar River watershed?" I did not have to wait for an answer.

So began our series of fieldwork trips to see firsthand where our tap water comes from and where it goes. Fridays became "Expedition Fieldwork" days, with a field trip almost every week. We visited the Cedar River watershed and had a tour from Ralph. We also visited the Alki sewage treatment plant, and the West Seattle water tower and reservoir, where water utility educator Mike Mercer showed us around. Educators from the county and city also came into the classroom and presented watershed-related programs for us. I was very impressed with the quality of interactions we had with all of the adults we met, not just the educators but also people such as the workers at the sewage treatment plant. Many of them were not used to school visits but were pleased that we were interested and were very well prepared for us. We followed up each of our field experiences by marking the jobs we had discovered on our map of the city's water system and discussing how these professionals acted as stewards of water.

I integrated our fieldwork into other parts of our weekly schedule as well. I used pamphlets I collected for reading activities, and facts and figures became the basis for math problems. I turned a map of the city water system into a math board game. On the Fridays when we were not doing fieldwork, we did activities back in class to fill in the gaps in our research. For example, on one Friday we built model watersheds out of rocks, aluminum turkey trays, and plastic wrap. This is one of the many great activities from the Project Wet curriculum (Watercourse and Western Regional Environmental Education Council, Bozeman, Montana, 1995).

Finally it was time for me to assess their learning. First I had them review what they knew about the water system by listing all of the jobs they had encountered that were required to get water to us, and then put them in order. Then I had each student write a narrative piece telling the journey of a droplet of water through the water cycle and the city water system, including as many steps as they could think of. We assess student writing in Seattle using the six-trait direct writing assessment, which asks students to become proficient in three different modes of writing. One of these is the narrative, so this piece of writing doubled as an assessment of their narrative writing as well. I gave it to the students as if it were a formal assessment, scored it and used it to report to parents at fall conferences, which take place just before Thanksgiving. I did not have to read their papers to know they had learned. All of them could easily list the six or seven steps required for water to get to us, and no one thought of water as coming from the ocean or a geyser anymore—our experiences had cleared that up. Moreover, their firsthand understanding of the water journey had at least two positive impacts on their writing: organization improved because sequencing was so clear and concrete in the water journey, and they understood the topic so well that they were freed up to be more creative with ideas and word choice. Many of them wrote very entertaining stories.

THE TURTLE CLAN: ELECTRICITY'S JOURNEY

The Monday after the "test," the Turtle Clan sat on its meeting carpet and considered chapter two of the Story. "Well," I asked the students, "Where does our electricity come from?" The students immediately identified the fuse box, which, in our 1949 one-time-portable classrooms, is located in easy reach above the counter around the sink. As we crowded around, some of the students shared with us that the little round things were fuses, and it was soon clear that the fuses must be connected to wires that were hidden in the walls.

I found and made copies of a basic blueprint of our school. We split into groups of two or three and spent the afternoon exploring the building, inside and out, trying to find evidence of electrical hardware and sketching it onto our maps. Two groups returned and informed us that they had found the place where the electricity entered the school grounds. We followed them outside, and they showed us a single, humble wire connecting the southern roof of the school with a gray trashcanlike thing at the top of a wooden telephone pole on the other side of Genesee Street.

"You mean all our lights and computers run on *that*?" students asked in surprise.

Since so much about electricity was new to us at this point, we had to invent a number of terms to describe things that we did not understand. These terms remained a part of our vocabulary even after we learned the standard electrical terms. The *trashcans* on the wooden poles were later identified as transformers (the "stepping-down kind"), the *fishbowls* on the side of every house as electric meters, and the *donuts* that the students saw where every wire encountered a power pole were later discovered to be ceramic insulators. We learned the standard terms of electrical power on Friday fieldwork trips to a coal-fired power plant, a hydroelectric power plant, and the Puget Power 24-hour Operations Center. As the teacher, I struggled to translate the explanations of our guides on these trips into words and patterns the students could understand. Happily, our guide on the tour of a substation caught on and explained as we stood in the rain outside the chainlink fence that "the higher the voltage, the more donuts you need, because there are a lot more electrons trying to jump to the poles and zoom into the ground. Follow me over here and you'll see the whole donut shop."

These facilities were so enormous that on our tours we did a lot of gaping. At the coal plant we walked on a catwalk twelve stories above the building floor, and peeked into boilers burning at 4,000 degrees. At the hydroelectric plant, students commented on how it was so much quieter than the coal plant, and that fewer people were working there. Fresh from their experience with the "test," the students asked many questions about power outages and what the people in the control room do in the case of storms or earthquakes.

During these weeks we did many in-class activities to support the students' growing understanding of the power system. To get a sense of the invisible phenomenon of electrons moving, we first experimented with direct-current circuits—the standard battery-and-bulb stuff of science labs, except with cheap flashlight bulbs and aluminum foil for wire. We studied the conductivity of different materials, which made the hardware of wires, switches, and insulators surprisingly accessible to these young children. One of my students came to me with an idea for an alternative type of wire: "You know how we have to get out of the swimming pool when there's lightning? Because water's a good conductor, right? And rubber is an insulator. So we could hang up garden hoses full of water and we'd have water-wires!"

I knew that we could not understand how a generator works without understanding AC power (alternating current). I had to begin learning about it myself by reading a high school science curriculum. I tried to explain it to the class with diagrams on the overhead projector with little success. Our breakthrough came at last when we went to the gym and made a "generator" with our bodies. Twenty students stood in a big circle—the electrons in a coil of copper wire. One student stood in the center with a long piece of wood—the magnet—and spun around. The minus pole coming by made all the electron-students jump back, and the plus pole made them jump forward. Suddenly we could imagine this happening sixty times a second, causing all the electrons in all the wires all the way from the power plant to our own toaster jumping back and forth together. As our understanding of the system grew, students were able to diagram the basic parts of a power plant, write a narrative from the point of view of an electron, and make big maps of imaginary towns, complete with yarn power lines of different voltages, substations, houses, coal mines to keep the power plant boiling, and water to drive those giant spinning magnets.

One impressive academic outcome of this part of the expedition was that the students learned to take notes. They took turns, in groups of two or three, making presentations to the class about some aspect of the power system they had researched. While their classmates presented, these second and third graders sat in two rows of chairs with their expedition journals on their laps, identifying the main ideas of the presentation and taking notes. Later, I gave them short-answer tests with only their own notes to depend on as study guides. The students surpassed my expectations in their ability to gather and retain information in this way.

Notwithstanding our teaching team's agreement to withhold any value judgments during this part of the expedition, I made sure on two occasions that our learning experiences were not limited to the perspectives of the power plant tour guides. On the day after the coal-plant tour, I taught a long teacher-directed lesson on the effects of invisible carbon dioxide and carbon monoxide. I also invited a member the Snoqualmie Nation to meet us at the top of Snoqualmie Falls following our tour of the hydroelectric plant to share his perspective on the various uses of this site that is sacred to his people.

THE ORCA CLAN: THE JOURNEY OF FOOD AND GARBAGE

The "test" taught us that our food does not just appear on our plate; many hands doing many jobs are required to feed us. And the garbage can is not the end of the journey for our food. So what are those jobs that bring us what we eat and take away what we throw out? For the next seven Fridays, we did fieldwork to find out, step by step.

Week One

We asked our cafeteria worker, "Where does our school lunch come from?"

"Cooper School," she said. So we hopped on a city bus, and down to Cooper we went. There we saw how our school lunches are made. Importantly, we saw that the carrots, beans, and flour for cookies all come in bags, boxes, and cans.

"Where does all this food come from?" we asked.

"From the district facilities warehouse," our tour guide said.

Week Two

We hopped on a city bus and went to the facilities warehouse. There we saw not only all the food, but all the classroom supplies, custodial supplies, every single thing every school in the district uses. Interestingly, all the food was still packed up.

"Where does all this food come from?" we asked.

"From Associated Grocers," our guide said.

Week Three

We located Associated Grocers, and off we went. It is an enormous warehouse that distributes food, from produce and meat to canned goods and everything in between. But they would not give us a tour, because there were too many huge forklifts, and we are too small. "Where does this food come from?" we asked. This time, it was not just one place. So we decided to concentrate on farms.

Week Four

We could not get to a farm—too far for a city bus, and not enough parent drivers. But out of our previous trips emerged many other objects we used from the earth: plastic, paper products, metal, etc. This week we explored the journey of plastic, from fossil fuels to refineries to factories to store shelves to homes to recycling plants. We also chronicled the journeys of paper and metal in great detail. Each student chose an everyday product which before had been thought of as just a consumer object. Armed with the new concept that everything we use comes from the earth, they constructed diagrams and flow charts from their notebook paper back to the seed of a fir tree and from the plastic on their "gigapet" back to deposits of oil in Kuwait, and farther back to prehistoric

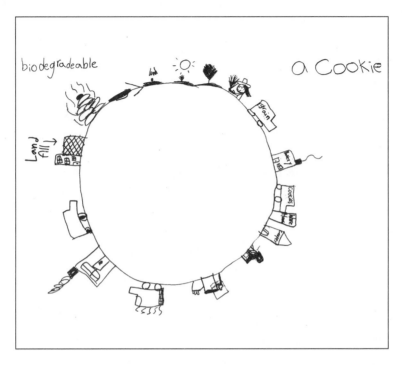

This diagram by Andie Weikert, a second grader at Pathfinder Elementary School in Seattle, Washington, shows the journey of a cookie—biodegradable material—from seeds of grain to the landfill.

plants. Because of our fieldwork, students included every truck, forklift, crate, and hand cart used along the way. Countless interesting questions emerged, and the students tried to research the answers. How come so many products we use are petroleum/fossil fuel-based? How many trees are cut down for all the paper products we use? How are so many cows raised for meat? How do farmers keep the bugs off the crops?

The chronicling of these journeys not only showed us how much effort it takes to get products to us; the exercise also had a significant impact on the students' writing. Second and third graders typically struggle with including enough information; they go from point A to C and skip B. By focusing on the details and by closely examining each other's work, the students learned the importance of organizing their thinking and their writing into discrete steps. Every student in the Orca Clan scored a three (out of five) or higher in organization and communication of ideas on the district's direct writing assessment, a significant improvement over their previous scores in these areas.

Week Five

The next three weeks focused on the other end of the journey. We throw our lunchroom waste in the garbage can. The students knew where the garbage can was emptied, but where do the contents of the dumpster go? We called the number on the side of the dumpster. "The transfer station," they said. We set out for the station, but we waited on the wrong side of the street for the bus we needed to take.

Week Six

The students started recycling what they could (which was not much). "We need to go to a recycling center," they said. So off we went. We had never seen anything like this place. There were so many bottles, so many cans, so much paper, building materials, vacuums, conveyor belts, electrostatic panels, forklifts, and bobcats. With the help of the employees there, we listed all the new products created by this recycling. The students then wanted to know what happens to the things we do not recycle.

Week Seven

We called the transfer station. "Where do you take your garbage?"

"The landfill." We took a school bus this time. We saw leachate pumps, methane burners, wires to confuse seagulls, lots of trucks, and garbage, garbage, garbage! We talked about how, if we lived in New York City, we would not be lucky enough to have a landfill nearby, and that our garbage would travel on barges to other countries to be buried—a startling thought, and the end of the journey.

CHAPTER THREE ARRIVES

One Thursday afternoon, when all our fieldwork had been completed, the three clans gathered in the Orca room. As members of the Turtle Clan finished giving their report, a familiar figure walked in and stood by the door. It was Grey Eagle, an Anishinabe elder and storyteller who comes to Pathfinder regularly to tell stories.

"A strange thing happened," he began. "I was down in Nisqually and a person came up to me and handed me this." He held up a rolled-up piece of paper. The children's eyes widened. He unrolled the paper and read the story.

> So there they were, standing at the edge of the woods looking onto rocks and water. And then it came. The Voice. It was a voice they had never heard before. It was strong, not loud, it was peaceful, it was larger than they could understand. It came from the rocks, the trees, the water, the air they were breathing.
>
> "Thank you for your help," it said. "And congratulations on helping yourselves, for you need me to live."
>
> "Who are you?"
>
> "You know me, you know me very well. You use my trees, my soil, my seeds, my water, the bones of those who lie dead inside me. You plant your food in me, live on me, dump your garbage on me. You know me very well."
>
> "Why are we here? "
>
> "You have spoken that you are my stewards. And as you have been told, you have more to learn before you become my stewards. You have done well, but now, answer me this: how do you use me? Why do you use me? How much of me do you use? Do you need all that you use? Answer me this."
>
> "Then will we be your stewards? Then will we be stewards of the elements? "
>
> The wind, the sea, the trees, they all began speaking in their normal voices.

THE EAGLE CLAN: USING WATER

After hearing chapter three, we met as a class to decide what to do. I turned the questions toward our school building. "How do we use water in our building?" "Where can we get water in our building?" We listed as many locations as we could think of first, and then went on a hunt to find more. The students thought of almost everything, including "those gray heat machines," which they learned were called radiators and do, indeed, use water. During our follow-up hunt, each student had a building map and made a mark every time a new water source was identified. As a group we counted sixty-four different taps and several hundred different water uses and sources in the building. It appeared that the students were no longer taking the element water for granted.

Our next task was to figure out *how much* water we use, which we initially turned into *how often*. Friday—expedition fieldwork day—rolled around, and teams of students from Room 10 were spread all over the building all day long, taking turns monitoring every water source. At the end of the day the tally marks were totaled and the results provided material for math problems for weeks afterwards. We made bar graphs and pie charts showing the least frequent use (brushing teeth) to the most frequent use (toilet) and learned how to make color graphs and pie charts on the computer, which we later presented to the school. The school district's resource conservation specialist David Broustis visited and taught us that the school's toilets use 4.5 gallons every time they are flushed, which led to one math problem, and that new, "low flow" toilets would use only 1.6 gallons per flush, which led to several more math problems. He also taught us that the urinals in the boys' bathrooms flush every five minutes, twenty-four hours a day, seven days a week, weekends and holidays included, which led to math problems and persuasive letter writing at a later stage of the expedition.

We spent the remainder of December on the technology used to make water accessible to us. A plumber friend of mine volunteered to show the students the tricks and tools of his trade. The students learned how to cut copper pipes with a pipe cutter and then put them together with a soldering iron. Every student was allowed to cut and add a section, and soon we had a pipe sculpture, with two faucets and a fountain that worked! We set it up outside the classroom.

Students rotated through the water "technology" projects; while one group was soldering pipes, another was trying to figure out how to move water from one bucket to another using only a piece of plastic tubing—soon they had all discovered the siphon. Both of these pieces of technology were to prove useful later in the expedition, though I did not know how useful at the time.

I was more focused on the academic element. I used our technology activities to practice the expository mode of the direct writing assessment. "Giving directions" is one type of writing within the expository mode, and is an expectation of the Seattle School District's third- and fifth-grade curriculum frameworks. After each activity, students were prompted to write instructions explaining how to use the technology, and after each prompt I gave examples of student work to elicit what made successful instructions. The students identified the traits quite naturally in their peers' work, but in their own words. For example, they noted clear organization ("It has an introduction") and sentence fluency ("She used connecting words like first, then and after that"). As they were required to write technology directions several times, I saw immediate improvement in these traits; many of them were using "connecting words" in their second set of directions, for example. The fact that they had all used the technology made it easy for them to talk about the writing. Students were constructing their beliefs about good writing from their own experience using and understanding the technology.

We also embarked on a related unit in math during December, focusing on measurement of liquid volume. We collected containers, compared standard units of measurement, and made our own measuring containers so students could measure their water use at home. The work culminated with a task that asked students to figure out the correct amount of water to make juice for an upcoming field trip, using various units of measurement and converting between them.

THE TURTLE CLAN: USING ELECTRICITY

At about this time our school librarian brought us two copies of *The Magic School Bus and the Electric Field Trip,* by Joanna Cole. The students were amazed to see a comic-book-style description of so many things they had already learned about and seen. Most useful to us, however, were several pages covering a new topic: various appliances and tools. I copied these pages, spread them out on the tables, and set the students to work, scavenger-hunt style, to answer the question: "What does electricity *do* in different kinds of appliances and machines?" When we shared our findings, four categories became clear to us. The electrical appliances we knew about all seemed to include either a filament, a heating element, a motor, or an "electron gun," which was the best term we could find to describe what happens inside a television screen or computer monitor.

We started to answer the question "How much do we use?" by counting. For homework, the students tallied up the light bulbs, electrical outlets, and electricity-using appliances in their homes. They had to categorize which appliances had filaments, motors, etc. During class time, we conducted a similar survey around the school. But to go further with this study, we realized we needed expert help. The Eagles could measure water using cups and gallons. The Orcas could collect garbage in bags, but no bag or bucket was useful in measuring electricity.

To the rescue came David, the school district's resource conservation specialist. He brought into our class one of the fishbowls we had seen many times, mounted on a piece of plywood for demonstration. He explained to us that the unit of measurement for electricity had to track not only how many electrons were moving—kilowatts—but also how long they moved—hours. The children saw in the meter a spinning wheel that counted all the kilowatt-hours that passed through the fishbowl. The abbreviation "KWh" soon appeared all over the board and in math problems that the students tackled with enthusiasm.

But David also had another demonstration for us. He plugged in a typical hundred-watt bulb and, beside it, another bulb made with a loop of glass tubing. As we investigated the several differences, one stood out: the regular bulb was too hot to touch, while the tube bulb stayed cool. Not only that; the regular bulb spun the counting wheel much faster than the other bulb.

David took us to see the school's main electrical meter, located in a secret closet by the gym. We had to lift the students up so they could see this deluxe fishbowl. All of our work in studying the electrical system made the meaning of this device suddenly clear. Every light, every computer, every electric pencil sharpener in the building, when it is on, makes this counting wheel spin ever faster as our school partakes in the dance of electrons that begins miles away in the big power plants. When everything is turned off, the wheel does not spin at all.

"Why do we have to count up the kilowatt hours, anyway?" I asked. The students stood and thought. "Do we have to pay for it?" asked one. "You got it," said David. "We send you the bill every month."

"How much does it cost?" asked another.

"Oh," said David, "only about seven thousand dollars last year."

During the next two weeks, while the students worked on reports of their findings to present to the Eagles and Orcas, a new area of inquiry emerged. During morning meeting, one of the students asked, "What about solar power? How does that work?"

I confessed that I did not know and sent a group of students to discover what they could in the library and over the Internet. The Internet materials they found were quite technical, and referred to other ways of making power as well: wind power and something called "micro-hydro." A yellow pages investigation revealed a distributor of solar and wind-power equipment called "The Power Company." We did not have time to arrange a field trip, but I went myself and met Dick Frost, a former oil company worker and an enthusiastic promoter of alternative energy. Dick enjoyed hearing about our expedition so much that he let me borrow a $500 wind generator to take back to show the students.

Unpacking, assembling, and examining this piece of equipment was a thrill for the students. Their understanding of how a generator works allowed them to make their own sense out of this device quickly:

"Hey, the propeller's just like the turbines in the power plant! It spins around. And it makes the magnet spin inside there."

"What's different?" I asked.

"This one's lots smaller."

"Oh, and this one uses wind to spin the magnet, not water!"

"Or coal."

"Not coal, steam. The coal makes steam, remember?" We walked outside and faced the device into the moderate wind. The three plastic blades began to rotate silently. Our minds were spinning as well.

THE ORCA CLAN: USING FOOD AND MAKING GARBAGE

The questions "How do you use me?" and "Why do you use me?" were pretty obvious to the Orca Clan studying Earth. We devoted a week to them. Interestingly, "How much of me do you use?" turned into "How much of me do you throw away?" and answering this question turned into a real eye-opening experience.

For a week, we took the garbage can and paper-recycling bin out of the room. The students were not to throw anything away in the lunch-room either, instead returning it to the classroom. After three days, our room was pretty cluttered. After a week, it was a downright mess. The students were trying to keep the room clean; they were extremely conscious of not adding to the pile, and they did an admirable job. When writing, the students filled up their entire paper and used both sides. Homework that week was done in their journals. But for all the effort we put into reducing the amount of garbage we made, there was garbage we could not help but produce. The next week, the students had plastic grocery bags tied to their waists in which they were to put all their personal garbage. Because of the previous week, the bags did not really fill up. But one thing became extremely clear—the students who had school lunch, because of the way it is packaged, were at a major disadvantage. This lead to an eye-opening study of packaging.

The final hands-on experience was one not many wanted to get their hands on. We took nine garbage bags from three days of the lunchroom waste of three hundred students and emptied them onto the cafeteria floor. Yuck. We then proceeded to sort it all: paper recycling, milk cartons, metal recycling, potential compost, and garbage. We sorted it into a physical pie chart. And the results were startling. What appeared to be 75 percent of the garbage could have gone somewhere else. At this point in the expedition, the students' motivation seemed to come from wanting to make a difference. Though their service projects had not begun, they seemed to already know that they had the power to bring about positive change. The students produced outstanding, careful work in our measurement and graphing assignments. But the standard had not been raised and imposed by me. They had raised their own standards because they knew that the information was real and, most importantly, that it might help them to do something good. This powerful motivation began to spread into all of the students' work.

CHAPTER FOUR ARRIVES

Once again, the three clans gathered together to share their findings. Right in the middle of one presentation, a tall hooded figure in a brown cloak slipped in the back door, strode up to some of the students who were sitting on the floor, and handed them a rolled-up piece of paper. When the students' startled babble died down, Bryan sat on the stage and read this fourth chapter of the Story. The three children had been led to a cave high in a cliff, where they spoke not only with their own animals, but with a whole council of the animals.

> The Bear spoke again. "Pathfinders! We have been watching you, and you have done well. You have learned a lot. You know where your water, electricity, and food come from. You have studied how you use the elements, and how much you use. In fact, you have learned more than we ever hoped." The children were feeling good now. "We believe you are ready for the next step. But first, we think it is time to tell you why you and your clans have been chosen. Frog?"

> Frog, the one who warns people of danger, spoke. "We are dying. Every day, somewhere in the world, an animal species goes extinct. You two-legged ones are in danger, too, as is the Earth

itself." Frog spoke again: *"I warn people of danger, but I also teach about things that are connected, because I connect the land and the water. You must ask yourselves: When you use Water, Earth, or Fire, does it affect the animals, the earth, even other people? How?"...*

Salmon spoke. "I teach about respect. Now, you should be able to answer your last two questions: "How can you use Water, Earth, and Fire more responsibly? What actions can you take in your homes and school to be more respectful toward and responsible with the elements? You must decide on something you think should change, write a proposal, and make it happen. When you have made change, then, and only then, will you be stewards of the elements."

With this fourth chapter of the Story, the groundwork was laid for student-initiated service projects. The story gave us the words "responsible" and "respectful" to guide us in choosing actions relating to our use of the elements. One of the guiding questions for the students in writing their Proposals for Change was, "Who will your project help, and how?" For many students, the answer was "the animals," "the air," or "the environment." This is broader than, and perhaps different from, the idea of service as an action directly helping a particular individual or group. We consider the projects the students developed to be true service. Perhaps our students, in imagining their projects in response to the request of Salmon, had already built for themselves a personal belief that stewardship anywhere is a service to us all.

THE EAGLE CLAN: PROPOSALS FOR CHANGE

After hearing the charge given to us in part four of the Story, we once again met as a class. This time we brainstormed potential projects according to the criteria mentioned in the chapter: "What actions can you take to be more respectful toward and responsible for water?" Some of the ideas came from guest speakers, like making nontoxic soap and turning the school into a "toxic-free" zone, and replacing nonnative plants with native species near a local stream. Others came from students' own interests, like designing a water Web page and building a three-dimensional model of a local park's watershed showing how people do and do not respect it. One student suggested building a "living machine," or biological wastewater treatment plant that would treat the classroom wastewater using bacteria, plants, and fish instead of chemicals. Several students wanted most of all to use our new plumbing knowledge to build a drinking fountain in the classroom. Though this idea did not represent respect or responsibility for water, it was the project those students loved, and it provided a service to their classmates, who were tired of trekking down the hall to get a drink. We narrowed it down to ten choices and then the students each wrote their top three on an index card, which I used to make project groups. But before the groups could begin their work, they had to write proposals for change.

Now we had the opportunity to really focus on persuasive writing, the third direct writing assessment. We had already practiced it in other contexts, such as writing letters to the school site council requesting that the building's urinals be turned off at night and weekends. We had discussed what makes good persuasive writing using samples of student work. Now we were ready to write something more serious.

I asked the school principal to stop by and hear about the students' ideas. He was impressed, but informed them that you cannot treat your own wastewater, replace all the toxic cleaners in the school, or build a permanent drinking fountain in the classroom without first getting permission. Each group had to decide on its audience. Some were writing to the school site council, others to the city parks department, still others to a local historical museum to request that their model be exhibited there. I realized at this point that before the students could go any farther, they needed to think through what would be involved in carrying out their ideas. So our next step was for each group to write an "action plan" detailing the problem they were trying to solve, the solution, the steps needed to carry out the solution, the materials required and whom it would affect. These action plans became the prewrite step for their proposals for change. Each student wrote his or her own proposal, and each proposal went through several drafts.

"Fieldwork Fridays," as well as Monday, Tuesday, and Wednesday mornings, were devoted to working on the proposals. The actual proposals grew out of the action plans. Although it quickly became clear that the audiences we were writing for would be interested in the problem, the solution, and whom it would affect, we left out the steps and the materials needed to complete the solution. We discussed "what makes a good proposal for change" and they came up with things like "convincing," "makes sense," "easy for the audience to understand," and "interesting." We thought of examples of how to make a persuasive piece demonstrate these criteria. For many students, the final drafts became the piece of writing they were most proud of for the year. Indeed, the defined audiences they were writing for and the connection to their work inspired more interest in multiple drafts and, in many cases, higher quality work than I had seen previously that year. As students finished their proposals for change (most of which were submitted to the proper audiences), they began to work on their projects.

"Fieldwork Fridays" became project days. If you had walked into the classroom on a typical Friday in late January, you might have seen only a few students: the living machine group clustered around their three fish tanks, trying to figure out how to pump water from one tank to another (their knowledge of how a siphon works ended up being very useful) and the legs of two members of the drinking fountain group sticking out from under the sink as they worked with a wrench. The plants group would have been down at the park, replacing nonnative English ivy and false bamboo with native plants donated by a local nursery. The watershed model group would have been with a parent volunteer at the parks department office downtown copying topographical maps. The play group would have been rehearsing onstage. The video group would have been filming with a parent in an empty classroom. The nontoxic soap group would have been going from classroom to classroom, doing a survey of the building's supplies to see what toxic cleaners need to be replaced. The water Web page group was in the library, researching other Web pages to get ideas for their own. I would have been running from group to group, discovering that I really was not needed for much. The students generally only asked for help

Proposal for Change

To: Pathfinder Staff and Facilities Committee
From: Kirstin Marie Tiede

We are trying to change our lights to fluorescent light bulbs. They are special because they don't use as much electricity as incandescent bulbs. Next we are writing a presentation to the classrooms about turning off their lights when they don't need them. We are also checking the classroom lights at lunch time and seeing if they're on. If they're on we will write the teacher a note about turning off their lights when they don't need them. We also are making stickers to put in the classrooms on the light switches. Our project will save electricity. It will help the classrooms because we will have more money to buy stuff we need. And we will not leave our lights on. And we would help the school. It will help the environment because if people don't leave their lights on there won't be as much pollution in the air and the coal won't run out at the power plants.

I hope you will let our class do our stuff that we want to do.

Third-grader Kirstin Marie Tiede wrote this proposal about her plans to help her school, Pathfinder Elementary in Seattle, conserve electricity.

when they had problems working together. When it came to the task at hand, they were determined to figure it out themselves. Students in the drinking fountain group, one of whom is commonly referred to as a behavior problem, spent two and a half hours under the sink, first wrestling with a stuck screw and then trying to figure out how the pieces of our new fountain fit together. They never wanted help, and successfully solved both problems themselves. They not only learned how a drinking fountain is constructed; they also learned about the rewards of perseverance. There were similar character-building experiences in every project group. By this time, the students had a passion for their projects—on many levels—and they were not going to let any social conflicts or technical difficulties get in the way. One of the most powerful aspects of this project for us as teachers was how well it motivated certain students who were struggling academically or who often displayed a negative attitude at school, or both. The student in the drinking fountain group mentioned above was also a low-level reader, but he managed to work his way through an instructions manual for installing a drinking fountain (with a little help from his group). One student in the living machine group had a reputation for years for having a negative attitude about school and doing very little work, particularly writing. But the other students in his group came to respect and rely on his resourcefulness and problem-solving skills when they were setting up the living machine—and he wrote with pride about how he used a piece from a jumprope to connect two tubes. He discovered how writing—and work—fit into his life.

THE TURTLE CLAN: ELECTRICITY—PROPOSALS FOR CHANGE

When we heard Salmon's instructions for us to write proposals and take action, the blades of the wind generator were still spinning in our heads. "Hey," someone asked. "Do you think we could put a wind generator or solar panels on the top of our school?"

None of us knew the answer. But we had all made the connections: using electricity from power plants costs a lot of money, causes air pollution and global warming, and causes the problems related to big hydro-power, notably its impact on salmon runs and its disturbing effect on such places as Snoqualmie Falls, which are important to many Indian nations and nonnative people. (These problems, incidentally, did not dampen our awe of the remarkable technologies and engineering feats that bring us our electric power.)

The students began to come up with possible projects, most of which related to the dream of generating our own clean energy right here at school. In a remarkable coincidence (a real one), a parent named John Schlick called to tell me that he was involved in drafting an alternative energy bill that was pending in the state legislature. I told him to please come right in and tell the students about it. He described how the bill, called "Net Metering," would make it much easier for citizens to link the power they generate, whether by wind, sun, or other means, directly to the public utility system. He explained that most people who make wind and solar power have to use expensive batteries to store that power. But it is possible, using machines called inverters, to generate power that flows directly into the big system without causing problems. With "Net Metering," a house with a wind generator could make its electric meter wheel spin *backwards,* reducing or eliminating its utility bill!

This sounds complicated, and it is, but thanks to John's clear explanations and the students' prior knowledge, they got it. One project group formed immediately: the new law group, consisting of five students who set to work writing speeches that they hoped to give to the state legislature in Olympia a week later. Our other six groups formed over the next week as our needs became clearer. To work on generating power at school, the wind group and the solar group formed. We realized that we would need to raise money to buy the equipment, so six students became the fund-raising group. Some students wanted to put on a presentation about saving electricity: the conservation group. Our last two groups to form were the meter group and the model group, the first because we decided that we wanted to put an electric meter right in our room to measure the power we made and saved, and the second because the students wanted to make a model of our Turtle-power system that could be taken around to show to people.

The members of the new law group each wrote a speech. I gave them minimal instructions: a good speech tells what you care about and why, and includes clear, accurate supporting details. They worked at the assignment vigorously, in class and at home. When they were done, they read their speeches to the class and received suggestions. I had doubted that one particular student, a second grader with a learning disability, could handle the assignment, and I had let her join the group with private reluctance. She came to class with her entire speech committed to memory, and delivered it with a confidence I had never seen from her before (though I have seen it since). The only editing I did on any of their work was to eliminate overlapping material.

A few days later, the five students headed for Olympia with John and another parent. Reports were unanimous that these five eight- and nine-year-olds were the shining stars of the proceedings. One parent told me that the students clearly believed that they *belonged* there. One citizen in the audience took issue with their portrayal of the problems of hydro-power, and debated with the students over lunch, but even from him they received congratulations on their efforts. Some of the students were able to return to Olympia two months later to witness Governor Gary Locke signing the Net Metering Bill into law.

Back at school, the wind group invented a wind meter: a large cardboard tube that funneled the wind onto a flap, and a series of lines and numbers to measure how far the flap was moved by the air. The principal accompanied us onto the roof to test the strength of the wind in various places and to determine the best site for a wind generator. The solar group made phone calls and looked through catalogues to find the prices for PV (photovoltaic) systems. The fund-raising group decided to raise money by selling compact fluorescent light bulbs, which, we discovered, use three-quarters less energy than regular incandescent bulbs. They built their store, a heavy-duty, lemonade-style stand with a giant plywood light bulb suspended overhead. They called local supermarkets to see if we could sell our wares in front of their stores. Light bulb sales began on Saturdays, with a lot of tricky math back in class to subtract our overhead costs (we had to buy the light bulbs) from our gross earnings to figure our real profit (which, in the end, amounted to $350).

The meter group made phone calls to Seattle City Light to see if they would donate an electric meter to our class. They agreed, but needed technical information that we did not yet have. The model group built small replicas of windmills, solar panels, and meters, and connected them all up with wire on a school building made of shoeboxes. The Conservation group made stickers for all the light switches in the school reminding people to turn them off.

At the same time, the students wrote their proposals for change. As with the Eagle Clan, the Turtles talked to the principal to help figure out who the audience of the proposals should be. Some were written to the central district facilities office. Some went to the school site council, and some to the resource conservation specialist. Most of the students selected these pieces for their student portfolios, attaching comments like, "This is the most important thing I ever wrote."

As this whole effort emerged, I was so impressed with the ambition and the elegance of it all that I felt I could happily retire in June at age 34 if we could pull it off. Sadly, I am still working. The vision of wind generators spinning on the roof and of a classroom, or even a whole school, "off the grid" encountered a series of difficulties insurmountable by us at that time. An inverter, which we thought we could get for under $500, in fact cost over $1500. The level of detailed technical knowledge required for our proposal to be approved by district facilities was not available to us. More than anything I felt the familiar crunch of too little planning time for a project that would essentially require its own general contractor. We had encountered our limits. And our limits, the disappointment notwithstanding, always have something to teach us.

THE ORCA CLAN: PROPOSALS FOR CHANGE

It was time for all we had done, all we had seen, all we had talked about, and all we had learned to become an action plan. So it was turned over to those who had been charged with becoming stewards of the elements. What can we do to treat Earth with more respect? The students generated ideas quickly, based on their own values and their own interests: compost our lunchroom waste, do a better job recycling, teach others about respecting Earth, adopt-a-street, start growing food organically.

I assumed they would suggest composting or the obvious recycling. I was hoping they would choose teaching others, for it had been a requirement of a small grant we had received. But organic farming?

Proposal for Change

To: Finance Committee
From: Ellen Bellows Teel

Our class is trying to raise money for a wind generator and solar panel by selling compact fluorescent light bulbs. We are selling them in front of Pcc and on Stewards of the Elements Night. The store is made out of plywood and is more of a little stand than a store. This is good because it gives us money for supplies. It doesn't make pollution. Why are fluorescent light bulbs a good thing to sell, instead of pizza or popcorn? I'll tell you why. The fluorescent light bulbs save electricity 75 percent! And popcorn and pizza don't. I hope you enjoy my proposal.

Thank you very much for reading it.

Ellen Teel, a third grader at Pathfinder Elementary School in Seattle, describes her class's plan to sell compact fluorescent light bulbs to raise funds for a wind generator and solar panel for the school.

That was a surprise. And I knew it involved a lot of work, but they were the stewards.

The students split themselves into groups by using a process we call "democracy in action." They put their heads down and raised their hand for the project they wanted to be a part of. Amazingly, the groups were evenly split from the first vote. Fueled by their desire to make a difference, the students worked hard on their proposals for change. Every idea, every word mattered to them, and the resulting writing took them to new heights.

Over the next four Fridays, the groups pursued their projects, some with parent helpers, some independently. The farming group learned how to build seed germination stands, and planted their "crops." They measured and cut plastic sheets to cover existing chemical-treated wood in garden beds so that any classroom could safely grow organic food. The compost group built their bin and created a schedule for gathering the school's compostable food waste. The teaching group made a model of our garbage pie on plywood and wrote a presentation to go along with it. And by the night of our culminating event, Stewards of the Elements Night, all our plans were either underway or in place, ready to be put into action.

CULMINATING EVENT: STEWARDS OF THE ELEMENTS NIGHT

On an evening in February, parents and students began to arrive in the Pathfinder School auditorium at 6:30 p.m. Distinguished guests, some of the city and county workers and educators who had helped us along the way, also came. Stewards themselves, they came to watch us become stewards. Three hundred people were assembled for the event.

At 7:00 p.m. the lights went off, the room fell silent, the curtain opened, and the first skit began. Each skit demonstrated what students had learned during their exploration of the elements, as well as adventures they had along the way. Next came the project groups with their proposals for change. Many parents commented later that they had no idea of the scope and the breadth of the studies and projects undertaken until that night.

It took a long time for all seventeen groups to present their work, and by the end everybody was tired and restless. Suddenly, a voice spoke from the back of the room: "I have a story." It was Grey Eagle, the storyteller. He walked to the front and once again the room fell silent. The children, who had been sitting for more than two hours, were suddenly still. They had developed a ritual for these expedition stories.

Grey Eagle's story came from the fifth chapter. It told of the three children who had started it all looking for some sign from the animals that they had learned enough, that they were finally stewards of the elements. But no sign came—the animals were gone and the elements were silent. The three children sat down, discouraged.

A frog plopped into the stream and disappeared in the water. They remembered standing before the Council of Animals and hearing Frog speak about the connection between the elements and the lessons to be taught.

Just then, they heard a howl, and thought of Wolf, the wise animal who was the last of the Council to speak.

"What was it that Wolf told us?" asked Eagle girl.

"Wolf said we should find Stewards who protect and preserve the Elements," Turtle boy answered.

"And Wolf also said that there are already Stewards here, people working every day to preserve Air, Earth, Fire, and Water," added Orca girl.

They were silent for a moment, thinking about the significance of what Wolf had said. Then it came to them and each began to speak.

"Our class is treating water with plants and animals instead of chemicals," said Eagle girl. "That's protecting the element Water."

"Our class is learning how to use the sun and wind to generate electricity," said Turtle boy. "That's protecting Air from pollution."

"And our class is recycling, composting, and growing plants organically," said Orca girl. "That's protecting and preserving the Earth."

The Three looked at each other in growing excitement and then their words began tumbling over each other:

"We have learned how the Two-Legged mistreat the Elements."

"We have worked out plans to better use the Elements."

"We are putting those plans into action."

"All three clans are teaching adults and other kids why it is so important to treat the Elements with respect."

The Three paused in surprise and wonder. Then they shouted in unison: "WE are the STEWARDS of the ELEMENTS!"

"Aaaaah," they sighed. "It's great to reach the end and have it over."

Then they heard a voice from above and looked up. It was Seagull. "You are Stewards of the Elements," Seagull said, "but it is not the end. In fact, your work has just begun."

The three who had gotten the whole thing started sighed, as the Seagull continued.

"All those in your clans must gather, with families and friends, for an Honoring Ceremony."

The Eagle, Orca, and Turtle clans gathered at Pathfinder for an evening program that started their lifetime responsibility of Sharing the Gift. They recounted their mysterious adventure with stories, skits, and suggestions for protecting and preserving the Elements.

SUCCESS AND FAILURES

As we the teachers reflect on the expedition, we are drawn to the Expeditionary Learning design principle Success and Failure. What had we achieved? Academically, the students had numerous experiences in three writing modes and had such a wealth of information to apply to their writing that it became easy for them to succeed. The quality of student work was excellent, and we could see, activity by activity, confidence in writing abilities grow. And with the deep immersion nature of what we were doing, children's confidence in reading also grew. The context of what they were reading was all about what they knew. One student, who has dyslexia and little confidence, received a pamphlet from the public utilities department. It was not written for students, but she plowed through it, largely because those "big words" were now an integral part of her vocabulary. After questioning her about what she read, it was easy to tell her without hesitation that she had become an excellent reader. She liked hearing that, but she already knew she was a success.

We feel that the academic accomplishments of the students in this expedition can be traced to two roots. First, they cared deeply about what they were doing. And second, the work was real, and the results were real. The Orca Clan reduced the amount of garbage we produced in the lunchroom by approximately 70 percent. The Eagle Clan treats all of the water they use in the classroom with their "living machine" instead of the sewage system, and waters the Orca Clan's plants. The Turtles' and Eagles' process of educating the school has helped reduce our utility bill by $4000 in eight months; under an agreement with the school district, 90 percent of this savings will remain in our building budget.

These successes make us wonder what could we have done differently? Certainly time constraints held us back. Although we had two snacks from it, the garden is not really flourishing. The project to teach others about respecting Earth, while well done, was not something other schools could use. The Turtles ran out of the money and time needed to truly power their class by wind and solar power. Outside of our three clans, no one ever saw the Eagle's skits or videos.

However, these unrealized plans speak directly to the intangibles— the experience, intelligence, and understanding that do not show up on a standardized test or essay questions. Real work teaches perseverance. In this culture of sound-bites and lightning-fast video edits, where so much is disposable and schools do one-month units and move on to the next "thing," these students learned through experience that one does not become an expert quickly. There is much learning to be done in order to grow and become someone who can share a gift that is meaningful.

And hard work is behind that perseverance. The real work of stewardship started when the expedition ended. Presented with real-life issues, these students now know how to address them.

𝒜PPENDIX

ABOUT THE AUTHORS

John Adelmann teaches history at Central Alternative High School in Dubuque, Iowa.

Jeanne Anderson teaches kindergarten and first grade, staying with her students for two years, at Audubon Elementary School in Dubuque, Iowa.

Michelle Brantley is a fellow at Expeditionary Learning Outward Bound.

Meg Campbell is the executive director of Expeditionary Learning Outward Bound, and a lecturer at the Harvard Graduate School of Education where she teaches a course on school design implementation.

Sally Carey was the service learning coordinator at Rocky Mountain School of Expeditionary Learning and Hill Middle School.

Emily Cousins is the service director at Expeditionary Learning Outward Bound. She is based at the New York City Outward Bound Center.

Carol Duehr teaches fifth and sixth grade, looping with her students for two years, at Fulton Intermediate Center in Dubuque, Iowa.

Bayan Ebeid teaches math and creative writing at the Brooklyn, New York, middle school I.S. 30.

Patricia B. Fisher teaches sixth-grade science and math at College Park Middle School in Hickory, North Carolina.

Deb Fordice teaches sixth grade at Audubon Elementary School in Dubuque, Iowa. She also cofacilitates the Expeditionary Learning service summit for educators, entitled "Writing Elders' Life Stories."

Christine Griffin is a sixth- and seventh-grade social studies teacher at King Middle School in Portland, Oregon. She is part of a team of five teachers who spend two years with their students, before looping again with another group.

Laura Kelly teaches art and English as a Second Language to middle school students at I.S. 30 in Brooklyn, New York.

Karen MacDonald is a sixth- and seventh-grade language arts teacher at King Middle School in Portland, Oregon. She is part of a team of five teachers who spend two years with their students, before looping again with another group.

Amy Mednick is the communications director at Expeditionary Learning Outward Bound.

Christina Nugent teaches fifth and sixth grade, looping with her students for two years, at Fulton Intermediate Center in Dubuque, Iowa.

Patricia O'Brien teaches second grade at Bonham Elementary School in San Antonio, Texas.

Chris Quigley teaches second and third grade at Pathfinder Elementary School in Seattle, Washington.

Paola Ruocco teaches humanities to middle school students at School for the Physical City in New York City.

Sheila Sanders teaches sixth-grade math and science at College Park Middle School in Hickory, North Carolina.

Cheryl Sims teaches science to middle school students at School for the Physical City in New York City.

Katherine Stevens teaches English at Central Alternative High School in Dubuque, Iowa.

Bryan Street teaches third and fourth grade at Pathfinder Elementary School in Seattle, Washington.

Carol Teague is a sixth-grade math, social studies, and language teacher at College Park Middle School in Hickory, North Carolina.

Wendy Ward teaches science to sixth, seventh, and eighth graders at Rocky Mountain School of Expeditionary Learning in Denver, Colorado.

Chris Weaver is a fifth- and sixth-grade teacher at Pathfinder Elementary School in Seattle, Washington. He has also taught second and third grade at Pathfinder.

Karen Wohlwend teaches kindergarten and first grade, staying with her students for two years, at Audubon Elementary School in Dubuque, Iowa.

SERVICE RESOURCES

"Addressing Issues of Race and Culture Through Service Learning." Rich Cairn and Wokie Roberts in *Generator,* Spring 1993. National Youth Leadership Council: Tel. 651-631-3672.

The Call of Service. Robert Coles. New York: Houghton-Mifflin, 1993.

Enriching Learning through Service. Kate McPherson. Project Service Leadership: Tel. 360-576-5070.

Growing Hope: A Sourcebook on Integrating Youth Service into the School Curriculum. Rich Cairn and James C. Kielsmeier. National Youth Leadership Council: Tel. 651-631-3672.

"How Would You Like to Visit a Nursing Home?" Peri Smilow. *Equity & Excellence in Education,* Volume 26, Number 2, September 1993.

"In the Service of What? The Politics of Service Learning." Joseph Kahne and Joel Westheimer. *Phi Delta Kappan,* May 1996.

Making a Difference: A Students Guide to Planning a Service Project. Washington Leadership Institute: Tel. 206-296-5630.

The National Indian Youth Leadership Model: A Manual for Program Leaders. McClellan Hall. National Youth Leadership Council: Tel. 651-631-3672.

"The Power of Community Service." Diane Hedin. *Proceedings of the Academy of Political Science,* Volume 37, Number 2, 1989.

A Practitioner's Guide to Reflection in Service Learning. J. Eyler, D. Giles, A. Schmiede. National Service-Learning Cooperative Clearinghouse: Tel. 800-808-SERV.

For more information contact the National Service-Learning Cooperative Clearinghouse, University of Minnesota, Tel. 800-808-SERV.

EXPEDITIONARY LEARNING DESIGN PRINCIPLES[1]

Learning is an expedition into the unknown. Expeditions draw together personal experience and intellectual growth to promote self-discovery and the construction of knowledge. We believe that adults should guide students along this journey with care, compassion, and respect for their diverse learning styles, backgrounds, and needs. Addressing individual differences profoundly increases the potential for learning and creativity of each student.

Given fundamental levels of health, safety, and love, all people can and want to learn. We believe Expeditionary Learning harnesses the natural passion to learn and is a powerful method for developing the curiosity, skills, knowledge, and courage needed to imagine a better world and work toward realizing it.

The Primacy of Self-Discovery

Learning happens best with emotion, challenge, and the requisite support. People discover their abilities, values, "grand passions," and responsibilities in situations that offer adventure and the unexpected. They must have tasks that require perseverance, fitness, craftsmanship, imagination, self-discipline, and significant achievement. A primary job of the educator is to help students overcome their fear and discover they have more in them than they think.

The Having of Wonderful Ideas

Teach so as to build on children's curiosity about the world by creating learning situations that provide matter to think about, time to experiment, and time to make sense of what is observed. Foster a community where students' and adults' ideas are respected.

The Responsibility for Learning

Learning is both a personal, individually specific process of discovery and a social activity. Each of us learns within and for ourselves and as a part of a group. Every aspect of a school must encourage children, young people, and adults to become increasingly responsible for directing their own personal and collective learning.

Intimacy and Caring

Learning is fostered best in small groups where there is trust, sustained caring, and mutual respect among all members of the learning community. Keep schools and learning groups small. Be sure there is a caring adult looking after the progress of each child. Arrange for the older students to mentor the younger ones.

Success and Failure

All students must be assured a fair measure of success in learning in order to nurture the confidence and capacity to take risks and rise to increasingly difficult challenges. But it is also important to experience failure, to overcome negative inclinations, to prevail against adversity, and to learn to turn disabilities into opportunities.

Collaboration and Competition

Teach so as to join individual and group development so that the value of friendship, trust, and group endeavor is made manifest. Encourage students to compete, not against each other, but with their own personal best and with rigorous standards of excellence.

Diversity and Inclusivity

Diversity and inclusivity in all groups dramatically increases richness of ideas, creative power, problem-solving ability, and acceptance of others. Encourage students to investigate, value, and draw upon their own different histories, talents, and resources together with those of other communities and cultures. Keep the schools and learning groups heterogeneous.

The Natural World

A direct and respectful relationship with the natural world refreshes the human spirit and reveals the important lessons of recurring cycles and cause and effect. Students learn to become stewards of the earth and of the generations to come.

Solitude and Reflection

Solitude, reflection, and silence replenish our energies and open our minds. Be sure students have time alone to explore their own thoughts, make their own connections, and create their own ideas. Then give them opportunity to exchange their reflections with each other and with adults.

Service and Compassion

We are crew, not passengers, and are strengthened by acts of consequential service to others. One of a school's primary functions is to prepare its students with the attitudes and skills to learn from and be of service to others.

---

[1] The above principles have been informed by Kurt Hahn's "Seven Laws of Salem," by Paul Ylvisaker's "The Missing Dimension," and by Eleanor Duckworth's *"The Having of Wonderful Ideas" and Other Essays on Teaching and Learning* (New York: Teachers College Press, 1987).

Outward Bound USA
One Mystery Point Rd.
Garrison, NY 10524-9757
(914) 424-4000

Expeditionary Learning Outward Bound
122 Mount Auburn St.
Cambridge, MA 02138
(617) 576-1260
info@elob.org
www.elob.org